STUDENT RESOURCE GUIDE TO THE INTERNET

STUDENT SUCCESS ONLINE

Cynthia B. Leshin

Illustrated by Bob McLaughlin

PRENTICE HALL
UPPER SADDLE RIVER, NEW JERSEY 07458

Library of Congress Cataloging-in-Publication Data
Leshin, Cynthia B.
    Student resource guide to the Internet : student success online /
Cynthia B. Leshin ; illustrated by Bob McLaughlin.
        p.   cm.
    Includes index.
    ISBN 0-13-621079-1
    1. Internet (Computer network) in education—Handbooks, manuals,
etc.
LB1044.87.L477   1998
025.04—dc21   97-22922
                                                                        CIP

Acquisitions editor: *Todd Rossell*
Editorial/production supervision: *Barbara Marttine Cappuccio*
Director of manufacturing and production: *Bruce Johnson*
Managing editor: *Mary Carnis*
Creative director: *Marianne Frasco*
Marketing manager: *Frank Mortimer, Jr.*
Manufacturing buyer: *Marc Bove*
Cover art and cover design: *Bob McLaughlin*
Interior design: *Kevin Kall*
Formatting/page make-up: *North Market Street Graphics*

 ©1998 by Prentice-Hall Inc.
Simon & Schuster / A Viacom Company
Upper Saddle River, New Jersey 07458

Printed in the United States of America

10   9   8   7   6   5   4   3   2   1

ISBN   0-13-621079-1

Prentice-Hall International (UK) Limited, *London*
Prentice-Hall of Australia Pty. Limited, *Sydney*
Prentice-Hall Canada Inc., *Toronto*
Prentice-Hall Hispanoamericana, S.A., *Mexico*
Prentice-Hall of India Private Limited, *New Delhi*
Prentice-Hall of Japan, Inc., *Tokyo*
Simon & Schuster Asia Pte. Ltd., *Singapore*
Editora Prentice-Hall do Brasil, Ltda., *Rio de Janeiro*

FOR MY SON TODD

CONTENTS

PREFACE   ix

ABOUT THE AUTHOR   xiii

PART I   UNDERSTANDING THE INTERNET   1

CHAPTER I
WHAT IS THE INTERNET?   3

What Is the Internet?   3
   History of the Internet   3
   What Does It Mean to "Be on the Internet"?   6
   Tool Kit of Internet Resources   11
   The Web and the Internet   13
   Connecting to the Internet   15

CHAPTER II
SURFING THE NET   19

Internet Navigation Using Browsers   19
   Browser Basics   20
   Navigating the Net Using Toolbar Buttons   22
Learning Adventure Using Browsers to Surf the Net   25
   Guided Tour 1: Surfing the Net   25
   Guided Tour 2: Surfing to Cool Web Sites   27
   Guided Tour 3: Saving Your Favorite Web Sites   28
   Guided Tour 4: Navigating With Frames   36
   Guided Tour 5: Customizing Your Browser   39
Multimedia-Oriented Web Environments   42
   Before You Begin. . .   42
   How Do Plug-ins and Viewers Work With My Browser?   43
   Installing a Plug-in Without an Install Program or a Helper Not
     Listed in General Preferences   50
   Cool Multimedia Web Sites   54

CHAPTER III

VIRTUAL COMMUNITIES   55

Listserv Mailing Lists 56
  What Is a Listserv Mailing List?   56
  How Does a Mailing List Work?   57
  How to Receive Documents From a Listserv   58
  How to Join a Listserv Mailing List   58
  Important Information Before You Begin   59
  Finding Listserv Mailing Lists   60
Usenet Newsgroups 61
  What Are Newsgroups?   61
  What Is the Difference Between Listserv Mailing Lists
    and Usenet Newsgroups?   61
  Browsers and Usenet Newsgroups   62
  Reading Usenet News Using Netscape Navigator   63
  Reading Usenet News With Netscape Navigator   64
  Reading Usenet News Using Explorer   65
Chats 70
MOOs and MUDs 71
Internet Phones 72
  How Do I Talk to Someone Using an Internet Phone?   73
  What Do I Need to Use an Internet Phone?   73
  Learning Adventures—Exploring Virtual Communities 75

PART II STUDENT SUCCESS AND THE INTERNET   77

CHAPTER IV

RESEARCHING INFORMATION AND RESOURCES ON THE INTERNET   79

Internet Research Tools   80
Basic Guidelines for Becoming a Cybersleuth   81
Research Guidelines   81
Search Directories   82
Other Search Directories   85
Other Subject-Oriented Directories   86
Search Engines 87
  Excite   87
  Infoseek   89

Other Search Engines   91
Internet Collections   92
Reference Resources   100
Virtual Libraries   103
Using Internet Sources for Research   105
Evaluating Internet Information   105
Recording Internet Information Sources   109
Referencing Electronic Media   110
Examples of APA Style   111
Using the Internet for Research and Finding Cool Things   123

CHAPTER V
USING CYBERSPACE FOR CAREER PLANNING AND FINDING A JOB   125

Self-Awareness Journey   126
Career Exploration   128
People as Information Resources   128
Publications as Information Resources   128
The Internet as an Information Resource   129
Professional Services as Information Resources   130
Using Cyberspace to Find a Job   131
How Do I Begin?   131
Preparing Your Résumé for the Internet   139
Finding Employment Opportunities on the Net   146
Career Planning and Finding a Job   165

CHAPTER VI
COOL WEB SITES   169

Preparing for College   169
Improving Your Grades   169
Extra Credit   170
Surfing Adventures—Cool Web Sites   170
Shareware and Software   170
Some Useful Internet Services   170
Preparing for College   170
Improving Your Grades   180
Using the Internet as a Communication Tool   180

Composition and Grammar   181
Learning Lab   181
Libraries   182
Reference Desk   183
Speeches and Speech Writing   185
Writing Resources   186
Extra Credit   188
Books and Literary Resources   188
Government   189
History of Internet and Computers   189
Maps   190
News Publications   191
Study Abroad   194
Substance Abuse   194
Weather   197
Virtual Universities   198
Surfing Adventures   198
Shareware and Software   205
Useful Internet Services   206

GEEK SPEAK   209

REFERENCES   217

APPENDICES   221

Finding Web Sites That Have Moved   221
What to Look for When Purchasing
a Computer—Performance and Pricing   225

INDEX   231

PREFACE

The Internet is a powerful medium for finding information, sharing information, and interacting with others. These capabilities offer new ways to access resources for school, college preparation, career planning, and finding a job. Some of the ways that you will find the Internet valuable as a tool for success in school, for improving your grades, and in preparing for a career include:

- finding the latest information on a subject for research papers;

- collecting data from others online;

- collaborating with others who share your research interests;

- cross-cultural exchanges with Netizens worldwide;

- meeting and learning from subject matter experts on virtually any topic;

- access to resources such as dictionaries, encyclopedias, and library catalogs worldwide;

- access to literature such as the classics and novels;

- access to news publications and electronic journals with resources for researching their databases for past articles or stories;

- access to databases of diverse information at universities, and government agencies; and

- learning about companies by visiting their Web sites.

In addition to helping you succeed in school, your understanding and knowledge about how to use the Internet provides you with important skills that employers value. In a time of rapid global change, companies realize that the Internet has an important role in their future. Most companies do not totally understand how the Internet will or can fit into their success, therefore they are looking for bright, knowledgeable, and enthusiastic individuals who will help pioneer this new electronic frontier. Many companies, in fact, are turning to the Internet to find employees, believing that the people who keep up with the most current information and technology advances in their field will be the best candidates for employment. These professionals are already cybersurfing, networking with peers, researching information, asking questions, and learning collaboratively from others around the world.

Student Resource Guide to the Internet has been designed to meet the needs of students preparing for college and college students who want to succeed both in college and in life. In this book you will find the following valuable resources:

- Practical, step-by-step guidelines for conducting research on the Internet;

- Internet educational reference and resource collections;

- Guidelines for evaluating Internet sources;

- Detailed examples of how to reference online media in your work;

- Valuable resources for career planning and finding a job;

- Guided tours with detailed examples of how to use the Internet to find a job;

- Resources for finding a college, applying to college, and for taking the required standardized tests;

- Valuable resources for financial aid—scholarships, fellowships, loans, and grants;

- Resources for helping you to improve your grades—communication, writing, learning, and research tools;

- Starting points for finding valuable resources for your classes; and

- Practical, easy-to-understand information on navigating and experiencing powerful multimedia electronic environments on the Internet.

Professors and others interested in learning how to use the Internet as a communication and information retrieval tool will also find this a valuable one-of-a-kind book.

Educated individuals understand that we are rapidly moving into a new world, a digital world where the way we live, work, and play is about to be changed forever. Those who want to be successful in this world are learning about the digital tools and resources that are transforming our lives. Those who do not join this webolution will be left behind.

The Internet is not a trend. It is like an ever-cresting wave being driven by the force and momentum of international currents, spraying its global magic from the monitor and inviting us to jump in—the world awaits. Travel, information-on-demand, and communication make the Internet a technology that is here to stay.

No one, not even corporate giants such as Microsoft, envisioned how the Internet would change our world. No one could have prophesied that the Internet of the 1970s and 1980s based at our educational institutions would become the fastest growing communication medium of all times. Today we are experiencing perhaps the greatest revolution in communication. Some have called the World Wide Web the fourth media, positioned to take a place with print, radio, and television as a mass market means of communication.

But we are still pioneers in exploring the uses of this powerful new tool. At home, at school, or at work, children and adults alike are fascinated with the entertainment and edification aspects of the Internet. Individuals and businesses—from Fortune 500 companies to small sole proprietorships—are establishing their links in cyberspace, browsing for new customers, new profits, a new way to do business, even a new way to live. Opportunities for commerce and the private sector to find good matches to their personal interests, in trade, and/or employment are quickly becoming unlimited.

Student Resource Guide to the Internet provides the foundation you need to begin using the Internet as a tool for success. You will explore and learn about many new opportunities available to you as we move into the digital age.

Happy Internet Adventures

ACKNOWLEDGMENTS

The creation of this book has involved many talented individuals that I would like to recognize.

I am most grateful to Todd Rossell for the opportunity to produce this book. Todd has supported my creative vision and has worked with me closely in the design and development process. As a partner in this process, our focus has always been on the creation of a special and valuable book for students.

To Bob McLaughlin for unique illustrations and creation of the book's cover art. Bob's creative talents have brought to life my vision for this book.

To Carrie Brandon for her continued support and creative input. Carrie has been an important part of our design and development team offering suggestions for the cover design, the creation of our character, and input on content.

To Barbara Cappuccio, Marianne Frasco, and all the other personnel at Prentice Hall who have transformed these words into this guide, especially those who read the manuscript and made valuable and most appreciated suggestions.

To my copy editor, Norma Nelson, for her many important and useful suggestions to improve my writing.

To Kathryn K. Kelly for her review of the book.

To my husband, Steve, for his continuing support and for helping to make this Internet adventure possible.

Cynthia B. Leshin

NOTE Figures 1.5, 2.3, 2.4, 2.5, 2.15, 2.16, 2.17, 2.18, 2.22, 2.23A, 2.23B, 2.24, 3.4, 3.5, and 3.6: *Screen shots reprinted by permission from Microsoft Corporation.*

Figures 4.5, 4.6, 4.7, 4.8, 5.6, 5.7, 5.17, and 5.19: *Reprinted by permission from Excite. Excite, Excite Search, Excite City.Net, City.Net, and the Excite Logo are trademarks of Excite, Inc. and may be registered in various jurisdictions. Excite screen display copyright 1995–1997 Excite, Inc.*

Figures 4.4, 4.8, and 5.17: *Reprinted by permission. Infoseek, Ultrasmart, Ultraseek, iSeek, Quickseek, Imageseek, Ultrashop, "proof of intelligent life on the net," and the Infoseek logos are trademarks of Infoseek Corporation, which may be registered in certain jurisdictions. Other trademarks shown are trademarks of their respective owners. Copyright © 1995–1997 Infoseek Corporation. All rights reserved.*

Netscape Communications Corporation has not authorized, sponsored, endorsed, or approved this publication and is not responsible for its content. Netscape and the Netscape Communications corporate logos are trademarks and trade names of Netscape Communications Corporation. All other product names and/or logos are trademarks of their respective owners.

Microsoft has not authorized, sponsored, endorsed, or approved this publication and is not responsible for its content.

NASA has not authorized, sponsored, endorsed, or approved this publication and is not responsible for its content.

# ABOUT THE AUTHOR

Cynthia Leshin is an educational technologies specialist with her doctorate in educational technology from Arizona State University. Dr. Leshin has her own consulting company—XPLORA. She consults with businesses and schools interested in learning about and implementing technology-rich environments for student success, improved learning, and customer support.

She has authored ten books for Simon and Schuster including *Internet Adventures—Step-by-Step Guide to Finding and Using Educational Resources; Netscape Adventures—Step-by-Step Guide to Netscape Navigator and the World Wide Web; Management on the World Wide Web;* and seven discipline-specific Internet books with Internet-based learning activities. She has also written a book, *Instructional Design: Strategies and Tactics.* Her expertise in educational psychology and theories of learning provides her with a unique background for translating complicated technical information into an easy-to-use, easy-to-understand, and practical learning resource.

Dr. Leshin has taught computer literacy and Internet classes at Arizona State University West and Estrella Mountain Community College. She has taught college-accredited Internet classes using distance learning technology for Educational Management Group, a Simon & Schuster company. The Internet serves as a tool for teaching and communicating with her students.

In Dr. Leshin's "other life" she rides mountain bikes and races for Cannondale's HeadShok team. She also enjoys organic gardening, hiking, skiing, scuba diving, and exploring southwestern trails with her three dread-locked Puli dogs and her husband, Steve.

PART I

UNDER-
STANDING
THE
INTERNET

CHAPTER I

WHAT IS THE INTERNET?

In this chapter, you will learn

- what the Internet is.
- the history of the Internet.
- what it means to "be on the Internet."
- the difference between the Internet and the World Wide Web.
- Internet addressing protocol—the URL.
- the three standards used by the World Wide Web.
- how to connect to the Internet.

WHAT IS THE INTERNET?

in'ter·net n

1. world's largest information network **2.** global web of computer networks **3.** inter-network of many networks all running the TCP/IP protocol **4.** powerful communication tool **5.** giant highway system connecting computers and the regional and local networks that connect these computers. *syn* **information superhighway, infobahn, data highway, electronic highway, Net, cyberspace**

A term frequently used to refer to the Internet is "information superhighway." This superhighway is a vast network of computers connecting people and resources around the world. The Internet is accessible to anyone with a computer and a modem.

History of the Internet

The Internet began in the 1960s at the height of the cold war when the United States Department of Defense was trying to figure out how U.S. authorities could communicate with each other in the aftermath of a nuclear attack. The foremost military think tank at the time, the Rand

Corporation, worked on the first communication network that evolved into today's Internet.

1962: The Rand Corporation begins work on the packet-switching network to facilitate the transfer of data over a network.

1969: ARPANET is created, connecting four U.S. campuses: Stanford Research Institute, the University of Utah, UCLA, and UC Santa Barbara.

ARPANET became an immediate success allowing military institutions and universities to share its research. In the 1970s, government and university networks continued to develop as many organizations and companies began to build private computer networks.

1971: ARPANET expands to include 23 university and government research centers.

1974: Telnet, the first commercial version of the ARPANET, is introduced.

1979: The first Usenet newsgroup is introduced by two graduate students at Duke University.

In the 1980s the ARPANET continues to grow at what soon will become a phenomenal pace. These early computer networks that made up the ARPANET evolve into the "internet" as TCP/IP (the protocol used today on the Internet to communicate and share information) is created. The explosion of the personal computer market in the 1980s and powerful network servers make it possible for the first time for companies to connect to the Internet.

1982: The word "internet" is used for the first time.

1984: The novel, *Neuromancer,* by William Gibson is published introducing the term "cyberspace."

1986: The National Science Foundation creates NSFNET when it establishes five super-computing centers at universities to provide powerful computing power.

1988: Internet Relay Chat (IRC) is developed by Jarkko Oikarinen.

1990: The ARPANET ceases to exist and is replaced by the Internet, whose backbone is the National Science Foundation's NSFNET.

1991: The National Science Foundation lifts its restrictions on the use of NSFNET for educational institutions only. Electronic commerce is born.

Mark McCahill leads a team from the University of Minnesota and releases *gopher.*

Tim Berners-Lee, working at CERN in Switzerland, introduces the World Wide Web.

1993: The first Web browser, Mosaic, is created by Marc Andreesen and a group of student programmers at the National Center for Supercomputing Applications (NCSA) at the University of Illinois at Urbana-Champaign.

1994: Netscape Communications Corporation introduces Netscape Navigator.

The age of the Internet arrives as a 30-year-old cold war concept explodes into the fastest-growing interactive communication medium that the world has ever known.

1995: The browser war between Microsoft and Netscape Communications Corporation begins as Microsoft introduces Internet Explorer in the summer of 1995.

Security—encryption, Internet viruses, secure online business transactions, and company security—becomes an important focus for Internet hardware and software.

1996: Microsoft continues the race for Net surfer's hard disk space as the war with Netscape escalates. The release of Explorer 3.0 matches Netscape 3.0 browser features and performance.

Most of the other Internet browsers collapse under the weight of the two most powerful browsers from Netscape and Microsoft.

The browser has developed into an extremely complicated and sophisticated software technology. Plug-ins and helper applications bring rich and creative multimedia environments to the Net surfer's desktop.

New buzzwords and computer jargon, called geek speak, are created by the *digerati.*

Issues related to free speech on the Internet are addressed. The Internet scores as three judges called Government attempt to regulate content on the Internet, a "profoundly repugnant" affront to the First Amendment (June 1996).

PointCast—free software delivering personalized news to the desktop over the Internet—overtakes the browser war to win the title of the year's most compelling innovation.

An interest in collaborative computing and groupware sparks the third generation of browsers.

1997: Intel introduces the next generation of fast and powerful computers with its MMX-technology PC.

Netscape brings groupware to the Internet with the introduction of its Netscape Communicator suite of group-friendly applications for sharing data and collaborating over the Net.

Microsoft integrates the Internet into the computer desktop as Web standards become a part of Windows and its software applications.

Visit the following Web sites for more information on the history of the Internet and computers. Additional sites can be found in Chapter 6.

COMPUTER HISTORY WEB SITE http://granite.sentex.net/~ccmuseum/hist_sites.html

HOBBES INTERNET TIMELINE http://info.isoc.org/guest/zakon/Internet/History/HIT.html

PUBLIC BROADCASTING SYSTEM—HISTORY OF THE INTERNET http://www.pbs.org/internet/history/

What Does It Mean to "Be on the Internet"?

"Being on the Internet" means having full access to all Internet services. Any commercial service or institution that has full Internet access provides the following:

- Electronic mail (email)
- Telnet
- File Transfer Protocol (FTP)
- World Wide Web

Electronic Mail

Electronic mail is the most basic, the easiest to use, and for many people, the most useful Internet service. Email services allow you to

- communicate with friends or new acquaintances
- interact with professional colleagues
- participate in electronic discussion groups—listserv mailing lists

- interact with others on bulletin boards such as Usenet newsgroups

- request information from an individual, company, or institution

- receive technical support for hardware and software

- send résumés to a company

- participate in electronic workshops or conferences

You can then easily reply to, save, file, and categorize received messages.

The type of electronic mail program you use will usually depend on how you are connected to the Internet. If you are connected to the Internet through a college, school, business, or government agency that is using a local area network (LAN) then you may be using an email program that runs on the network server such as Lotus's CCMail, Microsoft Exchange, or BeyondMail.

If you are connecting to the Internet with an organization with no LAN or from home, then you have more choices of which email software program to use. Home users most often use Eudora and Eudora Pro, shown in Fig. 1.1. Browsers such as Netscape Navigator and Microsoft Internet Explorer have email programs built in, eliminating the need for additional email software. Still, many Net users prefer the features and expanded capabilities of programs such as the highly rated and very popular Eudora Pro.

Notice the pop-up menus: File, Edit, Mailbox, Message, Transfer, Special, Window, and FaxMenu (available only if fax software is installed) for performing email operations. The toolbar below the pop-up menus provides easy access to the frequently used email operations: deleting a message, checking your In Box messages, accessing messages to be sent in the Out Box, checking for new messages, creating messages, replying to or forwarding messages, checking the spelling of a new message, accessing your address book, or printing a message.

Telnet

Telnet is one of the oldest Internet tools that allows users to log onto another computer and run resident programs. Although Telnet is not as visually interesting as the World Wide Web, it is essential to Internet travel. Telnet is a text-based environment requiring commands to navigate. Some Telnet access sites automatically link you to Web pages. Many Telnet sites, such as libraries, allow anyone to login without

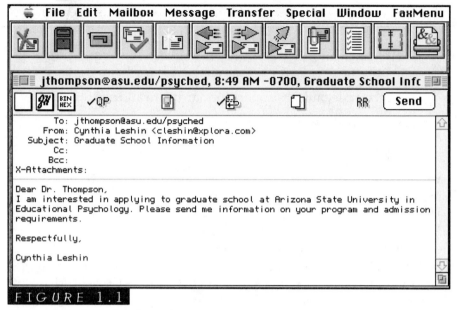

FIGURE 1.1

Electronic mail window for Eudora Pro (© 1997 QUALCOMM Incorporated. All rights reserved. Eudora Pro™ is a trademark of QUALCOMM Incorporated.)

having a special account. Others require users to have a valid account before accessing many of the resident programs.

There are things you cannot do on the Web that Telnet can do. For example, when you Telnet to a remote computer, frequently a mainframe supercomputer, you are working on another machine and are using that machine's speed and power. College students and business travelers dial a local Internet service provider and then Telnet to their college or business accounts to get their email. Telnet saves them the cost of a long-distance phone call.

Telnet also provides direct access to Internet services not always available from your Internet provider. Many of these services are exciting and interesting (see Fig. 1.2). Some open doors to alternative learning environments.

Some of the Internet services available using Telnet include

- databases (such as earthquake, weather, special collections)

- libraries (public, academic, medical, legal, and more)

- Free-Nets (noncommercial, community-based networks)

- interactive chats

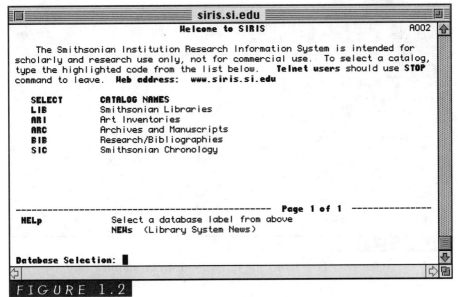

The Smithsonian Telnet site at **telnet://siris.si.edu**

- MOOs, MUDs

- bulletin boards

File Transfer Protocol (FTP)

FTP is a special method used to transfer files between two Internet sites. Files or data can be sent to another site—uploading a file—or can be retrieved from a remote site—downloading a file. Many servers that make files available to Internet users are known as *anonymous* FTP sites. Any Internet user can log onto these sites and retrieve files. Before Web browsers, users would connect to an FTP site and login using *anonymous* as their username, and their email address as their password. When using a Web browser such as Netscape or Explorer, this login procedure is taken care of by the browser software.

FTP resources contain computer software, databases, updates to most retail software, electronic texts, technical reports, journals, magazines, news summaries, books, images, and sound. One of the most widely used FTP services is to travel to FTP servers to download the most current versions of software such as Netscape, Explorer, Eudora, utility programs, or applications for experiencing multimedia environments on the Web. Using a browser makes file retrieval easy. FTP surfers just enter the URL for the FTP site or the Web site that has a link to the FTP server and follow the links (see Fig. 1.3).

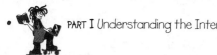

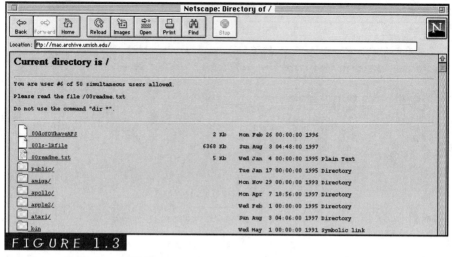

Gutenberg FTP Internet site at **ftp://mac.archive.umich.edu/**

Files that are sent using FTP are usually compressed to facilitate faster transfer over the Internet.

Most PC compression and decompression is done with a package called PKZIP. Macintosh compressed file extensions include

.hqx (BinHex or a textual representation of binary files)
.sit (files compressed using Stuffit)
.cpt (files compressed using Compact Pro)

One of the most commonly used decompression programs for Macintosh is Stuffit Expander. There are many Internet sites where you can find a copy of Stuffit Expander and download it to your computer by double-clicking on the Web link. After you obtain a copy of Stuffit Expander, place a copy on your desktop. When you receive files that need to be decompressed, drop them onto the Stuffit icon. Visit the following Web sites for free compression programs.

TUCOWS (WINDOWS ONLY) **http://www.tucows.com**

JUMBO **http://www.jumbo.com**

SHAREWARE **http://www.shareware.com**

NOTE Some files will be self-extracting which means that after they have been downloaded to your desktop, they can be opened by just double-clicking on their program icon.

World Wide Web

The World Wide Web (WWW or Web) is a collection of standards and protocols used to access information available on the Internet. This information is in the form of documents linked together in what is called a *hypermedia system*. Hypermedia is combined-use multimedia (text, images, video, and sound) in a Web presentation page.

Using the World Wide Web requires a "browser" to view Web documents and navigate through the intricate link structure. Today, the two premiere Web browsers are Netscape Navigator (shown in Fig. 1.4) and Microsoft Internet Explorer (Fig. 1.5). Both of these browsers combine a point-and-click interface design with an "open" architecture that is capable of integrating other Internet tools such as electronic mail, FTP, Gopher, and Usenet newsgroups. This architecture makes it relatively easy to incorporate images, video, and sound into text documents.

Tool Kit of Internet Resources

Although "being on the Internet" means that a user has access to email, Telnet, FTP, and the World Wide Web, there are many tools that Internet users have available to them to access these and other Internet resources. To better understand these tools and their uses, it is helpful to think of the Internet as a medium for

- information access,
- information sharing, and
- communication.

Information Access and Sharing Tools

Electronic tools that are actually software applications to help Internet users access and share information include:

- electronic mail (email)
- listserv mailing lists
- Usenet newsgroups
- Telnet

FIGURE 1.4

*Netscape Navigator browser showing a Home Page **http://www.prenhall.com/leshin** (Copyright 1996 Netscape Communications Corp. Used with permission. All rights reserved. This electronic file or page may not be reprinted or copied without the express written permission of Netscape.)*

- File Transfer Protocol (FTP)
- FreeNets
- Gopher
- World Wide Web

Communication Tools

Communication tools that make it possible to interact with other Net users include:

ELECTRONIC MAIL—delayed response media

LISTSERV MAILING LISTS—delayed response media

USENET NEWSGROUPS—delayed response media

FIGURE 1.5

Microsoft Internet Explorer showing Microsoft's Home Page
http://www.microsoft.com

INTERNET RELAY CHAT (IRC)—real-time media

MOOS, MUDS, AND MUSE—real-time media

INTERNET PHONES—real-time media

INTERNET VIDEOCONFERENCING—real-time media

Browsers such as Netscape and Explorer are most often used to access these Internet resources. Netscape's third generation browser introduced in January, 1997—Netscape Communicator (version 4.x series)—is a collaborative tool for expanded interaction, group discussions, and the sharing of multimedia data over the Internet. Microsoft has focused its development efforts on totally integrating the Internet into the desktop as its browser becomes a part of Windows and Microsoft software applications.

The Web and the Internet

The Web and the Internet are *not* synonymous. The World Wide Web is a collection of standards and protocols used to access information available on the Internet. The Internet is the network used to transport information.

The Web uses three standards:

- URLs (Uniform Resource Locators)

- HTTP (Hypertext Transfer Protocol)

- HTML (Hypertext Markup Language)

These standards provide a mechanism for WWW servers and clients to locate and display information available through other protocols such as Gopher, FTP, and Telnet.

URLs (Uniform Resource Locators)

URLs are a standard format for identifying locations on the Internet. They also allow an addressing system for other Internet protocols such as access to Gopher menus, FTP file retrieval, and Usenet news-groups. URLs specify three types of information needed to retrieve a document:

- the protocol to be used;

- the server address to which to connect; and

- the path to the information.

The format for a URL is: **protocol//server-name/path**

World Wide Web:	http://home.netscape.com/home/welcome.html
Document from a secure server:	https://netscape.com
Gopher:	gopher://umslvma.umsl.edu/Library
FTP:	ftp://nic.umass.edu
Telnet:	telnet://geophys.washington.edu
Usenet:	news:rec.humor.funny

FIGURE 1.6

Sample URLs

NOTE The URL for newsgroups omits the two slashes. The two slashes designate the beginning of a server name. Since you are using your Internet provider's local news server, you do not need to designate a news server by adding the slashes.

HTTP (Hypertext Transfer Protocol)

HTTP is a protocol used to transfer information within the World Wide Web. Web site URLs begin with the http protocol: **http://** and this Web URL will connect you to Netscape's Home Page: **http://home. netscape.com.**

HTML (Hypertext Markup Language)

HTML is the programming language used to create a Web page. It formats the text of the document, describes its structure, and specifies links to other documents. HTML also includes programming to access and display different media such as images, video, and sound.

Connecting to the Internet

Now that you have a basic understanding of the Internet, you are ready to begin your cyberspace adventure. Before you can travel and explore the information superhighway you will need the following:

 an Internet account

 a username and password (required to log onto your Internet account)

 instructions from your institution on how to log on and log off

There are three ways to obtain these requirements:

NETWORK Network connections are most often found in colleges, schools, businesses, or government agencies and use dedicated lines to provide fast access to all Internet resources. Special hardware such as routers may be required at the local site. If you are at one of these institutions you will only need to apply for an Internet account. Many of these institutions have opportunities for accessing your account from a home computer.

INTERNET SERVICE PROVIDER (ISP) Internet access providers offer SLIP (Serial Line Interface Protocol) or PPP (Point-to-Point

Protocol) connections (SLIP/PPP). This service is referred to as *Dial-Up-Networking* and makes it possible for your PC to dial into their server and communicate with other computers on the Internet. Once you have established a PPP, SLIP, or direct Internet connection, you can use any software that speaks the Internet language called TCP/IP. There are several TCP/IP software applications including Eudora, Netscape Navigator, and Explorer.

Internet services should give you the required TCP/IP software to get you connected to the Internet. Additionally, many will provide Internet applications such as Eudora, Netscape Navigator, or Microsoft Internet Explorer. Prices are usually based on hours of usage, bandwidth, and locality.

COMMERCIAL ONLINE SERVICE PROVIDERS Examples of online services include America Online (AOL), CompuServe, Prodigy, Delphi, and Microsoft Network (MSN). Online services are virtual communities that offer services to their subscribers including electronic mail, discussion forums on topics of interest, real-time chats, business and advertising opportunities, software libraries, stock quotes, online newspapers, and Internet resources (Gopher, FTP, newsgroups).

Finding an Internet Provider

There are several Web sites to help you find an Internet access provider:

http://thelist.com

http://www.clari.net/iap/iapcode.htm

http://www.primus.com/providers

To find the names of providers in your area, click on the link to your area code. You will find descriptive information of providers within your area code and a description of their services.

 NOTE All providers that service your area will be found by the area code listing.

TIPS FOR FINDING A PROVIDER

IF YOUR AREA CODE IS NOT LISTED

There are providers who have nationwide access. Some of the Web sites have information on these service providers.

IF THERE IS NO LOCAL DIAL-IN NUMBER

Look for service providers that are the closest to you or who have an 800 number dial-in access. Many providers are also listed on these Web sites.

CHOOSING A PROVIDER

Contact providers by phone, fax, or electronic mail. If you want to use Netscape or Explorer you will need to get a SLIP or a PPP account.

Ask about the following:

- Type of Internet accounts available.

- Price and hours of access. How much will it cost per month for a SLIP or PPP account? How many hours of Internet access are included? An average price is $20 per month for 150 hours of graphical access.

- Technical support. Does the provider offer technical support? What are the hours (days, nights, weekends, holidays)? Is support free?

- Software. Do they provide the TCP/IP software? Is the software custom configured? Do they provide free copies of an email program such as Eudora and a Web browser such as Explorer? Good Internet providers will supply custom-configured TCP/IP software and the essential Internet navigation and communication software.

CHAPTER II

SURFING THE NET

This chapter is a guided tour of the tools and resources you will use to surf the Net. In this tour, you will

- learn how to navigate the Internet using a browser.
- travel on a guided Net tour.
- surf to cool Web sites.
- save your favorite Internet sites (URLs).
- learn how to export and import your favorite URLs.
- learn how to use and navigate Web page frames.
- learn about the Web's multimedia-oriented environment.
- learn how to use and install helper applications and plug-ins.
- visit cool multimedia Web sites.

INTERNET NAVIGATION USING BROWSERS

A *browser* is a software program for viewing a Web document. In 1995 the browser war began between Netscape Communications Corporation (NCC) and Microsoft. At this time approximately 30 browsers had been developed for exploring the World Wide Web and the Internet. In 1996 the browser war between Microsoft and Netscape escalated with the release of Microsoft Internet Explorer, featuring browser capabilities to match those of Netscape Navigator. When 1996 drew to a close there were only two premier browsers—Netscape Navigator and Microsoft Internet Explorer—others collapsed under the weight of these two popular and powerful Net tools. In 1997 Netscape and Microsoft headed in different directions as the fourth generation browser was introduced. Netscape Communications Corporation (NCC) focused on providing network services for business and Microsoft integrated the Internet into the desktop.

NCC introduced the Netscape Communicator Suite featuring

- *Navigator 4.0*—for Internet browsing

- *Messenger*—an email application for local area networks

- *Collabra*—a tool for public and private discussions

- *Composer*—a more advanced HTML editing tool

- *Conference*—a collaboration tool for sharing multimedia files

- *CoolTalk*—Internet telephone for telephone conferencing

Higher-end packages also include a group calendar and administration tools.

Microsoft's Explorer 4.0 integrates Internet Explorer into the Windows operating system. This integration between the desktop and browser allows users to edit and work with documents from within the browser as they surf the Net. The software application and the browser are viewed simultaneously on the computer screen.

The one common thread between these two browsers is the increased ease of playing and viewing multimedia files on Web pages. For example, Netscape 4.0 has an automated plug-in installer. Microsoft's *ActiveX* supports many audio and video formats. Both browsers also feature more personal customization options such as the ability to create toolbar buttons and to hide or make visible icons and buttons.

IMPORTANT The browser war to determine who will control Net surfers' desktop and hard disk space makes one thing certain—new browser versions will be introduced every few months. What is important to remember is that their navigational functions will remain basically unchanged. Tools for communication and interaction such as email and Usenet news features may change slightly and take on a new appearance. New features may be added. HOWEVER, if you have a basic understanding of the browser it will be easy to transfer this knowledge and learn the new functions and enhancements. This section is designed to give you the basic information to use a browser—no matter which version. The basics for Netscape Navigator and Microsoft will be presented.

Browser Basics

When a browser is opened you will see a Web page or *window* that may contain text, images, movies, and sound. Each multimedia resource on a page has associated locational information to link you to the resource.

This locational information is called the URL. For example, the URL or address used to connect to the Home Page for the White House is **http://www1.whitehouse.gov/WH/Welcome.html** (see Fig. 2.1).

FIGURE 2.1

*Home Page for the White House using Netscape Navigator **http://www1.whitehouse.gov/WH/Welcome.html***

Netscape and Explorer include the following features to assist you with your Internet travels:

WINDOW TITLE BAR shows the name of the current document. In Fig. 2.1 note the title bar with the name *Welcome to the White House.*

PAGE DISPLAY shows the content of the Web window. A page includes text and links to images, video, and sound files. Links include highlighted words (colored and/or underlined) or icons. Click on a highlighted word or icon to bring another page of related information into view. In Fig. 2.1 the White House page has links to the president and vice president and commonly requested federal services.

ADDRESS LOCATION field shows the URL address of the current document. In Fig. 2.1 you see the address or URL for the Home Page for the White House.
http://www1.whitehouse.gov/WH/Welcome.html

STATUS BAR indicates the status of the document or file you are trying to transfer. The status bar displays three types of information from left to right: the Web address of the document; the progress indicator (displays downloading progress); and the progress bar (displays the completed percentage of your document layout as your page downloads).

TOOLBAR buttons activate browser features and navigational aids.

POP-UP menus also activate browser features and navigational aids. Many of these features perform the same functions as the toolbar buttons.

Navigating the Net Using Toolbar Buttons

A browser's toolbar has buttons (Figs. 2.2 and 2.3) that perform commands that you will use most frequently when surfing the Internet. You are probably already familiar with toolbar buttons from other software application programs, such as a word processing application.

FIGURE 2.2

Netscape Navigator (version 4.0) toolbar buttons (Copyright 1996 Netscape Communications Corp. Used with permission. All rights reserved. This electronic file or page may not be reprinted or copied without the express written permission of Netscape.)

FIGURE 2.3

Microsoft Internet Explorer (version 3.0) toolbar buttons (Screen shot reprinted by permission from Microsoft Corporation.)

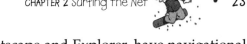

Notice that both browsers, Netscape and Explorer, have navigational buttons for

- taking you to a previous Web page—**Back** button.
- moving forward to the next page in your history list—**Forward** button.
- taking you back to the first opening page—**Home** button.
- finding information and newsgroups—**Search** button.
- saving your favorite URLs—**Bookmarks** button (Netscape); **Favorites** button.
- printing the currently displayed page—**Print** button.
- stopping the transfer of a Web document or file—**Stop** button.

Other tools include a button for

- reloading the same page that you were viewing—**Reload** button (Netscape) and **Refresh** button (Explorer). This tool is useful if you have used the **Stop** button and would like to view the entire document or page.
- using larger or smaller fonts on the Web page you are viewing—**Font** button (Explorer only).
- accessing the browser's email program—**Mail** button (Explorer only).

Netscape and Explorer share features for assisting the Internet traveler. Each of these browsers also has what their developers believe are other important and frequently used Internet commands that have been made into toolbar buttons. When you have used one browser it is very easy to transfer your knowledge of Internet navigation to other browsers.

Pop-Up Menus

Pop-Up Menus (see Fig. 2.4) appear when you point to something within your browser or page and click on it. For example, click on the **Help** menu and the following pop-up menu appears.

This menu gives options for finding help on Internet Explorer as well as other Microsoft services designed for the Internet.

Clicking on some objects, such as an image on a page (Fig. 2.5), presents a pop-up menu that lists things you can do to whatever you clicked, such as saving the image to your hard drive.

 NOTE If you are using a PC, your mouse will have two buttons. Use the right button to click on an image or menu.

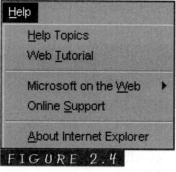

Help pop-up menu for Explorer

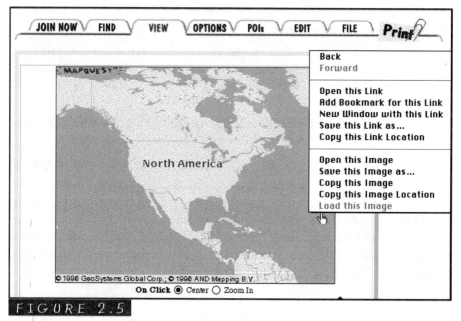

Clicking on MapQuest's map provides this pop-up menu for image options

Directory Buttons

Other toolbar buttons within browsers offer features to help you find information and resources on the Internet. For example, Netscape's **Places** buttons (version 4.0), as shown in Fig. 2.6, provide links to new Web sites (**What's New?**), interesting Web sites (**What's Cool?**), business and after-hour Web sites (**Destinations**), tools for helping you find people on the Net (**People**), and information on how to upgrade your browser or find plug-ins and viewers (**Software**).

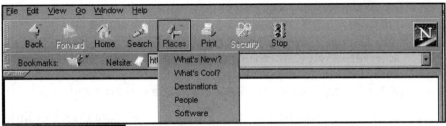

FIGURE 2.6

Netscape's buttons equip Net surfers with additional features (Copyright 1996 Netscape Communications Corp. Used with permission. All rights reserved. This electronic file or page may not be reprinted or copied without the express written permission of Netscape.)

LEARNING ADVENTURE USING BROWSERS TO SURF THE NET

In this section, you will practice using Netscape and/or Explorer for

- navigating the Internet.

- organizing and saving your favorite URLs.

- exploring the Internet.

GUIDED TOUR 1

Surfing the Net

In this guided tour you will use Netscape Navigator or Explorer to connect to World Wide Web sites and Home Pages; use pull-down menus and navigational toolbar buttons to navigate World Wide Web sites; and save bookmarks of your favorite pages.

1. *Log onto your Internet account.* When you have connected, open the Netscape or Explorer browser by double-clicking on the application icon.

Netscape Navigator Icon (Copyright 1996 Netscape Communications Corp. Used with permission. All rights reserved. This electronic file or page may not be reprinted or copied without the express written permission of Netscape.)

Microsoft Explorer Icon

You will be taken to a Home Page. Notice the Location/Address URLs in Fig. 2.1. This Home Page may belong to Netscape Communications Corporation (**http://home.netscape.com**) or Microsoft (**http://www.microsoft.com**), or it may have been designed by your college or university. Look at the top of the Home Page in the Title Bar to see whose Home Page you are visiting.

Notice the highlighted text on Web pages containing built-in URL information for linking to that information. You can also type in new URL text to link a page.

2. *Begin exploring.* Use your browser toolbar buttons and pull-down menus. Depending on which version of Netscape you are using, either click on the **What's New** button or the **Places** button to find **What's New** and **What's Cool.** You will see a list of highlighted underlined links to Web sites. Click on a link and EXPLORE. HAVE FUN! If you are using Explorer, investigate the Home Page that you are viewing or click the pop-up menu **Go** and select **Best of the Web.**

3. *Save your favorite pages.* When you find a page that you may want to visit at a later time, click on the pull-down menu, **Bookmarks,** or the **Bookmarks** button (in Netscape 4.0). Next, click on the menu item **Add Bookmark;** in Explorer select the **Favorites** menu.

Click on the **Bookmarks Favorites** pull-down menu or button again. Notice the name of the page you marked listed below the **View Bookmarks** menu item. To view this page again, select the **Bookmarks** pull-down menu and click on the name of the page you saved. Later you will learn how to organize your bookmarks.

4. *Explore* Home Pages and cool Web sites.

After you have linked to several pages, click on the **Go** pull-down menu. Notice the listing of the places you have most recently visited. If you want to revisit any of the pages you have already viewed, click on the name of the Web site.

Netscape and Explorer create a history list of the Web sites you have visited (select the **Go** menu). The history list in Netscape is available for your current working session only. Exit Netscape and the history list is gone. Explorer also creates a History list or folder that keeps track of your Internet visits for a user-definable number of days. To view your history list, select the **View** menu then the **Navigation** tab or, for a shorter list, select the Go menu. Use these history lists to revisit sites.

GUIDED TOUR 2

Surfing to Cool Web Sites

In this guided tour you will enter in URL addresses to link to World Wide Web (WWW) sites, but before you begin, remember:

- Do not capitalize the protocol string. For example, the HTTP protocol should be **http://** not **HTTP://**. Some browsers such as Netscape correct these errors; others do not.

- URLs are case sensitive, be sure to copy the address capitalization exactly.

- Don't place any spaces within an address.

- If you have trouble connecting to a Web site, check your URL to be sure you have typed the address correctly. Check to be sure you placed the slash marks in the right direction—forward slash (/), not backward slash (\).

- Netscape accepts abbreviated Net addresses, without the **http://www.** prefix. If you type a single word as your URL, Netscape adds the prefix **http://www.** and the suffix **.com**. For example, to connect to Netscape's Home Page, type **Netscape.**

  With Explorer you do not need to type **http://**. You will need to type the rest of the URL.

There are three options in Netscape for entering a URL:

- the **Netsite** text field (see Fig. 2.1);
- the **File** menu—**Open Location;** or
- the **Open** toolbar button (only in Netscape 2.x or 3.x series).

If you are using Explorer, you have two options:

- From the menu bar choose the **File** pop-up menu, then click on **Open.**
- Highlight the URL in the **Address** text field (see Fig. 1.5) and type your URL over the highlighted address.

Select one of the above options. It will take you to the window where you can enter your choice of URL text.

 NOTE If you type a URL and your browser cannot find the site, this probably means that the address was typed incorrectly. Refer to the previous page for URL tips.

Some of the best and coolest places on the Net are listed below. Practice using your browser and saving your favorite Web sites by entering the following URLs.

AWESOME LIST: http://www.clark.net/pub/journalism/awesome.html

CNET'S BEST OF THE WEB: http://www.cnet.com/Content/Reviews/Bestofweb

EXCITE REVIEWS: http://www.excite.com/Reviews

LYCOS TOP 5% SITES: http://point.lycos.com

NETGUIDE LIVE'S BEST OF THE WEB: http://www.netguide.com

PLACES TO SEE WINNERS PAGE: http://www.astep.com/award

THE RAIL: http://www.therail.com/cgi-bin/grand

WORLD WIDE WEB TOUR: http://www.derossi.com/tour/tour.tg

YAHOO INTERNET LIFE: http://www.zdnet.com/yil

GUIDED TOUR 3

Saving Your Favorite Web Sites

In this guided tour you will use Netscape Navigator or Explorer to organize, modify, save, and move bookmark files. If you are using Explorer, begin on page 34.

Netscape Navigator Bookmarks

Before you can organize and work with bookmark files, you must access Netscape's **Bookmark** window (Fig. 2.7). Go to the **Window** pull-down menu and select **Bookmarks** or use the Bookmark toolbar button.

 NOTE If you are using Netscape 4.0 you can also access your bookmarks for adding and editing from the toolbar or taskbar.

1. *Organizing your bookmarks.* Before you begin saving bookmarks, it is helpful to consider how to *organize* saved bookmarks. Begin by thinking of categories that your bookmarks might be filed under such as Software, Business, Education, Entertainment, Research, and so forth. For each category make a folder. These are the steps for making your bookmark folders.

Window	FaxMenu
Netscape Mail	
Netscape News	
Address Book	
Bookmarks	⌘B
History	
Macromedia - Shockwave Gallery	

FIGURE 2.7

*Netscape's Window pop-up menu for working with **Bookmarks** (Copyright 1996 Netscape Communications Corp. Used with permission. All rights reserved. This electronic file or page may not be reprinted or copied without the express written permission of Netscape.)*

a. Go to the **Window** menu and select **Bookmarks.**

Notice the Web sites saved in the Bookmarks folders in Fig. 2.8. This Bookmarks window gives you three new menus for working with your bookmarks: **File, Edit,** and **Item.**

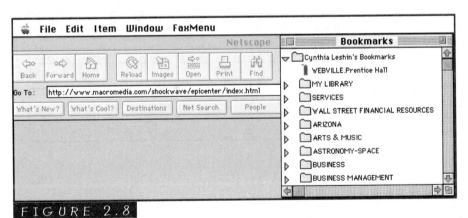

*Netscape's **Bookmarks** window (Copyright 1996 Netscape Communications Corp. Used with permission. All rights reserved. This electronic file or page may not be reprinted or copied without the express written permission of Netscape.)*

b. Create a new folder for a bookmark category by selecting the **Item** menu (Fig. 2.9).

c. Select **Insert Folder** (see Fig. 2.9).

Item	Window	FaxMenu

Edit Bookmark...   ⌘I
Go to Bookmark

Sort Bookmarks

Insert Bookmark...
Insert Folder...
Insert Separator

Make Alias

Set to New Bookmarks Folder
Set to Bookmark Menu Folder

FIGURE 2.9

*Opened **Item** menu from within the Bookmarks window (Copyright 1996 Netscape Communications Corp. Used with permission. All rights reserved. This electronic file or page may not be reprinted or copied without the express written permission of Netscape.)*

New Folder

Name: MUSIC

Location (URL):

Description:

Last Visited:

Added on: Fri Jan 10 14:16:42 1997

There are no aliases to this bookmark

[Cancel]   [OK]

FIGURE 2.10

Insert Folder window (Copyright 1996 Netscape Communications Corp. Used with permission. All rights reserved. This electronic file or page may not be reprinted or copied without the express written permission of Netscape.)

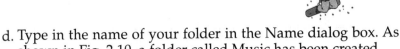

d. Type in the name of your folder in the Name dialog box. As shown in Fig. 2.10, a folder called Music has been created.

e. Enter in a description of the bookmark folder (optional).

f. Click OK.

2. *Add bookmarks to a folder.* Netscape provides an option for identifying the folder into which you would like to drop your bookmarks.

   a. Select the folder you would like to add your new bookmarks to by clicking on the name of the folder once. The folder should now be highlighted.

   b. Go to the **Item** menu and select **Set to New Bookmarks Folder** shown near the bottom of Fig. 2.9.

   c. Go back to the Bookmarks window and notice how this newly identified folder has been marked with a colored bookmark identifier. All bookmarks that you add will be placed in this folder until you identify a new folder.

3. *Modify the name of your bookmark.* Bookmark properties contain the name of the Web site and the URL. You may want to change the name of the bookmark to indicate more clearly the information available at this site. For example, the bookmark name *STCil/HST Public Information* has very little meaning. Changing its name to *Hubble Space Telescope Public Information* is more helpful when later selecting from many bookmarks.

   a. To change the name of a bookmark, select the bookmark by clicking on it once.

   b. Go to the **Item** menu from within the Bookmarks window.

   c. Select **Properties.** (For the Macintosh, select **Edit.**)

   d. Enter in the new name for your bookmark by either deleting the text shown in Fig. 2.11, or begin typing the new name when the highlighted text is visible.

   e. Notice the URL for the bookmark; you can also enter a new description for the URL.

4. *Make copies of your bookmarks.* Occasionally you will want to save a bookmark in several folders. There are two ways to do this:

   a. Select the bookmark that you would like to copy. Go to the **Edit** menu from within the Bookmark window and select **Copy.** Select the folder where you would like to place the copy of the bookmark. Go to the **Edit** menu and select **Paste.**

Hubble Public Pictures

Name:	Hubble Space Telescope Public Information
Location (URL):	http://www.stsci.edu/pubinfo/Pictures.html
Description:	

Last Visited: Tue Jul 23 07:06:52 1996

Added on: Sat Feb 10 14:34:34 1996

There are no aliases to this bookmark

Cancel   OK

FIGURE 2.11

Properties window from *Item* options *(Copyright 1996 Netscape Communications Corp. Used with permission. All rights reserved. This electronic file or page may not be reprinted or copied without the express written permission of Netscape.)*

b. Make a copy of your bookmark for another category folder by selecting **Make Alias** from the **Item** menu. When the alias of your bookmark has been created, move the alias bookmark to the new folder (see "Note").

NOTE Bookmarks can be moved from one location to another by dragging an existing bookmark to a new folder.

5. *Delete a bookmark.* To remove a bookmark:

a. Select the bookmark to be deleted by clicking on it once, then pressing the *delete* key; or

b. Go to the **Edit** menu from within the Bookmarks window and choose either **Cut** or **Delete.**

6. *Export and save bookmarks.* Netscape provides options for making copies of your bookmarks either to save as a backup on your hard drive, to share with others, or to use on another computer. Follow these steps for exporting or saving your bookmarks to a floppy disk.

a. Open the **Bookmarks** window.

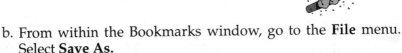

b. From within the Bookmarks window, go to the **File** menu. Select **Save As.**

c. Designate where you would like to save the bookmark file—on your hard drive or to a floppy disk—in the **Save in** box (Fig. 2.12).

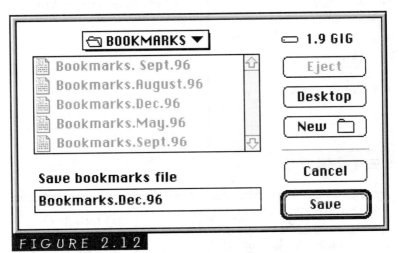

FIGURE 2.12

Netscape Bookmarks window for saving bookmark files (Copyright 1996 Netscape Communications Corp. Used with permission. All rights reserved. This electronic file or page may not be reprinted or copied without the express written permission of Netscape.)

d. Enter a name for your bookmark file in the **File name** dialog box.

e. Click **Save.**

7. *Import Bookmarks.* Bookmarks can be imported into Netscape from a previous Netscape session saved on a floppy disk.

a. Insert the floppy disk with the bookmark file into your computer.

b. Open the **Bookmarks** window.

c. From within the Bookmarks window, go to the **File** menu and select **Import** (Fig. 2.13).

d. Designate a location for the bookmark file: The **Look in** window displays a floppy disk or you can click on the scroll arrow to bring the hard drive into view.

e. Click on **Open,** shown in Fig. 2.14. The bookmarks will now be imported into your Netscape bookmark list.

```
File   Edit   Item   Window   F
New Web Browser          ⌘N
New Mail Message         ⌘M
Open Bookmark File...    ⌘O
Import Bookmarks...
What's New?

Close                    ⌘W
Save As...

Page Setup...
Print...                 ⌘P

Quit                     ⌘Q
```

FIGURE 2.13

*Netscape **File** menu from within Bookmarks (Copyright 1996 Netscape Communications Corp. Used with permission. All rights reserved. This electronic file or page may not be reprinted or copied without the express written permission of Netscape.)*

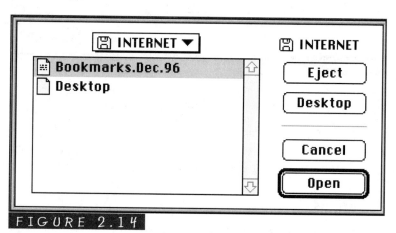

FIGURE 2.14

***Import** window allows a bookmark from a floppy disk to be imported into your Netscape application (Copyright 1996 Netscape Communications Corp. Used with permission. All rights reserved. This electronic file or page may not be reprinted or copied without the express written permission of Netscape.)*

Internet Explorer Bookmarks

1. *Organize your bookmarks.* Before you begin saving bookmarks, it is helpful to consider how to organize saved bookmarks. Begin by thinking of categories that your bookmarks might be filed under such as Software, Business, Education, Entertainment, Research, and so forth. For each category make a folder. These are the steps for making your bookmark folders.

a. Go to the **Favorites** menu and select **Organize Favorites** (Fig. 2.15).

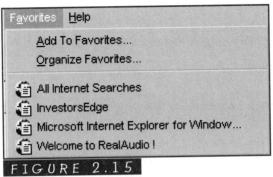

FIGURE 2.15

Explorer's menu for adding, organizing, and viewing favorite URLs

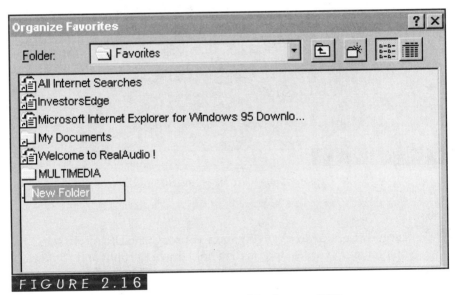

FIGURE 2.16

Explorer creates a New Folder for your URLs

b. Click on the **Folder** icon. A new folder will be created (see Fig. 2.16). Type a name for the folder in the highlighted folder box.

c. To save a URL, click on the **Favorites** menu and select **Add to Favorites.**

d. Use this same **Organize Favorites** option for organizing, renaming, or deleting your favorite URLs (see Fig. 2.17).

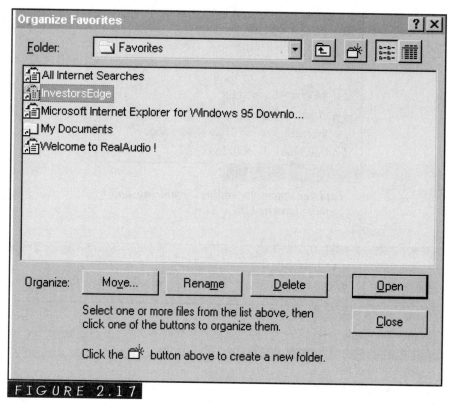

FIGURE 2.17

Explorer dialog box for organizing URLs

 NOTE Another option to use to organize your favorite URLs is to select the Organize Favorites option, then hold down the Shift and Alt keys. The standard Explorer window appears (see Fig. 2.18) offering easier drag-and-drop reorganization.

GUIDED TOUR 4

Navigating With Frames

In this guided tour you will visit Web sites with *frames* and learn how to navigate and work with frames. Frames were introduced as a new feature of Netscape Navigator 2.0. Frames make it possible to create multiple windows on a browser page. Figure 2.19 is an example of a Web page divided into several windows called *frames*.

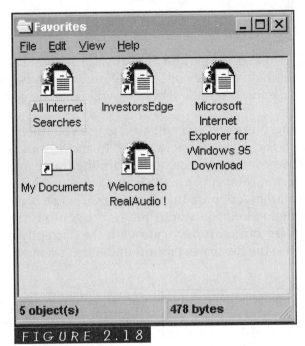

FIGURE 2.18

Another option for organizing favorite URLs in Explorer

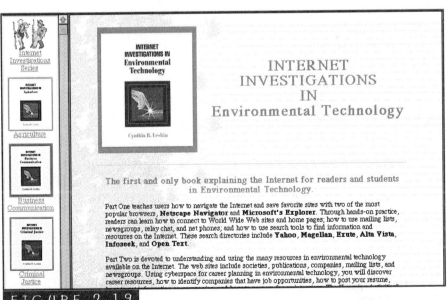

FIGURE 2.19

A Prentice Hall Web site using frames to organize information (Source: Internet Investigations in Environmental Technology by Leshin, copyright 1997. Reprinted by permission of Prentice Hall, Inc., Upper Saddle River, NJ.)

Frames are used to organize and display information. The icons in the left margin are the categories of information that can be linked. Click on an icon and information on that book will be displayed in the right foremost frame.

If you are using Netscape you will need to use your mouse to navigate within frames and to save bookmarks. To move forward and back within frames, position your cursor within the frame and hold down the mouse button (Macintosh users); Windows users hold down the right mouse button. A pop-up menu appears. Choose **Back** or **Forward.** If you are using Explorer, only one frame is active at a time. Click on the **Back** or **Forward** button to navigate with the currently active frame. You can also use the history list found under the **Go** menu.

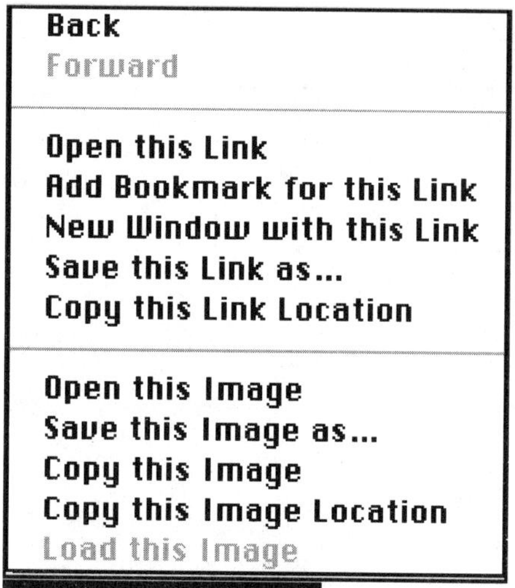

Back
Forward
Open this Link
Add Bookmark for this Link
New Window with this Link
Save this Link as...
Copy this Link Location
Open this Image
Save this Image as...
Copy this Image
Copy this Image Location
Load this Image

FIGURE 2.20

The pop-up menu from within Netscape displaying frame navigation (Copyright 1996 Netscape Communications Corp. Used with permission. All rights reserved. This electronic file or page may not be reprinted or copied without the express written permission of Netscape.)

To bookmark a frame in Netscape, place your cursor over the link to the frame and hold down the mouse button. The pop-up as seen in Fig. 2.20 appears. Select **Add Bookmark for this Link.** In Explorer the active frame will be marked as a Favorite.

To print a frame, click the desired frame and select **Print Frame** from the **File** menu.

Now that you know about frames, let's visit several Web sites where you can interact with Web pages that have multiple panes:

CNN INTERACTIVE: **http://www.cnn.com**

DISCOVERY CHANNEL: **http://www.discovery.com**

NETSCAPE'S LINKS TO COMPANY WEB SITES USING FRAMES
http://home.netscape.com/comprod/products/navigator/
version_2.0/frames/frame_users.html

WIRED: http://www.wired.com

1. Explore the links in the frame table of contents. If you are using Netscape, use your mouse to move forward and back within frames by positioning your cursor within the frame and holding down the mouse button (Macintosh users); Windows users hold down the right mouse button. A pop-up menu appears. Choose **Back in Frame** or **Forward in Frame.**

   If you are using Explorer, click on the **Back** or **Forward** button to navigate with the currently active frame or the history list under the **Go** menu.

2. Save bookmarks of your favorite Web documents by placing your cursor over the link to the frame and holding down the mouse button. A different pop-up menu appears. Select **Add Bookmark for this Link.**

3. Print a frame that you would like to save by clicking the desired frame and selecting **Print Frame** from the **File** menu.

4. Point at a border between a frame. If your pointer changes to two parallel lines with two arrows you can drag the frame border or reposition it.

GUIDED TOUR 5

Customizing Your Browser

Navigator and Explorer allow you to personalize your Net surfing preferences. If using Netscape, select the **Options** menu, then **General Preferences** (Netscape 4.0 select **Edit** menu, **Preferences, General Preferences**). Notice that you can enter your favorite starting Home Page (Fig. 2.21).

For Explorer, select the **View** menu, then the **Options** tab. Explorer also allows you to customize your toolbar by making your favorite Web sites into toolbar buttons. By default, the Links toolbar contains buttons that reconnect to Microsoft—services, product updates, Web tutorial, and favorite links (Fig. 2.22).

To change the **Links** toolbar sites:

1. Select the **View** menu, then **Options** (see Fig. 2.23A), then click on the **Navigation** tab.

Netscape's **General Preferences** for customizing Net travel (Copyright 1996 Netscape Communications Corp. Used with permission. All rights reserved. This electronic file or page may not be reprinted or copied without the express written permission of Netscape.)

Explorer toolbar buttons showing the default Quick Links to Microsoft services (Copyright 1996 Netscape Communications Corp. Used with permission. All rights reserved. This electronic file or page may not be reprinted or copied without the express written permission of Netscape.)

2. Select the **Page** box. The default is Start Page. You can then select a Quick Link button that you want to change; they are numbered from 1–5 (see Fig. 2.23B).

3. In the **Page** box, type the name for the button (see Fig. 2.24).

4. In the **Address** box, type the URL for the site that you want to become a button.

5. Click the **Use Current** button.

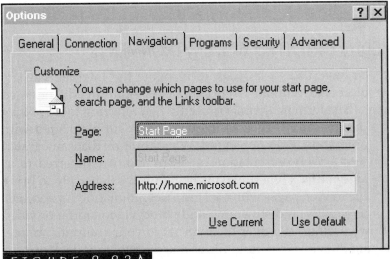

FIGURE 2.23A

Explorer Navigation tab dialog box for working with toolbar buttons

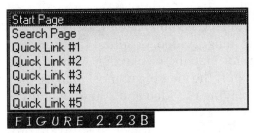

FIGURE 2.23B

*Options for selecting and changing the Quick
Link button*

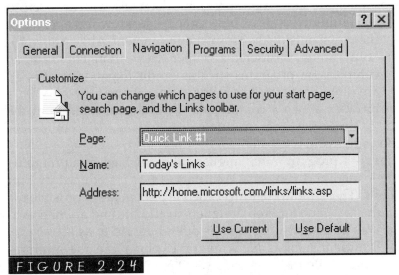

FIGURE 2.24

Dialog box for changing toolbar buttons

MULTIMEDIA-ORIENTED WEB ENVIRONMENTS

Now that you have used a browser to navigate the Internet, you are ready to explore the ultimate Web experience—multimedia-oriented environments. The term *multimedia* is used when referring to more than one medium—such as the use of text supplemented with animation, video, or sound. When multimedia is integrated into a Web presentation or document, it is referred to as *hypermedia*. Hypermedia is being used extensively to bring life to Web pages with cool graphics, animation, live objects, 3D video, interactivity, and streaming audio and video (audio or video files that flow continuously over the Internet to your computer, immediately playing the video or sound file as it arrives to your desktop).

Before You Begin . . .

Before you can experience multimedia Web environments you will need some basic information about *plug-ins* and *helper* or *viewer applica-* *tions*. When a graphic image, video, or sound file is created it requires a program for viewing or playing. Although the first browsers did support the viewing of most images, they did not support the playing of video and sound. Net users had to obtain copies of external viewer applications to experience Web audio and video. These external viewer software programs are written by companies other than Netscape or Microsoft and are necessary to experience cool multimedia effects.

Helper applications are stand-alone programs that work with browsers to play or display multimedia files. These same helpers can also operate on their own outside the browser environment. Almost any program can be considered a Helper Application. For example, compression programs such as Stuffit Expander or PKZIP are often configured as helper applications to work with a browser. When a compressed file is downloaded from the Internet the compression program automatically starts to decompress or open it upon successful completion of the download.

In 1995 Java—a programming language that enabled miniprograms to be downloaded and run on a Web page—was introduced by Sun Microsystems. These miniprograms called *applets* made it possible for the first time for Web designers to add life and animation to Web pages, creating what is often referred to as *live objects*. Browsers such as Netscape or Explorer ran the miniprogram while the Web page was being displayed. To experience Java visit the following Web sites.

GAMELAN: http://www.gamelan.com

JAVA CENTER: http://www.java.co.uk

Shortly after Java was introduced, *plug-in* applications were developed and became the hottest new Web technology for adding special effects to Web pages. Plug-ins are software programs designed to play a multimedia file from within the browser window or page, running as a system resource for as long as they are needed.

 Microsoft's response to Java was the *ActiveX* development platform. This technology, available in Explorer 3.0 or later, has also opened new doors for moving and animating Web objects, creating live audio, scrolling banners, and interactivity.

Today plug-ins and viewer applications are widely used and required to experience cool graphics, animations, video, and sound on Web pages. Most plug-ins and viewers are free and can be obtained at Web sites with shareware such as

TUCOWS (FOR WINDOWS) http://www.tucows.com

JUMBO http://www.jumbo.com

SHAREWARE http://www.shareware.com

or connect to Netscape's Plug-in page at **http://home.netscape.com/comprod/products/navigator/version_2.0/plugins/index.html.**

Newer versions of Netscape and Explorer have a few plug-ins and viewers already built-in.

How Do Plug-ins and Viewers Work With My Browser?

After you type in a URL requesting a Web page from a server, the components of that page—text, image, video, or sound—begin downloading to your computer. The server where the requested Web document resides sends a message to your browser with the *MIME* (Multipurpose Internet Mail Extension) type of the requested file. If the file is a MIME *text* type, the browser displays the file. If the file contains an image with an extension such as .JPEG, .GIF, JPG, JPE, or XMB, it is a MIME *image* type and the browser displays the image on the Web page using a built-in image viewer. Sound or video MIME types may or may not be able to be played depending on whether your browser has the required plug-in or viewer built in. For example, Netscape 3.0 and later can play sound files ending in .AU, .AIF, and SND.

If the MIME type is none of these, the browser looks for a plug-in or helper to see if it has been configured with your browser to run the file. If no plug-in or helper is found, you will be shown a dialog box such as Fig. 2.25 from Netscape Navigator.

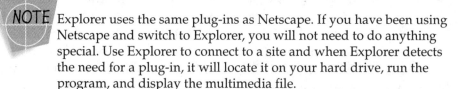

> ⚠ **This page contains information of type "video/vdo" that can only be viewed with the appropriate plug-in. What do you want to do?**
>
> [**Plug-in Info**] [**Cancel**]

FIGURE 2.25

Dialog box from Netscape indicating that the plug-in cannot be found (Copyright 1996 Netscape Communications Corp. Used with permission. All rights reserved. This electronic file or page may not be reprinted or copied without the express written permission of Netscape.)

 NOTE Before a plug-in or helper can play or display a multimedia file it must be installed or configured for your browser. Microsoft Internet Explorer supports many audio and video formats without requiring plug-in installation and configuration.

This message allows two options:

- Link to information on the plug-in you need to view the multimedia file by clicking on **Plug-in Info,** or

- Cancel the downloading of the file by clicking on the **Cancel** button.

 NOTE Explorer uses the same plug-ins as Netscape. If you have been using Netscape and switch to Explorer, you will not need to do anything special. Use Explorer to connect to a site and when Explorer detects the need for a plug-in, it will locate it on your hard drive, run the program, and display the multimedia file.

If you have never used Netscape and downloaded plug-ins, just open Explorer and visit multimedia sites. Explorer's *ActiveX* platform performs many of the same functions as Netscape's plug-ins.

Cool Plug-ins and Helpers for the Net

There are many plug-ins and helpers used by Web developers to permit cool graphics, animation, scrolling banners, and streaming audio and video to be added to Net pages. The best site to visit for the latest and hottest plug-ins is Netscape's site at **http://home.netscape.com/ comprod/products/navigator/version_2.0/plugins/index.html**

Listed below are a few of the more popular and frequently used plug-ins.

ACROBAT READER BY ADOBE SYSTEMS **http://www.adobe.com** Acrobat Reader documents created in word processing, desktop publishing, spreadsheet, graphics, or database files can be saved as Acrobat PDF files and viewed on any kind of computer even if the software and the fonts used to create the application are not present.

APPLE QUICKTIME PLUG-IN **http://www.quickTime.apple.com/dev/ devweb.html** This plug-in lets you experience QuickTime animation, music, audio, video, and virtual reality panoramas and objects on Web pages.

BUBBLEVIEWER **http://www.omniview.com** Bubbleview by Omniview lets you experience a 360-degree environment.

COSMO PLAYER **http://www.sgi.com** Experience 3D worlds on the Web with Silicon Graphics's Cosmo Player.

LIVE3D **http://home.netscape.com/comprod/products/navigator/ live3d/index.html** Live3D lets you experience a rich world of 3D spaces and the ability to interact with text, images, animation, sound, music, and even video on the Web.

MOVIESTAR BY INTELLIGENCE AT LARGE **http://www.ialsoft.com** An alternative plug-in for QuickTime Multimedia, Moviestar enables the viewing of video, sound, background music, animation, and more.

NETSCAPE MEDIA PLAYER **http://home.netscape.com/comprod/ mirror/media/download_mplayer.html** Netscape Media Player brings streaming audio and synchronized multimedia to your desktop.

THE POINTCAST NETWORK **http://www.pointcast.com** Personalize your own news broadcasting system using Pointcast Network. Options include world, national, business and political news as well as weather, sports, investments, lifestyle, or other topics of interest.

REALAUDIO http://www.realaudio.com RealAudio is a real-time streaming audio plug-in that lets you listen to live music, news, live events and much more.

SHOCKWAVE http://www.macromedia.com Shockwave is one of the hottest applications for bringing streamed movies and inter-action to your desktop. Shockwave plays files created in Macro-media Director.

VIVOACTIVE PLAYER http://www.vivo.com A streaming video player, Vivoactive brings video clips to your Web pages.

VR SCOUT http://www.chaco.com Immerse yourself in real-time virtual communities with Chaco Communications's VR Scout.

Installing Plug-ins—Netscape Navigator

You have learned that you need a plug-in or helper application before displaying or playing multimedia files on the Internet. At the time this book went to press it was necessary to download and install many plug-in applications. Future versions of Netscape and Explorer will make the playing of plug-ins easier with automatic installers (Netscape) or the built-in capability to play many audio and video files (*ActiveX* in Explorer).

 NOTE Choose a plug-in for a multimedia file, if it is available, over a helper application. It will take longer for a helper to display or play a file since the helper must first launch, then open the file. However, check to see if a helper has additional features that the plug-in may not.

The following guidelines are for installing a plug-in with Netscape Navigator. Most plug-ins come with installation programs that will place the plug-in in the appropriate folder and set up your browser to use it. If the plug-in does not have an install program, read the README file.

 **IMPORTANT** Read any README files that have been installed with the plug-in application. Many times they contain valuable information to help you with any problems you may encounter with the plug-in and having it work as intended

with your browser or computer system software. Since plug-ins and viewers are free, there is NO TECHNICAL SUPPORT. You will find that the README files may have all the information you need to solve your problems.

STEP 1

After you have found a plug-in that you would like to use with your browser, visit a Web site where you can obtain a copy of a free plug-in. The best site is Netscape's **http://home.netscape.com/comprod/ products/navigator/version_2.0/plugins/index.html.**

STEP 2

Download the plug-in from a Web site.

STEP 3

Run the program and an install or set-up will begin. Follow the instructions and the plug-in will be installed. If the plug-in does not have an install or set-up program, read the instructions that accompany the file.

STEP 4

After the plug-in is installed, click on the multimedia object and the plug-in takes over launching the file.

STEP 5

Restart your computer after you have installed the plug-in.

NOTE Many plug-ins and helpers require the latest system software to play or display the multimedia file. If you are having problems with a plug-in or helper, read the README file. There will probably be information on requirements for running the program.

Netscape Navigator 4.0 has a plug-in install feature built in.

Installing Helper (Viewer) Applications

One important helper application is the program to decompress files sent over the Internet. For the Macintosh, the most popular compression program is Stuffit Expander; for Windows, PKZIP is most commonly used. In this example we will use Netscape Navigator to install a compression utility.

STEP 1

Visit a shareware Web site and find the helper application you are looking for, in this case, either Stuffit or PKZIP.

STEP 2

After the program is downloaded to your hard drive, follow the instructions to install it or use the set-up feature.

STEP 3

Open Netscape and select **General Preferences** from the **Options** menu. Click on the **Helpers** tab. (With Version 4.0, go to the Edit menu, select Preferences, General Preferences, then Helpers.)

 NOTE Although different versions of Netscape may present different dialog boxes for these operations, the procedure is the same for installing helpers.

This tab displays the descriptions and names of helpers and plug-ins for text, image, sound, and video, as well as other applications that you many want to use with Netscape (i.e., a compression program). The files are listed under **Description** (see Fig. 2.26) using a naming standard known as **MIME** (Multipurpose Internet Name Extension).

 NOTE MIME types consist of two parts: the *main type* and the *subtype*. For example, the main type for a NASA image would be *image* and the *subtype* might be *jpeg.* The file name extension indicates the subtype for the file. You will find the main type and subtype for many of the different types of files you might encounter on the Net under the **Description** listing.

STEP 4

From within the Helper listing, look for the application you are trying to install, in this case, *application/x-zip compressed* (for the PC) or *application/x-stuffit* (for the Macintosh) (Fig. 2.27). Click on the application, then on the **Edit** button.

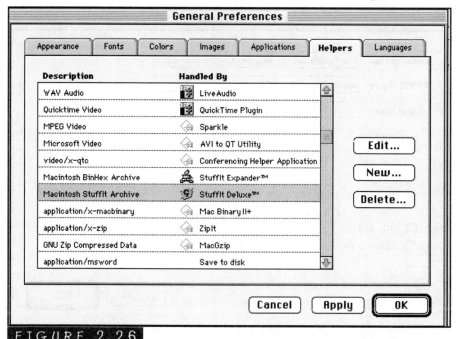

| Appearance | Fonts | Colors | Images | Applications | **Helpers** | Languages |

Description	Handled By
WAV Audio	LiveAudio
Quicktime Video	QuickTime Plugin
MPEG Video	Sparkle
Microsoft Video	AVI to QT Utility
video/x-qtc	Conferencing Helper Application
Macintosh BinHex Archive	StuffIt Expander™
Macintosh StuffIt Archive	StuffIt Deluxe™
application/x-macbinary	Mac Binary II+
application/x-zip	ZipIt
GNU Zip Compressed Data	MacGzip
application/msword	Save to disk

Edit...

New...

Delete...

Cancel   Apply   OK

FIGURE 2.26

The Helpers tab showing viewers and plug-ins for Navigator (Copyright 1996 Netscape Communications Corp. Used with permission. All rights reserved. This electronic file or page may not be reprinted or copied without the express written permission of Netscape.)

HELP . . . Please translate this geek speak

What this means is that when your browser, Netscape, encounters a computer file with the suffix or extension indicated in the **Edit Type Helper** dialog box, it will look for a software program referred to as *helper application* or *viewer* to open it so the file will be made available for you to use, view, or hear. In the above example, you want Netscape to decompress files that are downloaded to your computer from the Internet with a file extension of *sit*, indicating that they need to be decompressed.

🏃 STEP 5

You must now let Netscape know where to find this helper application on your computer hard drive.

Edit Type

Description: Macintosh Stufflt Archive

MIME Type: application/x-stuffit

Suffixes: sit

Handled By

○ Navigator

○ Plug-in:

◉ Application: Stufflt Deluxe™

    File type: SIT! ▼

[Browse...]

○ Save to disk

○ Unknown: Prompt user

[Cancel] [OK]

FIGURE 2.27

*The **Edit Type** dialog box from within **Helpers** (Copyright 1996 Netscape Communications Corp. Used with permission. All rights reserved. This electronic file or page may not be reprinted or copied without the express written permission of Netscape.)*

Click on the **Browse** button. Find the application that you want to use as a helper with Netscape, then click on the **Open** button (see Fig. 2.28). This action indicates to Netscape what file you would like to run from within Netscape whenever a file with the indicated extension is encountered. In this case, if a file from the Internet that needs to be decompressed—indicated by the file extension *.sit*—is encountered by Netscape, the browser will look for the application, open it, and perform the program action.

Installing a Plug-in Without an Install Program or a Helper Not Listed in General Preferences

There will be times when you may want to install a helper that cannot be found under the Helper listing or when a plug-in does not have an install program. Read the plug-in or helper README file. You will find that these documents usually have the information you need, such as the mime type and subtype.

Some general steps include the following:

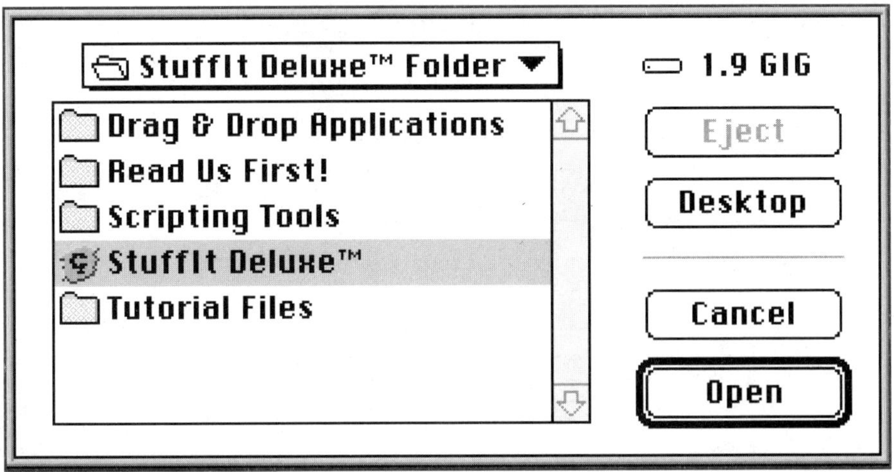

```
┌─────────────────────────────────────────────────────────┐
│  ┌──────────────────────────────┐    ┌──────────┐        │
│  │ 🗁 Stufflt Deluxe™ Folder ▼ │    ⊂═ 1.9 GIG         │
│  └──────────────────────────────┘                         │
│  ┌──────────────────────────────┐┌─┐  ┌──────────────┐   │
│  │ 🗀 Drag & Drop Applications  ││⇧│  │    Eject     │   │
│  │ 🗀 Read Us First!            ││ │  └──────────────┘   │
│  │ 🗀 Scripting Tools           ││ │  ┌──────────────┐   │
│  │ 📀 Stufflt Deluxe™          ││ │  │   Desktop    │   │
│  │ 🗀 Tutorial Files            ││ │  └──────────────┘   │
│  │                              ││ │  ┌──────────────┐   │
│  │                              ││⇩│  │    Cancel    │   │
│  └──────────────────────────────┘└─┘  └──────────────┘   │
│                                       ┌──────────────┐   │
│                                       │     Open     │   │
│                                       └──────────────┘   │
└─────────────────────────────────────────────────────────┘
```

FIGURE 2.28

The dialog box for finding the helper application on the hard drive (Copyright 1996 Netscape Communications Corp. Used with permission. All rights reserved. This electronic file or page may not be reprinted or copied without the express written permission of Netscape.)

🖎 STEP 1

Drag the plug-in into your browser's Plug-In Folder. You may need to use your computer operating system's **Find** feature to locate where this folder is kept on your hard drive.

🖎 STEP 2

Open Netscape and go to the **General Preferences;** select the **Helper** tab.

🖎 STEP 3

Scroll through the list of plug-ins and helpers to see if the program is already there. Netscape may be pre-configured for some plug-ins and helpers even if you do not have them.

🖎 STEP 4

If the program is not there, select the **New** button (in Fig. 2.26). A new dialog box will appear (Fig. 2.29). You will need the data from the README file to enter the information.

The example below illustrates these steps. We will configure Netscape to play the RealAudio helper application for listening to streaming audio.

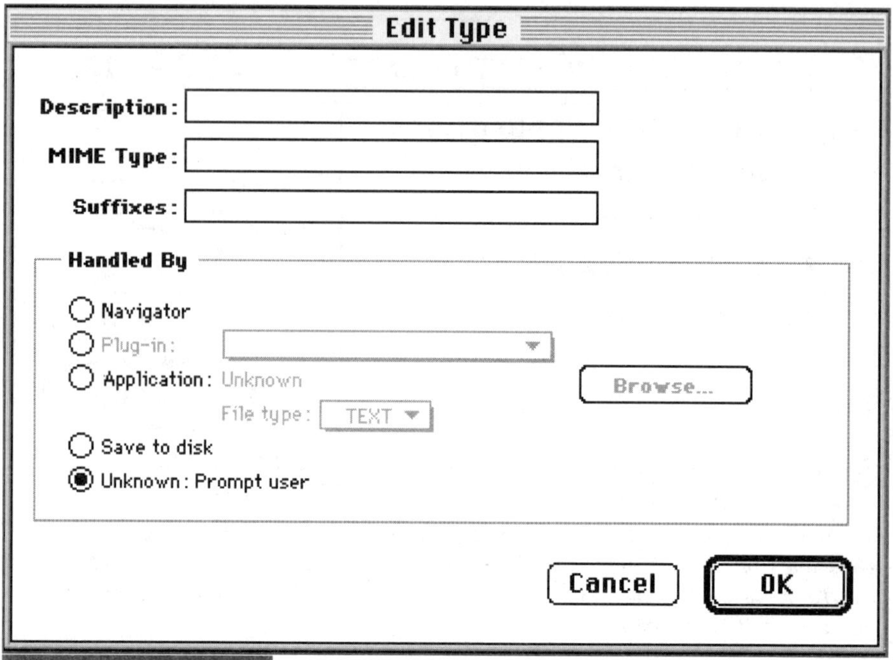

Edit Type

Description: [_____]

MIME Type: [_____]

Suffixes: [_____]

Handled By

○ Navigator
○ Plug-in: [_____ ▼]
○ Application: Unknown   [Browse...]
       File type: [TEXT ▼]
○ Save to disk
◉ Unknown: Prompt user

[Cancel] [OK]

FIGURE 2.29

*The **New** dialog box for adding a new Helper/Viewer to Netscape (Copyright 1996 Netscape Communications Corp. Used with permission. All rights reserved. This electronic file or page may not be reprinted or copied without the express written permission of Netscape.)*

a. Complete the information on the helper that is requested. In the **Description** box enter information about the application—it doesn't matter what you name the program. In this case the helper is RealAudio.

The **MIME Type** is *audio* and the subtype is *x-pn-realaudio*.

The files that RealAudio will open have the file extension of *.ra* and *.ram*. Enter these extension types in the **Suffixes** dialog box, as shown in Fig. 2.30.

IMPORTANT When you enter the extension in the **Suffixes** box, do not add a period (.) before the extension name.

b. Choose from the three options to indicate how the program is to be handled: by Netscape, as a plug-in, or as a helper application.

c. Click on the browse button to show Netscape where the application is located on your hard drive (see Fig. 2.31).

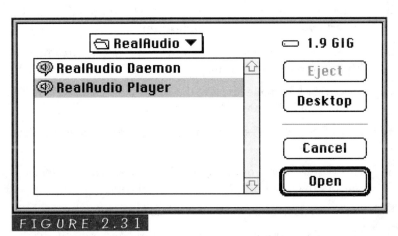

Edit Type

Description: RealAudio

MIME Type: audio/x-pn-realaudio

Suffixes: ra,ram

Handled By

○ Navigator
○ Plug-in:
● Application: RealAudio Player   **Browse...**
    File type: [PNRM ▼]
○ Save to disk
○ Unknown: Prompt user

[Cancel] [OK]

🔻 **RealAudio** ▼   ▭ 1.9 GIG

🔊 **RealAudio Daemon**   [Eject]
🔊 **RealAudio Player**   [Desktop]

[Cancel]

[Open]

NOTE Virtually any software program that runs on your computer can be used as a helper application. For example, you may want to use a word processing program such as Microsoft Word to read Internet files ending in a **.doc** extension.

Cool Multimedia Web Sites

Now that you better understand how to play and display multimedia files using plug-ins and viewers, step out boldly and visit the following sites for the ultimate Web experience.

ABC.COM—ABC news heard by RealAudio and viewed by Vivo-active **http://www.abc.com**

Alternative Entertainment Network **http://www.cummingsvideo.com**

Artists Underground—the place to discover new artists and their music **http://www.aumusic.com**

AudioNet—news, sports, events, and a cool CD jukebox **http://www.audionet.com**

Auto Channel—live broadcasts of races from around the world **http://www.theautochannel.com**

CNN Interactive—The latest world news **http://www.cnn.com**

Cybertown—a virtual community in cyberspace **http://www.cybertown.com/cybertown/index.html**

Cybervdo—experience some of the Net's coolest streaming video **http://www.cybervdo.com**

Discovery Channel—explore the world with Discovery's interactive channel **http:www.discovery.com**

ESPN SportsZone—a multimedia sports experience **http://espnet.sportszone.com**

Hot Wired—home of the *digerati* where you can experience sensory overload **http://www.hotwired.com**

MTV—an electronic MTV experience **http://www.mtv.com**

National Geographic—explore the world and multimedia **http://www.nationalgeographic.com**

National Public Radio—RealAudio at its best **http://www.npr.org**

Shockwave Gallery—a gallery of the coolest Shockwave experiences **http://www.macromedia.com/shockwave/epicenter/index.html**

CHAPTER III

VIRTUAL COMMUNITIES

If you enjoy surfing on the Net you may enjoy chatting and interacting with people from all over the world. In this chapter you will learn how to communicate with others using

- listserv mailing lists.
- Usenet newsgroups.
- Chat Worlds.
- MOOs and MUDs.
- Internet phones.

Although the Internet was created as a research network, it soon became popular for chatting and discussing work-related topics and hobbies. Online services such as America Online, CompuServe, and Prodigy popularized live events and chats. Live events featured guests whom online subscribers could talk with. Chats hosted discussions on current events or any topic that subscribers were interested in discussing within the global community of subscribers.

The popularity of live interactive events fostered new technological developments for Internet communication. Today more and more companies are introducing software to make Internet communication easier. For example, Netscape's Communicator Suite features new options for interaction, collaboration, and sharing information within a business or local area network; Web sites such as Yahoo, CNET.COM, the Discovery Channel, Time Warner, and The Palace offer free chat software for live interactive discussions on their site; Internet phones are the hottest new Internet service making real-time transmission of voice possible; desktop videoconferencing is becoming more popular as a communication tool with powerful possibilities for business interaction; and multi-user voice technology products are turning the Web into a virtual community where people can socialize, communicate, and collaborate with others one-on-one or in small groups.

People today are on the Internet because they value and enjoy the interactivity and the relationships they build within the virtual community of cyberspace. The way companies, institutions, and individuals communicate has changed. Internet communication involves five major services: electronic mail, electronic discussion groups (listservs and Usenet), Internet Relay Chat (IRC) or chats, Internet phones, and desktop Internet videoconferencing. Email and electronic discussion groups are delayed response media. IRC, Net phones, and desktop videoconferencing are real-time media. Net phones and videoconferencing are usually used for private conversations; IRC is typically used as a public forum; however, many chat clients offer options for private discussions. Electronic mail is most often used for private conversations; electronic discussion groups are used for public conversation.

LISTSERV MAILING LISTS

With so much attention on the World Wide Web, many new Internet users miss learning about electronic mailing lists (also referred to as lists, listservs, or discussion groups) as an Internet resource for finding and sharing information. Electronic mailing lists began in the 1960s when scientists and educators used the Internet to share information and research. Early programs, known as *listservs,* ran on mainframe computers and used email to send reports or studies to a large group of users.

Today, listservs perform the same function—the sharing of information. There are hundreds of special interest lists where individuals can join a virtual community to share and discuss topics of mutual interest.

What Is a Listserv Mailing List?

A *listserv* is the automated system that distributes electronic mail. Email is used to participate in electronic mailing lists. Listservs perform two functions:

- distributing text documents stored on them to those who request them, and

- managing interactive mailing lists.

Listservs and Text Documents

A listserv can be used to distribute information in the form of text documents to others. For example, online workshops may make their course materials available through a listserv. The listserv is set up to distribute the materials to participants at designated times. Other examples of documents available through a listserv include: a listing of all available electronic mailing lists, Usenet newsgroups, electronic journals, and books.

Interactive Mailing Lists

Interactive mailing lists provide a forum where individuals who share interests can exchange ideas and information. Any member of the group may participate in the resulting discussion. This is no longer a one-to-one communication like your email, but rather a one-to-many communication.

Electronic mail written in the form of a report, article, abstract, reaction, or comment is received at a central site and then distributed to the members of the list.

How Does a Mailing List Work?

The mailing list is hosted by a college, university, or institution. The hosting institution uses its computer system to manage the mailing list. Here are a few of the management functions of a listserv:

- receiving requests for subscriptions to the list;

- placing subscribers' email addresses on the list;

- sending out notification that the name has been added to the list;

- receiving messages from subscribers;

- sending messages to all subscribers;

- keeping a record (archive) of activity of the list; and

- sending out information requested by subscribers to the list.

Mailing lists have administrators that may be either a human or a computer program. One function of the administrator is to handle subscription requests. If the administrator is human, you can join the mailing list by communicating in English via an email message. The administrator in turn has the option of either accepting or rejecting your subscription request. Frequently lists administered by a human are available only to a select group of individuals. For example, an executive board of an organization may restrict its list to its members.

Mailing lists administered by computer programs called listservs usually allow all applicants to subscribe to the list. You must communicate with these computer administrators in listserv commands. For the computer administrator to accept your request, you must use the exact format required. The administrative address and how to subscribe should be included in the information provided about a list.

How to Receive Documents from a Listserv

Email is used to request text documents distributed by a listserv. The email is addressed to the listserv *administrative address.* In the body of the message a command is written to request the document. The most common command used to request a document is "send" or "get." The command is then followed by the name of the document that you wish to receive. A command to request a list of interesting mailing lists might look like this:

"get" or "send" <name of document>

or

get new-list TOP TEN

How to Join a Listserv Mailing List

To join an interactive mailing list on a topic of interest, send an email message to the list administrator and ask to join the list. Subscribing to an electronic mailing list is like subscribing to a journal or magazine.

- Mail a message to the journal requesting a subscription.

- Include the address of the journal and the address to which the journal will be mailed.

All electronic mailing lists work in the same way.

- Email your request to the list administrator at the address assigned by the hosting organization.

- Place your request to participate in the body of your email where you usually write your messages.

- Your return address will accompany your request in the header of your message.

- Your subscription will be acknowledged by the hosting organization or the moderator.

- You will then receive all discussions distributed by the listserv.

- You can send in your own comments and reactions.

- You can unsubscribe (cancel your subscription).

The command to subscribe to a mailing list looks like this:

subscribe <name of list> <*your name*>
or
subscribe Dave's Top Ten Cynthia Leshin

The unsubscribe command is similar to the subscribe command.

unsubscribe <name of list> <*your name*>

Active lists may have 50–100 messages from list participants each day. Less active mailing lists may have several messages per week or per month. If you find that you are receiving too much mail or the discussions on the list do not interest you, you can unsubscribe just as easily as you subscribed. If you are going away, you can send a message to the list to hold your mail until further notice.

Important Information Before You Begin

Mailing lists have two different addresses:

1. An *administrative address* that you will use when you
   - subscribe to the list.
   - unsubscribe from the list.
   - request information or help.

2. A *submission address* used to send your messages to the list.

The Administrative Mail Address

Most listserv mailing lists use software such as listserv, majordomo, or listproc that automatically processes users' requests to subscribe or unsubscribe. Some examples of administrative addresses used for subscribing and unsubscribing are:

listserv@uga.cc.uga.edu
majordomo@gsn.org
listproc@educom.unc.edu

NOTE Requests for subscriptions are usually processed by computers, therefore type the commands without any changes. Be sure to enter the exact address that you have received, duplicating spacing and upper- and lowercase letters. Do not add any other information in the body of your message. If your email package adds a signature, be sure to take it off before sending your request.

After you join a listserv mailing list, you will usually receive notification of your subscription request and an electronic welcome. This message will provide you with information such as the purpose of the list, the names of the listserv's owners, how to subscribe and unsubscribe, and other commands to use for the list.

TIP

Save a copy of this listserv welcome message. Later you may want to refer to it for information on how to unsubscribe or perform other operations related to the list.

The Submission Mail Address

Mail sent to the submission address is read by all of the subscribers to the list. This address will be different and should not be used for communicating with the list administrator. Here is an example of an address for sending your messages to the mailing list participants:

itforum@uga.cc.uga.edu

For this mailing list, the first word is the name of the list, *itforum* (instructional technology forum). Any mail sent to this address will be sent to all subscribers to the list. This address is used to communicate with subscribers to the list.

Finding Listserv Mailing Lists
World Wide Web Site for Finding Mailing Lists

Two of the best resources for helping you to find mailing lists are these World Wide Web sites:

http://www.liszt.com

http://www.tile.net/tile/listserv/index.html

Email a Request for Listservs on a Topic

To request information on listserv mailing lists for a particular topic, send an email message to **LISTSERV@vm1.nodak.edu.** In the message body type: **LIST GLOBAL / *keyword*.** To find electronic mailing lists you would enter: *LIST GLOBAL / environment.*

USENET NEWSGROUPS
What Are Newsgroups?

In the virtual community of the Internet, Usenet newsgroups are analogous to a café where people with similar interests gather from around the world to interact and exchange ideas. Usenet is a very large, distributed bulletin board system (BBS) that consists of several thousand specialized discussion groups. Currently there are more than 20,000 newsgroups with 20 to 30 more added weekly.

You can subscribe to a newsgroup, scan through the messages, read messages of interest, organize the messages, and send in your comments or questions—or start a new one.

Usenet groups are organized by subject and divided into major categories.

Category	Topic Area
alt.	no topic is off limits in this alternative group
comp.	computer-related topics
misc.	miscellaneous topics that don't fit into other categories
news.	happenings on the Internet
rec.	recreational activities/hobbies
sci.	scientific research and associated issues
soc.	social issues and world cultures
talk.	discussions and debates on controversial social issues

In addition to these categories there are local newsgroups with prefixes that indicate their topic or locality.

Some newsgroups are moderated and reserved for very specific articles. Articles submitted to these newsgroups are sent to a central site. If the article is approved, it is posted by the moderator. Many newsgroups have no moderator and there is no easy way to determine whether a group is moderated. The only way to tell if a group is moderated is to submit an article. You will be notified if your article has been mailed to the newsgroup moderator.

What Is the Difference Between Listserv Mailing Lists and Usenet Newsgroups?

One analogy for describing the difference between a listserv mailing list and a Usenet newsgroup is to compare the difference between having a few intimate friends over for dinner and conversation (a listserv) vs. going to a Super Bowl party to which the entire world has been invited (newsgroups). A listserv is a smaller, more intimate place to discuss issues of interest. A Usenet newsgroup is much larger and much more open to "everything and anything goes." This is not to say that both do not provide a place for valuable discussion. However, the size of each makes the experiences very different.

A listserv mailing list is managed by a single site, such as a university. Subscribers to a mailing list are automatically mailed messages that are sent to the mailing list submission address. A listserv would find it difficult to maintain a list for thousands of people.

Usenet consists of many sites that are set up by local Internet providers. When a message is sent to a Usenet site, a copy of the message that has been received is sent to other neighboring, connected Usenet sites. Each of these sites keeps a copy of the message and then forwards the message to other connected systems. Usenet can therefore handle thousands of subscribers.

One advantage of Usenet groups over a mailing list is that you can quickly read postings to the newsgroup. When you connect to a Usenet newsgroup and see a long list of articles, you can select only those that interest you. Unlike a mailing list, Usenet messages do not accumulate in your mailbox, forcing you to read and delete them. Usenet articles are on your local server and can be read at your convenience.

Browsers and Usenet Newsgroups

Netscape and Explorer support Usenet newsgroups. You can subscribe to a newsgroup, read articles posted to a group, and reply to articles. You can determine whether your reply is sent to the individual author of the posted article or to the entire newsgroup. Additional features include the scanning of related references and their associated URL. These URLs are shown as active hypertext links that can be accessed by clicking on the underlined words. News reader buttons and pull-down menus provide the reader with controls for reading and responding to articles.

Newsgroups have a URL location. These URLs are similar, but not identical, to other pages. For example, the URL for a recreational back-country newsgroup is **news:rec.backcountry.** The server protocol is **news:** and the newsgroup is **rec.backcountry.**

Newsgroups present articles along what is called a "thread." The thread packages the article with responses to the article (see Fig. 3.1). Each new response is indented one level from the original posting. A response to a response is indented another level. Newsgroups' threads, therefore, appear as an outline.

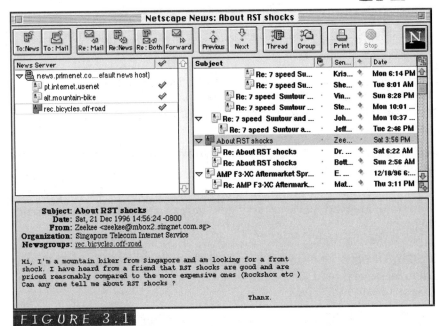

*The Netscape **News** window displaying groups subscribed to (left window) and article threads (right window) (Copyright 1996 Netscape Communications Corp. Used with permission. All rights reserved. This electronic file or page may not be reprinted or copied without the express written permission of Netscape.)*

NOTE Information on Explorer's news reader begins on page 65, however, you may want to read this section on Netscape newsgroups for general information. This section provides only basic information to get you started with Usenet newsgroups.

Reading Usenet News Using Netscape Navigator
Netscape News Window for Usenet News

To display the News window in Netscape, go to the **Window** menu and select **Netscape News.**

Notice that you have new options in the form of toolbar buttons (Fig. 3.2) and pulldown menus for receiving, reading, replying to, and sending messages to newsgroups. Netscape News works in much the same way as Netscape Mail.

This example also illustrates the newsgroup thread where articles are presented in an outline format with their accompanying response.

To: News: Displays a Message Composition window for creating a new message posting for a newsgroup.

FIGURE 3.2

Netscape News window buttons (Copyright 1996 Netscape Communications Corp. Used with permission. All rights reserved. This electronic file or page may not be reprinted or copied without the express written permission of Netscape.)

To: Mail: Displays a Message Composition window for creating a new mail message.

Re: Mail: Click on this button to reply to the current newsgroup message (thread) you are reading. Your reply goes only to sender of original message.

Re: News: Selecting this button replies to the entire newsgroup.

Re: Both: Displays a Message Composition window for posting a reply to the current message thread for the entire newsgroup and to the sender of the news message.

Forward: Displays the Message Composition window for forwarding the current news message as an attachment. Enter the email address in the **Mail To** field.

Previous: Brings the previous unread message in the thread to your screen.

Next: Brings the next unread message in the thread to your screen.

Thread: Marks the message threads you have read.

Group: Marks all messages read.

Print: Prints the message you are reading.

Stop: Stops the current transmission of messages from your news server.

Netscape News Menus

When you select Netscape News you will receive not only new toolbar buttons but also different pull-down menus for interacting with the Netscape news reader: File, Edit, View, Message, Go, Options, Window, and Help.

Reading Usenet News With Netscape Navigator

Netscape Navigator provides four ways to access newsgroups.

- If you know the name of the newsgroup, type the URL in the location field of the Netscape main menu.

- From within the Netscape News window, go to the **File** menu and select **Add Newsgroup.** Enter the name of the newsgroup in the dialog box.

- From within the Netscape News window, go to the **Options** menu (see Fig. 3.3) and select **Show All Newsgroups.** From this list, select a newsgroup and check the **Subscribe** box beside the newsgroup name.

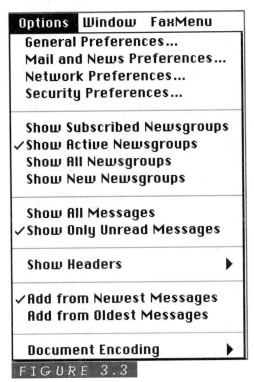

FIGURE 3.3

*Netscape News window **Options** menu (Copyright 1996 Netscape Communications Corp. Used with permission. All rights reserved. This electronic file or page may not be reprinted or copied without the express written permission of Netscape.)*

- From a World Wide Web site (i.e., **http://www.cen.uiuc.edu/ cgi-bin/find-news**) click on a link to a newsgroup or a newsgroup message.

Reading Usenet News Using Explorer

If you are using Microsoft Internet Explorer and want to read Usenet newsgroups you will need Microsoft's Internet Mail and News software. This software may already be installed and available if you are at a school, college, or university. Internet Mail and News can also

be downloaded at no cost from Microsoft's Home Page **http://www
.microsoft.com** or from within Explorer by selecting the link to
Microsoft Products. To determine if the news reader has been installed
and configured, select **Read News** from Explorer's **Go** menu. If a news
window opens (see Fig. 3.4), you know that the news reader has been
installed. If nothing happens, you will need to download and install
Internet Mail and News.

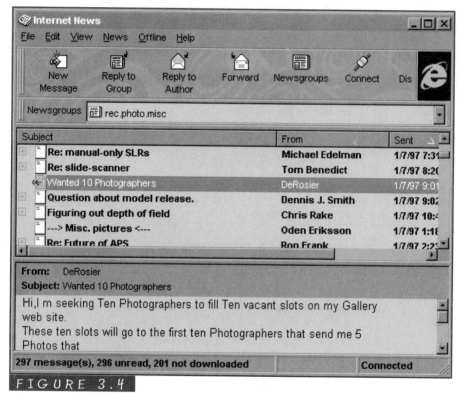

FIGURE 3.4

Explorer news reader window

Explorer's News Reader

When you open Explorer's news reader by selecting **Read News** from
the **Go** menu you will see this window.

Notice that the news reader has pull-down menus and toolbar buttons for using the reader.

TIP

> *Drag and reposition the toolbar and folder list by using your mouse to
> place the cursor over the borders. The cursor becomes a handle for drag-
> ging the frame up, down, left, or right.*

Before you can view newsgroups the name of your Internet Service Provider's news server must be entered into the news reader. To add a news server, follow these steps.

🦝 STEP 1

Open the news reader by selecting **Read News** from the **Go** menu.

🦝 STEP 2

You will now see the news reader window (Fig. 3.4). Select **Options** from the **News** pull-down menu, then click on the **Servers** tab. Click on the **Add** button to enter in the news server name. If you don't know the news server name, check with your Internet provider.

Once your news server name has been entered you are ready to either view newsgroups that your Internet provider has subscribed to, view newsgroups in a subject area, or subscribe to a newsgroup (see Fig. 3.5). Go to the **News** menu from within the news reader and select the **Newsgroup** options. This window provides you with options for viewing newsgroups. If this is the first time you are using the news reader, the window displaying available newsgroups will most likely be blank. You will need to tell the news reader what newsgroups you would like to view.

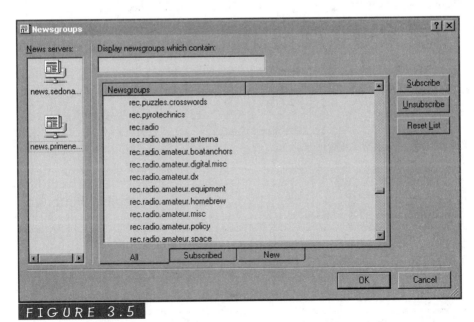

FIGURE 3.5

Explorer news window for downloading newsgroups

To view the news in a listed newsgroup, click on the newsgroup to select it and then click the **OK** button (see Fig. 3.5). You will see the articles that have been posted to this group. For example, in Fig. 3.4 the news group selected is **rec.photo.misc**. This example shows a few of the news articles posted. To view the newsgroup, click once on the news article; the contents will be displayed at the bottom of the news reader (see Fig. 3.4). To see an expanded version of the news article, double-click on the name of the news article (Fig. 3.6).

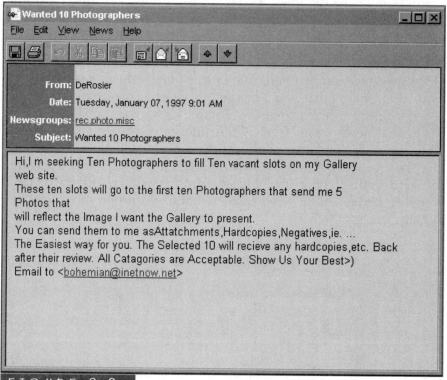

FIGURE 3.6

The expanded news reader window for reading and replying to a Usenet news article

To respond to the author of the article, use the toolbar buttons as shown in Figs. 3.4 and 3.6.

NOTES If your response is appropriate only for the author of the news article, send your response to the author and not to the entire group. There may be times that the information you want to share will be appreciated by all the readers of this group, in which case, post your response to the entire newsgroup.

Use search engines such as Infoseek Ultra, Excite, and Lycos to find newsgroups of interest. After entering keyword(s), select the newsgroup option for the search.

TIPS FOR NEW USERS OF NEWSGROUPS AND LISTSERVS

TIP 1 . . .

After you subscribe to a list or newsgroup, don't send anything to it until you have been reading the messages for at least one week. This will give you an opportunity to observe the tone of the list and the type of messages that people are sending. Newcomers to lists often ask questions that were discussed at length several days or weeks before. Begin by reading the Frequently Asked Questions.

TIP 2 . . .

Remember that everything you send to the list or newsgroup goes to every subscriber on the list. Many of these discussion groups have thousands of members. Before you reply or post a message, read and review what you have written. Is your message readable and free from errors and typos? When necessary, AMEND BEFORE YOU SEND.

TIP 3 . . .

Look for a posting by someone who seems knowledgeable about a topic. If you want to ask a question, look for their email address in the signature information at the top of the news article. Send your question to them directly rather than to the entire newsgroup or listserv.

TIP 4 . . .

Proper etiquette for a mailing list is to not clog other people's mail boxes with information not relevant to them. If you want to respond to mail on the list or newsgroup, determine whether you want your response to go only to the individual who posted the mail or you want your response to go to all the list's subscribers. The person's name and email address will be listed in their posting signature.

TIP 5 . . .

The general rule for posting a message to a list or newsgroup is to keep it short and to the point. Most subscribers do not appreciate multiple-page postings.

If you are contacting an individual by electronic mail, identify yourself, state why you are contacting them, and indicate where you found their posting. Again, be as succinct and to the point as possible.

CHATS

A popular Internet cartoon shows a dog sitting in front of a computer. The caption reads, "On the Internet, nobody knows you're a dog." This cartoon reveals the Internet's unique ability for individual anonymity and opens many communication doors for individuals who otherwise may feel inhibited with live face-to-face interaction. For many, chatting on the Net and creating alternative identities has become a new way of life and for some, an addiction. In fact a Usenet newsgroup has been formed called **alt.irc.recovery.**

Individuals participating in a chat create a name, known as *nickname,* or a *screen name* that identifies them to others in the chat room; some chats go even further and have users create an entire identity; some such as MOOs and MUDs have users role-playing in virtual reality worlds created by the users. Newer chat worlds have users interacting and traveling in 3D environments.

Before you can participate in a chat world you will need to have a software client. For example, MOOs and MUDs require a Telnet client. Some Web sites, such as The Palace, have a link to a client program that you will need if you want to participate in their live events. Other Web sites have chats that do not require you to download any additional software. For example, Time Warner's Pathfinder Web site has a chat room for discussing news of the day. *Wired* magazine has a chat room open for discussion, and the Discovery Channel Online has perfected online narrative making the audience part of the stories. Other requirements may include powerful multimedia PCs for 3D chats.

Conversations within chats are text-based. Users type in their message line by line. As a line is being typed, others on the channel see the message. Messages cannot be edited before they are sent to others on the channel. Anyone on the channel can respond to a message as it is revealed on their computer screen by merely typing in their response line by line.

Commercial services such as America Online, CompuServe, Prodigy, and Microsoft Network offer chat rooms for their members to communicate and meet others who have similar interests. Chat rooms with these services can be public or private. Public rooms are created by the service provider and tend to have focused discussion topics. Some of these rooms are hosted and others are not; some are available on a regular basis, while others are created for special events such as a guest who is online for a forum for several hours.

Private chat rooms are created by members and can hold between 2 and 25 or more registered online users. Private chat rooms may be used for a meeting or just a casual chat between friends. There is no way as yet to view a list of private chat rooms. New interactive software for forming live interactive chat worlds makes it possible for users to create both public and private forums for communicating online.

To experience chat using the World Wide Web, explore these sites:

WEBCHAT BROADCASTING SYSTEM http://wbs.net

DISCOVERY CHANNEL http://www.discovery.com

CNET.COM http://www.cnet.com

HOTWIRED http://www.hotwired.com

TIME WARNER'S PATHFINDER http://www.pathfinder.com

YAHOO CHAT http://chat.yahoo.com

THE PALACE http:www.thepalace.com

GLOBE http://globe1.csuglab.cornell.edu/global/homepage.html

To experience 3D Chat Worlds, visit these Web sites:

ALPHAWORLD http://www.worlds.net

COMIC CHAT http://www.microsoft.com/ie/comichat/download.htm

TIKKILAND http://mtv.com/tikkiland

V-CHAT http://www.msn.com/v-chat

WORLD'S CHAT http://www.worlds.net

MOOs AND MUDs

MOO (*Multi-User Shell, Object Oriented*) and **MUD** (*Multi-User Domain*). MOOs and MUDs put visitors into a space where they are able to navigate, communicate, and build virtual environments by using computer commands. Each

of these environments uses a different type of software, but is very similar in that users Telnet to a remote computer to create, communicate, and navigate in a text-based environment. Some MOOs and MUDs offer alternative learning environments such as Diversity University; others feature fantasy role-playing games. New identities are created and experimented with.

MOOs are very similar to MUDs, but use a more sophisticated programming language than MUD. A MOO lets users build things in a simulated environment by creating objects that are linked to a parent object. MUDs and MOOs are interactive systems suited to the construction of text-based adventure games and conferencing systems. The most common use, however, is multi-participant, virtual reality adventure games with players from all over the world.

Listed below are Internet sites to visit to explore MOOs and MUDs.

http://www.butterfly.net/~pyro/moo_page.html

http://www.bushnet.qld.edu.au/~jay/moo/

http://www.io.com/~combs/htmls/moo.html

DIVERSITY UNIVERSITY
http://www.academic.marist.edu/duwww.htm
telnet://moo.du.org:8888

LAMBDA MOO telnet://lambda.parc.xerox.com:8888/

HTMUD (A GRAPHICAL MUD) http://www.elf.com/~phi/htmud/

HYPERTEXT MUD LISTS PROVIDE LINKS TO MUDS ALL OVER THE WORLD
http://www.eskimo.com/~tarp3/muds.html

INTERNET PHONES

The Internet has made possible the global transmission of text, graphics, sound, and video. Now, a new service has come upon the Internet shore making the real-time transmission of voice possible. Products known as Internet phones let you use your computer as a telephone. Internet phones are the hottest new Internet service to talk with another person anywhere in the world at no more than the cost of your local Internet access. Internet telephones can operate over cable, satellite, and other networks.

However, Internet phones are still in their infancy and not yet a substitute for conventional phones. At this stage in their development, they are a novelty and far from practical to use as a business tool or for routine communication. Many IPhones require both parties to be running the same software and be online at the same time when the call is made, otherwise the phone won't ring. Currently, most Internet phone software is similar to Internet Relay Chat programs that help users running the same program find and communicate with each other.

Part of the appeal of the Internet phone is the capability to talk to anyone in the world without the cost of a long distance phone call. For the monthly cost of an Internet account two people anywhere in the world can talk for as long and as often as they choose. When one compares this to the cost of national and international phone calls, many are willing to overlook the current limitations and difficulties imposed on its users by this new technology.

How Do I Talk to Someone Using an Internet Phone?

There are two ways that you can communicate with Internet users on Net phones:

- through a central server, similar to an Internet Relay Chat server

- connect to a specific individual by using their IP (Internet Protocol) address

Some Internet users have their own IP addresses; others are assigned an IP address every time they log on. Check with your Internet provider for information on your IP address.

What Do I Need to Use an Internet Phone?

Hardware

Before you can chat using Internet phones you will need the following hardware:

- a sound card for your Macintosh or Windows system

- speakers on your computer

- a microphone for your computer

SOUND CARD To have a conversation where both parties can speak at the same time, you will need to have a sound card that supports full duplexing. Many Macintosh computers (including the Power Macs) support full-duplex sound. If you are using a PC, check your existing sound card. Full-duplex drivers are available if your sound card does not support full duplexing.

SPEAKERS The speakers that come with your computer are adequate for the current Net phones. The audio quality of this new technology is not yet what you are accustomed to with traditional telephones.

MICROPHONE Many computers come with microphones that will be suitable for use with the Internet phones. If you need to purchase a microphone, do not spend more than $10 to $15 on a desktop microphone.

Software

Netscape Communicator 4.x series and Microsoft Internet Explorer 4.0 have IPhones built into their Internet software. If you are not using these versions you may want to consider the following.

- VocalTec's Internet Phone
- Quarterdeck Corp's Web Talk
- CoolTalk

INTERNET PHONE (IPHONE) was the first Net phone introduced to Internet users in early 1995. After the release and testing of many versions in 1995, the IPhone is considered one of the better Net phones with highly rated sound quality. IPhone is easy to use and resembles the chat environments. When you begin the program you log onto a variety of Internet servers and have the option of joining a discussion group. Once you have joined a group you can call an online user simply by double-clicking on the user's name. This capability is considered to be one of IPhone's strongest points.

The disadvantage of IPhone is that you cannot connect to a specific individual using their IP address. All connections must be made by first connecting to IPhone's IRC-style servers. Both individuals must be online at the same time and connected to the server.

Internet Phone has a free demo version with a one-week trial period. For more information visit their Web site at **http://www.vocaltec.com** or call (201) 768-9400.

WEB TALK is the software program of choice for Internet users with their own IP address. To connect to a specific individual, just enter their IP address. The person you are trying to connect with must also be online at the same time. To talk with other online users, connect to WebTalk's server. To learn more about WebTalk visit its Web site at **http://www.webtalk.qdeck.com** or call (301) 309-3700.

COOLTALK Netscape 3.0 and 4.0 incorporate CoolTalk into their Navigator software. It is distributed by Netscape Communications Corp. and has a useful feature that sets it apart from other Internet phone programs. The "whiteboard" option becomes available after you have connected to another individual by either logging onto their global server or entering an individual's IP address. The whiteboard begins as a blank window. Using standard paint program tools you can enter text, sketch out ideas, draw, or insert graphics. The whiteboard makes this Net phone most attractive for Internet business users.

To learn more about CoolTalk, connect to Netscape's Home Page at **http://www.netscape.com** or call (717) 730-9501.

NOTES Keep an eye on Intel's Internet Phone. This software is free and has the advantage of allowing users to talk with those using different phone software. MCI has plans to launch a service in partnership with Intel to provide telephone and video services to businesses. You can contact Intel at **http://www.intel.com**

You can also chat across the Internet using video-conferencing programs such as CU-SeeMe. This program makes it possible for interaction with one individual, small groups, or hundreds in a broadcast. Not only do you hear individuals, but you also can see them in full color on your computer monitor. This program has a whiteboard feature for document collaboration.

CU-SeeMe runs on Windows or Macintosh over a 28.8 modem. If you have a 14.4 modem, only audio is possible. To learn more, visit their Web site at **http://www.cu-seeme.com/iw.htm** or call (800) 241-PINE.

Learning Adventures—Exploring Virtual Communities

In this section you will have the opportunity for HANDS ON exploration of virtual communities.

1. Visit this Web site and search for a listserv in your field of study.
http://www.tile.net/tile/listserv/index.html

   Use email to send a request to **LISTSERV@vm1.nodak.edu.** In the message body, type **LIST GLOBAL/keyword,** for example, LIST GLOBAL/music.

2. Subscribe to several listserv mailing lists.

3. Use your browser to explore Usenet newsgroups. Look for 5–10 groups related to your field of study.

   Visit this Web site for a listing of Usenet newsgroups.
http://ibd.ar.com/ger

   Use search engines such as Infoseek Ultra, Excite, or Lycos to search for newsgroups on a topic of interest.

   Visit this Web site and use a simple search tool to locate Usenet newsgroups of interest.

   http://www.cen.uiuc.edu/cgi-bin/find-news

4. Visit these Web sites to experience Internet chat:

   WebChat Broadcasting System **http://wbs.net**

   Cnet.com **http://www.cnet.com**

   HotWired **http://www.hotwired.com**

   Time Warner's Pathfinder **http://www.pathfinder.com**

   The Palace **http:www.thepalace.com**

   Globe **http://globe1.csuglab.cornell.edu/global/homepage.html**

   Yahoo Chat **http://chat.yahoo.com**

5. Visit Discovery Channel Online (**http://www.discovery.com**) where you can discuss great stories about the world. Their online narratives are wonderful places to learn something new.

PART II

STUDENT SUCCESS AND THE INTERNET

CHAPTER IV

RESEARCHING INFORMATION AND RESOURCES ON THE INTERNET

S earching for information is like a treasure hunt. Unless a researcher has knowledge of all the resources and tools available, then the search for useful information may be a time-consuming and frustrating process. In this chapter you will learn about resources on the Internet that will facilitate the search for information of interest to you, your career, and your field of study. Careful thought about the desired knowledge sought, the best place to begin to look for that knowledge, and extensive exploring and searching in layers of Web links usually provides the desired reward—the gold nugget Web site.

The tools that you will learn about and use to conduct research include

- search directories

  Yahoo
  Magellan
  Galaxy
  Excite
  Infoseek
  Subject directories

- search engines

  Excite
  Infoseek
  Alta Vista
  Image Surfer
  Lycos

HotBot

      Inktomi

      Open Text

      Wired Source

- Internet collections

      Archeology

      Art

      Business

      Criminal Justice

      Environmental

      Geography

      Government

      History

      Literature

      Mathematics

      Music

      News

      Science

- Reference resources

- Virtual libraries

You will also learn

- how to evaluate information you find on the Internet as to its content validity;

- how to record Internet information sources; and

- how to reference electronic media.

Internet Research Tools

The Internet contains many tools that speed the search for information and resources. Research tools called "search directories" and "search engines" are extremely helpful.

Search Directories

Search directories are essentially descriptive subject indexes of Web sites. They also have searching options. When you connect to their page, you will find a query box for entering keywords. The search engine at these sites searches only for keyword matches in the directories' databases. Directories are excellent places to begin your research.

Search Engines

Search engines are different from search directories in that they search World Wide Web sites, Usenet newsgroups, and other Internet resources to find matches to your descriptor keywords. Many search engines also rank the results according to a degree of relevancy. Most search engines have options for advanced searching to refine your search.

Basic Guidelines for Becoming a Cybersleuth

Search directories and search engines are marvelous tools to help you find information on the Internet. Search directories are often the best places to begin a search, as they frequently yield more relevant returns on a topic than a search engine, which may produce a high proportion of irrelevant information.

Search engines can be frustrating to use and may not be the best Internet resources to begin with, often supplying thousands of links on your keyword search. Although these search tools have advanced options for refining and limiting a search, researchers may discover that finding the desired information is not easy and that search results frequently offer a high percentage of irrelevant and useless information. For example, using a search engine for a search with the keywords *business management* returned 500,000 occurrences (*hits*) of the words *business* and *management*. Many of the occurrences of these words were in job listings or companies that were advertising their services. This is why search directories are frequently an excellent resource to begin with when starting your research. The search directory may lead you to the goldmine collection of electronic resources you are searching for.

Research Guidelines

When researching information on the Internet, it is essential that you use several search tools. The basic approach to finding information involves the following steps:

1. Use search directories such as

    YAHOO (http://www.yahoo.com),

    EXCITE (http://www.excite.com),

    GALAXY (http://galaxy.einet.net/galaxy.html),

MAGELLAN (http://magellan.mckinley.com), or

INFOSEEK (http://guide.infoseek.com)
to search for the information under a related topic or category. Explore the links that seem relevant to your topic, and make bookmarks of the ones you would like to investigate further. Look for one site that has a large collection of links on your topic. This is the resource goldmine that you are looking for.

2. Use search engines to further research your topic by determining one or more descriptive words (keywords) for the subject. Enter your keywords into the search dialog box.

3. Determine how specific you want your search to be. Do you want it to be broad or narrow? Use available options to refine or limit your search. Some search engines permit the use of Boolean operators (phrases or words such as "and," "or," and "not" that restrict a search). Others provide HELP for refining searches, and some have pull-down menus or selections to be checked for options.

4. Submit your query.

5. Review your list of hits (a search return based on a keyword).

6. Adjust your search based on the information returned. Did you receive too much information and need to narrow your search? Did you receive too little or no information and need to broaden your keywords?

7. Use several search directories and search engines for your research. No one search tool will provide a complete resource list.

Search Directories

Yahoo

Yahoo is one of the most popular search tools on the Internet and is an excellent place to begin your search. Although Yahoo is more accurately described as a search directory, this Web site has an excellent database with search options available. There are two ways to find information using Yahoo: search through the subject directory, or use the built-in search engine. Yahoo can be accessed from your browser's **Search** button or by entering this URL: **http://www.yahoo.com.**

Follow these steps to use Yahoo to search for information:

STEP 1

Begin by browsing the subject directory. For example, if you were searching for information on environmental online resources you would first select the *Society and Culture* directory, then follow the *Environment and Nature* category. Explore categories and see if the information you are searching for can be found under the categories (see Fig. 4.1).

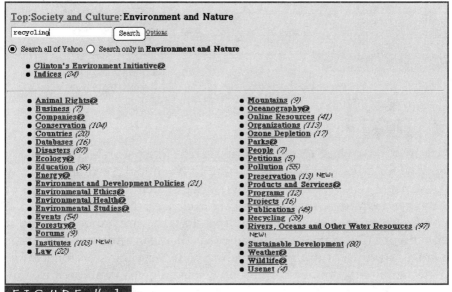

FIGURE 4.1

Yahoo's Environment and Nature *subject index search form in which the keyword* recycling *has been entered*

STEP 2

Yahoo's search engine can also be used to find information. Enter a descriptive keyword for your subject, one that uniquely identifies or describes what you are looking for. It is often helpful to do a broad search first, though results often present the need to change descriptive keywords or to refine your query.

Perhaps you are looking for information on recycling and were not able to find it easily under one of the Environment categories. Enter the keyword, in this case *recycling*, in Yahoo's query box (see Fig. 4.1).

STEP 3

Click on the **Search** button and review your query results (see Fig. 4.2).

> Found **6** Category and **332** Site Matches for **recycling**.
>
> ### Yahoo! Category Matches (1 - 6 of 6)
>
> <u>Business and Economy: Companies: Environment: **Recycling**</u>
>
> <u>Society and Culture: Environment and Nature: **Recycling**</u>
>
> <u>Business and Economy: Companies: Industrial Supplies: Machinery and Tools: **Recycling**</u>
>
> <u>Regional: Countries: Canada: Business: Companies: Environment: **Recycling**</u>
>
> <u>Regional: Countries: United States: Dependent Areas: Puerto Rico: Business: **Recycling**</u>
>
> <u>Regional: Countries: United Kingdom: Business: Companies: Environment: **Recycling**</u>

FIGURE 4.2

Yahoo search results from the keyword recycling

STEP 4

You may now want to refine your search. Most search engines have options for advanced searching using Boolean logic or more carefully constructed database queries. Review the search page for **Options** or **Advanced Options.** When using Yahoo, click on the **Options** button. If you are using two or more keywords, do you want Yahoo to look for either word (Boolean **or**), both keywords (Boolean **and**), or all words as a single string? For example, to refine your recycling search for information only on commercial recycling, select Boolean **and** because you want to find resources that contain the words "commercial" **and** "recycling" in their titles (see Fig. 4.3). Otherwise the search would be too broad and would find all resources that contained any of the keywords "commercial" **or** "recycling."

TIP

Yahoo suggests putting a phrase in quotes, such as "commercial recycling."

STEP 5

Further limit or expand your search by selecting a search method, search area (Yahoo categories, Web sites, Today's News, or Net Events), a period of time for the listing to have occurred, and the number of results returned per page.

STEP 6

Submit your query.

YAHOO!

New Cool Today's News More Yahoo

Search Options | Help on Search | Advanced Search Syntax

[ ] [Search] help

◉ Yahoo!   ○ Usenet   ○ E-mail addresses

For **Yahoo!** search, please use the options below:

Select a search method:
◉ Intelligent default
○ An exact phrase match
○ Matches on all words (AND)
○ Matches on any word (OR)
○ A person's name

Select a search area:
◉ Yahoo Categories
○ Web Sites
○ Today's News
○ Net Events

Find only new listings added during the past [3 years]

After the first result page, display [20] matches per page

Please note that most of the options selected will not be carried over to other search engines.

Search Tip: To search for phrases, put query words in double quotes.
Phrase example: "Jackie Chan" "martial arts"

FIGURE 4.3

*Yahoo **Options** for refining a search*

STEP 7

Review your return list of hits and adjust your search again if necessary.

STEP 8

Review your return list for other descriptive words that have been used when summarizing search results. For example, when using the keyword "recycling," search result summaries produced other important descriptive words such as "recycling consumer," "pollution," or "waste management in the home."

STEP 9

Conduct a search using other descriptive words.

Other Search Directories

Explore the following subject directories. You will find that their subject categories vary; most have advanced search options for refining your search and several (Infoseek and Excite) have powerful search engines built-in.

MAGELLAN http://magellan.mckinley.com

GALAXY http://galaxy.einet.net/galaxy.html

EXCITE http://www.excite.com

INFOSEEK http://guide.infoseek.com

Notice the option in Fig. 4.4 for connecting to its powerful search engine—Ultraseek.

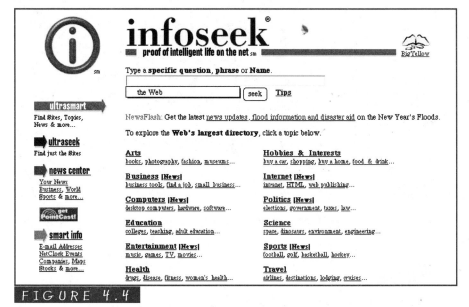

FIGURE 4.4

Home page for Infoseek showing search directory

Other Subject-Oriented Directories

In addition to search directories, subject-oriented directories are excellent sources to find information on a topic. These directories are usually compiled by individuals rather than a search service such as Yahoo.

THE ARGUS CLEARINGHOUSE http://www.clearinghouse.net/ searching/find.html Links to Internet directories, search tools, and virtual libraries. Select the link to The Argus Clearinghouse and you will connect to a subject-oriented research library.

ENCYBERPEDIA http://www.encyberpedia.com/ency.htm#menu
http://www.encyberpedia.com/ency.htm The HOTTEST encyclopedia from cyberspace designed to help you find good stuff
in the jungle of over two million Web Sites.

INTER-LINKS http://www.nova.edu/Inter-Links Inter-Links was
created and maintained by Rob Kabacoff from Nova Southeastern University. Internet resources are offered in broad categories
such as topical resources, fun and games, news and weather,
library resources, and reference resources.

THE INTERNET SERVICES LIST http://www.spectracom.com/islist An
impressive collection of Internet resources organized in over 80
categories. This popular site is an excellent place to begin a
search.

LIBRARY OF CONGRESS http://lcweb.loc.gov A large and impressive collection of resources including research tools and library
services to assist you with finding information.

LOOKSMART http://mulwala.looksmart.com Don't let this sim-
plistic interface turn you away from exploring this site that has
valuable subject-oriented resources.

WORLD WIDE WEB VIRTUAL LIBRARY http://www.w3.org/pub/
DataSources/bySubject/Overview.html A MUST VISIT search
resource for finding Internet resources. A go to the top of the
bookmark list site.

SEARCH ENGINES

Search engines require a keyword(s) or phrase that is descriptive of the
information you are looking for. Begin by listing keywords or phrases
on your topic. When you connect to a search engine look for its Search
Tips or Advanced Search Options to help you conduct a more efficient
and effective search. Taking this step will save time and help to prevent
information overload frustration.

Excite

Excite is one of the most widely used search engines offering a full
range of services (see Fig. 4.5). Excite searches scan Web pages and
Usenet newsgroups for keyword matches and create summaries of
each match. Excite also has a Web directory organized by category.

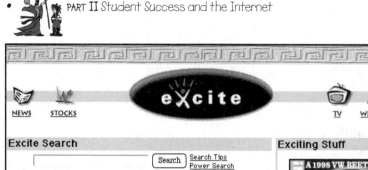

FIGURE 4.5

Excite Web page displaying services

Searching With Excite

STEP 1

Type a word or phrase that fits your information need. Be as specific as you can, using words that uniquely relate to the information you are looking for, not simply general descriptive words. For example, if you are looking for information on health and healing outside of traditional medicine you might begin by using keywords such as *holistic health*. When using more than one word, read the **Help** information to find the best way to enter multiple words or a phrase.

STEP 2

If the search result does not contain the information you are looking for, or if the returns have too much irrelevant information, use the Advanced Search option (as shown in Fig. 4.6).

STEP 3

Advanced features include the use of a plus sign (+) in front of a search word to ensure that all the returns contain that word. Use a minus sign

Excite Search

holistic AND health	Search	Search Tips
		Power Search

People Finder · Email Lookup · Yellow Pages · Maps
Stock Quotes · Book Flights · Newsgroups · Shareware

FIGURE 4.6

Search query for holistic health

(–) in front of a search word and Excite will make sure that *no* documents contain the word. Excite also supports the use of Boolean operators (**AND, OR, NOT**). Search engines also may suggest the use of double quotation marks around the words or phrase.

🎋 STEP 4

Excite lists 10 search results at a time in decreasing order of confidence. Each result lists a title, a URL, and a brief summary of the document. The percentage to the left of the return is the confidence rating (Fig. 4.7), with 100% being the highest confidence rating attainable. To see the next listing of documents related to your phrase or keywords, click the "next documents" button. Click the "sort by site" button to view the Web sites that have the most pages relevant to your search.

Infoseek

Infoseek provides search and browse capabilities of Web pages, Usenet newsgroups, FTP, and Gopher sites. You can even sign up for personalized news. Infoseek offers two free services: Infoseek Guide and Ultraseek. Of all search engines, Ultraseek seems to find the highest number of relevant matches to keywords.

INFOSEEK GUIDE (http://guide.infoseek.com) is one of Infoseek's earliest services introduced in early 1996. At that time, the company also offered a subscription-based service, Infoseek Professional. Infoseek Guide integrates a browsable directory of Internet resources located on World Wide Web sites, Usenet newsgroups, and other popular Internet resource sites. Users can choose to use the search engine and enter keywords or phrases, or browse the navigational directories.

Ultraseek (http://www.infoseek.com), under development for two years at Infoseek and introduced in the fall of 1996,

---

Excite Search found **16138** document(s) about : **holistic AND health**.
Documents **1-10** sorted by **Relevance**. Sort by Site.

84% About the American Holistic Medical Asso... [More Like This]
URL: http://www.doubleclickd.com:80/about_ahma.html
Summary: Later, associate membership was expanded to include all state-licensed holistically oriented practitioners, such as chiropractors, naturopaths, nurses, psychologists, dentists, etc. The mission of the AHMA is to support physicians in their evolving personal and professional development and to promote an art and science of health care which acknowledges all aspects of the individual, the.

82% Holistic Healing Web Page [More Like This]
URL: http://www.tiac.net:80/users/mgold/health.html
Summary: The holistic health-related information presented on this WWW page is not meant as medical advice. Environmental Issues Relating to Human & Planetary Health.

81% HOLISTIC CONCEPTS OF HEALTH AND DISEASE ... [More Like This]
URL: http://www.med.auth.gr:80/~karanik/english/vet/holist6.htm
Summary: HOLISTIC CONCEPTS OF HEALTH AND DISEASE #6. HOLISTIC CONCEPTS OF HEALTH AND DISEASE Answers.

81% Holistic Health Link [More Like This]
URL: http://www.kdcol.com:80/~daniel/prolink.htm
Summary: ....Holistic Health Services Holistic Health Care Practitioners Holistic Health Care Manufacturers, Distributors, and Suppliers. [Natural Connection] [Holistic Health Care] [Health Food Store] [Books] [E-Mail].

81% The Fosters: Holistic Health and Native ... [More Like This]
URL: http://www.blvl.igs.net:80/~bfoster/
Summary: The Fosters: Holistic Health and Native Herbs. A Homepage for Kristina and Bob Foster.

FIGURE 4.7

Search results with a percentage of confidence rating for finding relevant information

utilizes the next generation of search technology. Ultra promises new levels of speed, accuracy, and currency unmatched by other search technologies. Features of Infoseek Ultra include the following:

- the use of a highly accurate relevance ranking algorithm that is intended to provide highly relevant search returns;
- the ability to recognize proper names and phrases;
- permits case sensitive queries, full and partial phrase queries, and name variants;
- fast search returns for complex queries or during periods of high usage;
- an index of over 80 million URLs, with indexing of the text of over 50 million; and
- frequent updates of its Web pages' index to help ensure that you do not get a dead or obsolete link when you click on a search return URL.

Ultra recommends using quotes around words that must appear next to each other (see Fig. 4.8). Check the Tips link for more information on how to do efficient searches with Ultra.

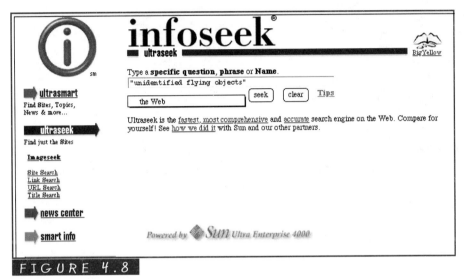

Infoseek Ultra showing a search for more than one keyword

Other Search Engines

There are many search engines to help you find information. You will need to use each of them at least several times before you can select the ones that best meet your needs. Listed below are additional search engines to explore.

ALTA VISTA (http://altavista.digital.com) by Digital is an excellent search engine with one of the largest Web-search databases.

IMAGE SURFER (http://isurf.interpix.com) differs from most search tools in that it focuses on finding images on the Web.

LYCOS (http://www.lycos.com) one of the older search tools, has recently expanded its services with new search capabilities for images and sounds, information on cities, road maps, companies online, stock quotes, and an excellent link to the top five percent Web sites (Fig. 4.9). Lycos moves to the top of the bookmark list.

HOTBOT (http://www.hotbot.com) is a new and very HOT search tool.

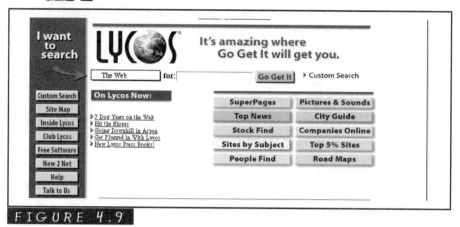

FIGURE 4.9

Lycos Home Page (The Lycos "Catalog of the Internet" Copyright 1994–1997 Carnegie Mellon University. All rights reserved. Lycos is a trademark of Carnegie Mellon University. Used by permission.)

INKTOMI (http://inktomi.berkeley.com) a search engine from Berkeley.

OPEN TEXT (http://www.opentext.com) has one of the most comprehensive collections of search tools and is one of the best designed search engines on the Internet.

WIRED SOURCE http://www.wiredsource.com/wiredsource has a collection of search engines to use for your research.

Internet Collections

Internet collections, compiled by an individual or group of individuals, are often goldmine resources for your research. One collection may give you all the Internet resources that you will need on a particular topic. For example, one excellent collection of business resources—Madalyn— has been compiled under a University of Delaware MBA program. Madalyn (**http://www.udel.edu/alex/mba/main/netdir2.html**) has links to accounting, corporate information, economics, entrepreneurship, ethics, finance, international business, management, marketing, quality, and more. Internet collections are your goldmine resources. If you are lucky you may be able to find your goldmine using a search directory. Listed below are some excellent collections and directories to explore.

ARCHEOLOGY

ARCHEOLOGY AND http://www.cr.nps.gov/archeo.html The National Park Service Archeology and Ethnography program is a leading authority on archeological and cultural resources in the United States. This site has a link to the National Archeological Database—a computerized communications network for the archeological and historical preservation community.

ART COLLECTIONS

ART HOTLIST http://sln.fi.edu/tfi/hotlists/art.html A collection of links to art galleries, museums, and artists.

ART SOURCE http://www.uky.edu/Artsource/artsourcehome.html This site offers a collection on art and architecture resources on the Net including original materials submitted by librarians, artists, and art historians. For electronic exhibitions select the link to Exhibitions.

INTERNET ARTRESOURCES http://artresources.com A complete guide to the visual arts with links to galleries, museums (over 1100 listed worldwide), art schools, artists, and much more.

BUSINESS COLLECTIONS

ALL BUSINESS NETWORK http://www.all-biz.com The All Business Network site (Fig. 4.10) has a pull-down menu of business topics. Select a topic you are researching, and click the **Find It** button. You will then be given a list of descriptive links on the subject to explore.

GTE SUPERSITE http://superpages.gte.net An excellent business resource with two research services: Yellow Pages and Business Web Site Directory. The Yellow Pages has a search tool to help you find comprehensive business information from more than 11 million listings found in over 5,000 Yellow Pages directories from virtually every city in the United States. The Business Web Site Directory features links to 60,000-plus business Web sites worldwide.

I.O.M.A. http://www.ioma.com/ioma/direct.html Links to business resources, including financial management, legal resources, small business, human resources, and Internet marketing.

MADALYN http://www.udel.edu/alex/mba/main/netdir2.html Maintained by the University of Delaware's MBA program,

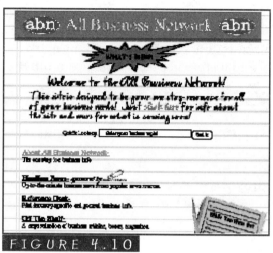

FIGURE 4.10

Home page for All Business Network

Madalyn has links to accounting, corporate information, economics, entrepreneurship, ethics, finance, international business, management, marketing, and quality resources.

CRIMINAL JUSTICE

DR. CECIL GREEK'S CRIMINAL JUSTICE LINKS http://www.stpt.usf .edu/~greek/cj.html This award-winning Web site has one of the most comprehensive listings of criminal justice resources on the Internet.

JUSTICE FOR ALL http://www.hotsites.net/fightback/jfa A comprehensive Web site with links to resources for victims of crime.

JUSTICE INFORMATION CENTER (NCJRS) http://www.ncjrs.org The National Criminal Justice Reference Service is one of the most extensive sources of information on criminal and juvenile justice in the world, providing services to an international community of policymakers and professionals. This site has many excellent links to criminal justice resources.

ENVIRONMENTAL COLLECTIONS

AMAZING ENVIRONMENTAL WEB DIRECTORY http://www. webdirectory.com The directory is a GOLDMINE of online environmental resources.

ENVIROLINK http://www.envirolink.org A virtual community that unites hundreds of environmental organizations and volunteers around the world and is dedicated to providing the most comprehensive, up-to-date environmental resources.

ENVIRONMENTAL SITES ON THE INTERNET http://www.lib.kth.se/~lg/ eindex.htm This is the GOLDMINE site for environmental resources on the Internet. It is sponsored by the Royal Institute of Technology in Sweden. In June 1996 it was selected as the Best Comprehensive Environmental Directory by CESSE (Center for Economic and Social Studies for the Environment), Brussels, Belgium.

INDIGENOUS PEOPLES RESOURCES http://www.halcyon.com/FWDP/ othernet.html The Internet has many other sources of information regarding indigenous peoples. This is an AWESOME list of resources.

GEOGRAPHY

CIA WORLD FACT BOOK http://www.odci.gov/cia/publications/ 95fact/index.html Published by the Central Intelligence Agency (CIA), The World Fact Book has a subject index for researching facts about countries.

GEOGRAPHIC NAME SERVER http://www.mit.edu:8001/geo Type the name of a place you want to look up and this search tool will get the information.

GEOGRAPHY RESOURCES http://www.ipl.org/ref/RR/GEN/ geography-rr.html The Internet Public Library has a wonderful collection of geography links.

THE GREAT GLOBE GALLERY http://hum.amu.edu.pl/~zbzw/glob/ glob1.htm This AWESOME site has links to every type of map or globe imaginable.

NATIONAL GEOGRAPHIC http://www.nationalgeographic.com Use the boarding pass to National Geographic's adventure travel online.

WORLD WIDE WEB VIRTUAL LIBRARY—GEOGRAPHY http://www .icomos.org/WWW_VL_Geography.html A collection of geography resources.

GOVERNMENT

FEDERAL GOVERNMENT AGENCIES http://www.lib.lsu.edu/gov/ fedgov.html A collection of over 200 government sites.

GOVERNMENT AGENCY LINKS http://www.fjc.gov/govlinks.html Links to the federal courts and other government agencies.

GOVERNMENT DOCUMENT LINKS http://thorplus.lib.purdue.edu/ reference/gov.html Purdue University has an impressive collection of online U.S. Government documents.

LIBRARY OF CONGRESS http://www.loc.gov Access the Library of Congress's databases, historical collections, exhibitions, publications, links to other electronic libraries, information on copyright, and much more.

PRESIDENT http://sunsite.unc.edu/lia/president A Web site with a collection of presidential resources and an exhibit on the First Ladies of the United States.

TEXAS A&M's WHITE HOUSE ARCHIVES http://www.tamu.edu/ whitehouse A collection of information about the White House and those who have resided there dating back to 1992.

THE WHITE HOUSE http://www1.whitehouse.gov/WH/Welcome .html Visit this site and explore the virtual library for a collection of presidential documents, speeches, and photos.

HISTORY

THE AMERICAN CIVIL WAR HOME PAGE http://funnelweb.utcc.utk .edu/~hoemann/warweb.html An AWESOME collection of Civil War resources.

THE ANCIENT WORLDS META INDEX http://atlantic.evsc.virginia.edu/ julia/AW/meta.html A GOLDMINE of resources on the ancient world.

BYZANTINE & MEDIEVAL STUDIES http://www.fordham.edu/ halsall/med/medweb.html Anything you ever wanted to know about Byzantine and Medieval history can probably be found in this amazing collection.

FROM REVOLUTION TO RECONSTRUCTION http://www.let.rug.nl This award-winning site has original source materials on American history from the colonial period until modern times.

GATEWAY TO WORLD HISTORY http://neal.ctstateu.edu/history/ world_history/world_history.html This site features a collection of history archives and historical resources on the Internet.

LITERATURE

AUTHOR'S PEN http://www.books.com/scripts/authors.exe A large collection of links with comprehensive resources to more than 625 authors. Author areas contain one or more home pages plus interviews, biographies, and complete bibliographies.

THE COMPLETE WORKS OF WILLIAM SHAKESPEARE http://the-tech.mit .edu/Shakespeare/works.html This site not only has an electronic version for each work of Shakespeare but also links to related resources and discussion forums.

THE GUTENBERG PROJECT ftp://mrcnext.cso.uiuc.edu http://www.w3.org/pub/DataSources/bySubject/Literature/ Gutenberg/Overview.html http://www.cs.waikato.ac.nz/~nzdl/gutenberg/text/query.html A collection of great works of English-language literature. Gutenberg's goal is to make 10,000 texts available online by the year 2001.

ULTIMATE BOOK LIST AND WRITER'S PAGE http://www.acpl.lib.in.us/ information_resources/ultimate_book_list.html A collection of book-related sites on the Internet. The ULTIMATE!

WORLD WIDE WEB VIRTUAL LIBRARY OF LITERATURE RESOURCES http://sunsite.unc.edu/ibic/guide.html A collection of book-related resources on the Internet.

MATHEMATICS

EINET MATH GUIDE http://galaxy.einet.net/galaxy/Science/ Mathematics.html A collection of mathematic resources from the search directory EINet Galaxy.

MATH AND SCIENCE GATEWAY http://www.tc.cornell.edu/Edu/ MathSciGateway This collection of math and science resources for students in grades 9–12 is maintained by Cornell University. Resources include astronomy, biology, chemistry, engineering, medicine, physics, meteorology, mathematics, earth, ocean, and environmental resources.

MATH PAGES http://www.seanet.com/~ksbrown This site contains over 300 articles on a variety of mathematical topics, including number theory, combinatorics, geometry, algebra, calculus, differential equations, probability, statistics, physics, and the history of mathematics.

MATH RESOURCES http://forum.swarthmore.edu/math.topics.html Selected math resources by subject. Math subjects are divided into K–12, College, and Advanced.

MATHEMATICS INFORMATION SERVERS http://www.math.psu.edu/ OtherMath.html An impressive collection of worldwide math resources.

TREASURE TROVE OF MATHEMATICS http://www.astro.virginia.edu/ ~eww6n/math/math0.html Although this collection has been compiled by an individual who provides a disclaimer at the top of his home page, the alphabetical listings are impressive.

THE VIRTUAL MATHEMATICS CENTER http://www-sci.lib.uci.edu/ ~martindale/GradMath.html Martindale's award-winning graduate and undergraduate mathematical center has an impressive collection of math resources. DEFINITELY MUST EXPLORE site.

MUSIC

CLASSICAL NET http://www.classical.net The site provides an extensive collection of classical music resources—over 2,000 in all—as well as more than 1,800 links to other interesting Web sites.

INTERNET MUSIC RESOURCES http://www.music.indiana.edu/ music_resources A collection of Internet music resources from Indiana University.

YAHOO MUSIC RESOURCES http://www.yahoo.com/Entertainment/ Music An extensive collection of music resources.

NEWS

ELECTRONIC NEWSSTAND http://www.image.dk/~knud-sor/en A collection of news publications including newspapers, magazines, radio and television stations, money and economy, sports, weather, and much more.

SCIENCE

ASTRONOMY LINKS FROM NASA http://quest.arc.nasa.gov/lfs/ other_sites.html An AWESOME collection of astronomy links from NASA.

CHEMISTRY RESOURCES http://www.rpi.edu/dept/chem/cheminfo/ chemres.html A collection of resources related to chemistry and associated fields.

EARTH PAGES http://starsky.hitc.com/earth/earth.html Earth Pages, sponsored by NASA, is a search and index tool to help navigate the Internet for data, information, and resources related to earth science.

EINET GALAXY http://galaxy.einet.net/galaxy/Science.html A collection of science and math resources.

GEOLOGICAL TIME MACHINE http://www.ucmp.berkeley.edu/help/ timeform.html Hop into this virtual time machine and experience time travel from the very early Precambrian to Quaternary present day.

INFOSEEK SCIENCE http://guide.infoseek.com/Science Infoseek's collection of science resources.

SCIENCE HOBBYIST http://www.eskimo.com/~billb This COOL site is an example of how individuals can contribute valuable information for the global universe. There are many unusual places to explore. A DEFINITELY MUST VISIT site.

SCIENCE TABLES AND DATABASES http://www.sci.lib.uci.edu/ ~martindale/Ref3.html Another Martindale site with an AWESOME collection of science tables and database resources.

VIRTUAL ASTROPHYSICS AND SPACE CENTER http://www-sci.lib .uci.edu/~martindale/GradSpace.html Martindale's award-winning graduate and undergraduate space center has an impressive collection of resources. DEFINITELY MUST EXPLORE site.

VIRTUAL BIOSCIENCE CENTER http://www-sci.lib.uci.edu/ ~martindale/GradBioscience.html A Martindale site with an exhaustive collection of bioscience resources including genetics, proteins, biology, botany, ecology, marine biology, genetics, and other resources such as periodic tables, dictionaries, and publications.

VIRTUAL CHEMISTRY CENTER http://www-sci.lib.uci.edu/ ~martindale/GradChemistry.html Martindale's graduate and undergraduate center for chemistry resources.

WINDOWS TO THE UNIVERSE http://www.windows.umich.edu An AWESOME astronomy collection from the University of Michigan is heavily designed with beautiful graphics. Although it seems to be designed for K–12, it is definitely worth a visit.

YAHOO SCIENCE RESOURCES http://www.yahoo.com/Science An extensive collection of science resources.

Reference Resources

The Internet is the newest and perhaps largest reference library. This rich source of information is available to Net users. Listed below are a few reference resources that you will find useful.

ASK AN EXPERT http://njnie.dl.stevens-tech.edu/curriculum/aska .html This Web site provides opportunities for you to interact with experts on topics such as computers, economics, literature, and science by sending questions via email.

BARTLETT'S FAMILIAR QUOTATIONS http://www.ccc.columbia.edu/ acis/bartleby/bartlett/index.html Looking for a quote for your class presentation or paper? Connect to this Web site and search by keyword or choose from a list of people.

BRITANNICA ONLINE http://www.eb.com For a minimal fee you can subscribe to the Britannica Online and Merriam-Webster's

Collegiate Dictionary. Some of the encyclopedia text is linked to Internet sites.

CIA WORLD FACT BOOK http://www.odci.gov/cia/publications/95fact/index.html Published by the Central Intelligence Agency (CIA), The World Fact Book has a subject index for researching facts about countries.

DICTIONARIES & THESAURI http://www.arts.cuhk.hk/Ref.html#dt A GOLDMINE collection of cyberdictionaries, thesauri, and other subject-oriented references.

ENCYBERPEDIA http://www.encyberpedia.com/ency.htm The HOTTEST encyclopedia from cyberspace designed to help you find good stuff in the jungle of over two million Web sites.

MEGACONVERTER http://www.megaconverter.com MegaConverter.com is an ever-growing set of weights, measures, and units conversion/calculation modules.

MY VIRTUAL REFERENCE DESK http://www.refdesk.com/main.html Links to many excellent reference resources including a link to a subject directory of resources—My Virtual Encyclopedia (see Fig. 4.11).

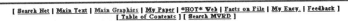

MY VIRTUAL ENCYCLOPEDIA

ARTS - CULTURE	HARDWARE	MOVIES	SHOPPING
AUTOMOTIVE	HEALTH	MUSIC	SOFTWARE
BOOKS - LITERATURE	HISTORY	PERSONAL FINANCES	SPACE
BUSINESS - CAREER	HUMOR	PETS - ANIMALS	RECREATION
EDUCATION	INTERNATIONAL	PHILOSOPHY	TELEVISION - RADIO
ENVIRONMENT	INTERNET	PHOTOGRAPHY	TRAVEL
FAMILY MATTERS	KIDS' STUFF	POLITICS	WEATHER
FOOD - RECIPES	MAGAZINES	RELATIONSHIPS	WOMEN'S ISSUES
GOVERNMENT	MENTAL HEALTH	SENIORS ONLINE	
GRAPHICS	MILITARY	SCIENCE	

FIGURE 4.11

My Virtual Reference Desk's link to a subject directory of resources

NOBLE CITIZENS OF PLANET EARTH http://www.tiac.net/users/
parallax This dictionary contains biographical information on
more than 18,000 people who have shaped our world from
ancient times to the present day. Information contained in the
dictionary includes birth and death years, professions, positions
held, literary and artistic works, and other achievements.

ONELOOK DICTIONARIES http://www.onelook.com Type in a word
and this search tool will look for multiple definitions from a
variety of online dictionaries: computer/Internet dictionaries,
science, medical, technological, business, sports, religion,
acronym, and general.

REFERENCE CENTER http://www.ipl.org/ref This virtual library
helps to make finding valuable information online easy. Click on
a reference shelf and be linked to resources (see Fig. 4.12).

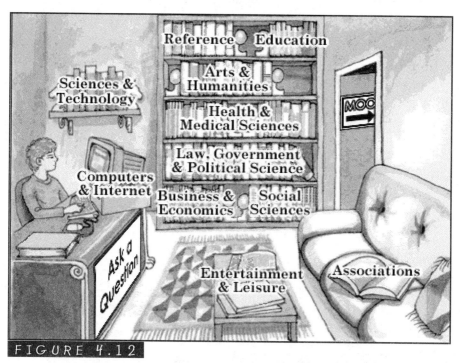

FIGURE 4.12

Online Reference Center Home Page

REFERENCE DESK http://www-sci.lib.uci.edu/~martindale/Ref.html
This GOLDMINE site has won multiple awards for its SUPERB
resource collection. A go to the top of the bookmark list site.

REFERENCE INDEXES http://www.lib.lsu.edu/weblio.html Links to online references such as dictionaries, library catalogs, newsstand, and subject collections.

REFERENCE SHELF http://gort.ucsd.edu/ek/refshelf/refshelf.html The University of California, San Diego, sponsors this collection of online reference resources.

RESEARCHPAPER.COM http://www.researchpaper.com/directory .html This award-winning online research tool offers an archive of thousands of magazines, newspapers, books, and photographs.

THE VIRTUAL REFERENCE DESK http://thorplus.lib.purdue.edu/ reference/index.html Purdue University's links to an AWESOME list of valuable online resources.

WIRED SOURCE http://www.wiredsource.com/wiredsource A collection of search engines to use for your research.

Virtual Libraries

Libraries from around the world can be accessed for research. Some libraries require a Telnet connection and the use of commands to find and retrieve information. Some libraries provide Help menus to assist you; others do not. Many libraries now have World Wide Web access, thus eliminating the need for commands to find information. Listed below are library resources on the Web.

ELECTRIC LIBRARY http://www.elibrary.com The Electric Library is a virtual library where you can conduct research online. Submit a question and a comprehensive search is launched of over 150 full-text newspapers, 800 full-text magazines, two international newswires, two thousand classic books, hundreds of maps, thousands of photographs, as well as major works of literature and art.

INTERNET PUBLIC LIBRARY http://www.ipl.org The Internet Public Library is the first public library of the Internet created by librarians committed to accommodating that world. The goal of this project is to provide library services to the Internet community, to learn and teach what librarians have to contribute in a digital environment, to promote librarianship and the importance of libraries, and to share interesting ideas and techniques with other librarians. Their mission directs them to serve the public by finding, evaluating, selecting, organizing, describing, and creating quality information resources.

LIBCAT http://www.metronet.lib.mn.us/lc/lc1.html An AWESOME guide to library resources on the Internet.

LIBRARY OF CONGRESS http://www.loc.gov http://lcweb.loc.gov Access the Library of Congress databases, historical collections, exhibitions, publications, links to other electronic libraries, information on copyright, and much more (see Fig. 4.13).

FIGURE 4.13

Library of Congress Home Page

LIBWEB http://sunsite.Berkeley.EDU/Libweb A collection of online libraries worldwide.

SMITHSONIAN INSTITUTION http://www.si.edu/newstart.htm A valuable online research service, the Smithsonian Institution features over one million resources. Click on the link to Resources and Tours to begin your journey.

WEBCHATS http://library.usask.ca/hywebcat/
http://library.usask.ca Library catalogs on the Web.

USING INTERNET SOURCES FOR RESEARCH

Internet resources provide valuable information that you can use for class presentations, papers, research, dissertations, and theses. However, the Internet should never be your sole source of information but rather another resource that you use to find information on a topic. The Internet can access

- information collections and databases,
- government documents,
- exhibitions,
- research papers,
- publications,
- news,
- online educational events,
- the latest and most current information on a topic, and
- communication with experts on your topic.

In this section you will learn

- how to evaluate Internet information sources.
- how to record information sources.
- how to reference Internet sources.

Evaluating Internet Information

The Internet is analogous to a wilderness frontier that is wild and untamed. With an estimate of 20 to 50 million pages of data created from a variety of sources—individuals, businesses, corporations, non-profit organizations, schools, special interest groups, or illicit if not illegal sources—it is inherent that not all the information is accurate, unbiased, reputable, scientifically valid, or up-to-date. Unlike scholarly publications, there is no editorial board for most Internet information. It is therefore essential that you understand how to evaluate information you research on the Net.

How strict you are with your evaluation will depend on your purpose. For example, if you are writing a factual report, dissertation, thesis, or paper that others will rely on for accurate content, it will be essential that you are judicious in choosing what information will be reported from the Net.

The first thing you must do when using the Internet for your studies is to determine which resources to use. The following guidelines will assist you with evaluation.

 Information Source. Where does the information come from— an individual, organization, educational institution, or other source? One way to quickly determine the source of the information is to look at the URL—Net site address. The first address protocol often will give you the source of the information—name of institution and domain. For example, an address such as **http://gort.ucsd.edu** tells the name of the institution—University of California, San Diego—and the *edu* ending indicates an educational institution. An educational institution has a good chance of being a reputable source. Other address endings that are highly likely to be reputable are *gov* for government or *mil* for military. Naturally, you will want to evaluate the information further. Just because the information is from an educational institution, government, or military source does not ensure that the content is factual and reliable.

Check to see if the document resides in an individual's personal Internet account or is part of the organization's official Internet site. This information can often be determined by looking at the URL address pathway.

Is the organization that publishes this document recognized in the field you are studying? Is the organization qualified to be an expert in this topic?

 Authorship. Closely related to the information source is the reputation of the data and the reliability of its source. Although the information may be from an educational institution, who wrote and compiled the data—a professor, a student, or other source?

Information on an educational institution Web site may be compiled by a student or graduate student who is not as yet an authority on the subject and may enter in written errors or present incorrect data without realizing it. The content may not have been reviewed for accuracy and reliability.

Who is the author? Does the author have credentials to be an expert on the topic? Consider educational background, experience, and other published writings. Have you encountered the author's name in your reading or in bibliographies?

Does the Internet document furnish information on the author such as institutional affiliation, position, experience, and credentials? If none of this is provided, is there an email address or a mailing address from which you can request biographical information? Correspond with the author to obtain more information about the source of his or her content.

 Accuracy. Is the data accurate? Check to see if there is a reference for the information. Where does the information come from—a published research paper or report, historical document, news publication, or is it a personal viewpoint? Does the document include a bibliography? Does the author acknowledge related sources?

Although information may be written from a personal viewpoint, don't invalidate it. Bias is to be expected especially if one is a participant in an event. If the writing seems biased, look for inconsistencies or incorrect thinking. Does the author acknowledge that his treatment of the subject is controversial? Are there political or ideological biases? Can you separate fact from opinion? Do any statements seem exaggerated or overly simplified? Has the author omitted any important details? Is the writer qualified to be authoritative?

One example of inaccuracy in Web writing is the use of the words *endangered species* when referring to animals that may in fact be only threatened or vulnerable. Many authors loosely use the words *endangered species.* To cross check this information, a reliable source such as the Convention on International Trade and Endangered Species (CITES) and the International Union for the Conservation of Nature (IUCN) must be used. These international organizations keep the working lists of which species are categorized as either extinct, endangered, threatened, vulnerable, indeterminate, or out of danger.

 Verifiable. Can the data be verified? Does it appear to be well-researched? Does the author make generalizations without proof or validation? Always be thinking "Show me why or how." In some instances you may need to ask if the data has statistical validity—supported by statistical testing. Watch for errors or omissions.

When numbers or statistical information is reported, it is critical that the data be cross-checked with a reliable publication source. For example, some Web factual data contain errors due to carelessness in copying and transposing numbers from a print version to a

Web site. Reporting that 17,000 areas of rain forest are destroyed daily when the correct number is 700 acres is an inexcusable error in sloppy copy.

Consistency of data. Is the data consistent or does it reflect contradictions with other information on the topic? Are definitions used consistently throughout?

For example, our search for reputable Web sites on the rain forest led to the discovery of Public Broadcasting System (PBS) and the Rain Forest Action Network as excellent online references to cross-check the consistency of data.

Quality. Is the text error free; is it well organized and grammatically correct? Check for the misspelling of names or carelessness and lack of attention to details in other areas. Information that contains these types of careless errors probably should not be relied on.

Is the tone scholarly, technical, factual, authoritative, or personal?

Currency. Is the information current and up-to-date? Does the document include a publication date or a date of copyright? Does it appear to be appropriate and relevant for today? Information that was reported in 1985 is probably not valid today. Look for the most current information unless currency is not an issue.

Bonus guidelines—other important suggestions

Whenever possible, check online information against other sources. Never use information that you cannot verify.

Question everything that you read. Learn to be critical and skeptical.

Information found on the Internet should complement information from traditional research resources. Never use Internet information as your sole source of knowledge.

"When in doubt, leave it out."

TIP

If you don't know where to find a reliable source to cross-check your information, talk with a resource librarian, teacher, or professor. These individuals can be excellent resources for finding publications to verify your data. You can also call a reputable organization.

Recording Internet Information Sources

As you browse the Internet reviewing resources that are informative and valuable, it is important to make note of where these resources can be found. You will need this information for referencing your work. In your writing you may want to indicate to your readers that information has come from the Internet by making a reference note.

TIP . . .

When you find an Internet resource that you think you would like to use in a class paper or project, make note of where this information can be found and make a bookmark within your browser. You may want to create a special browser folder for your URLs that you will be using for the paper or project.

The following information should be recorded as you select Internet information resources.

☑ title of the Internet document or resource (located in the title bar at the top of your browser's page)

☑ author (if no author is listed look for an email address at the bottom of the page)

☑ Internet address (URL) including all pathways

☑ date of publication (this date may be listed as the date of the latest revision or modification)

☑ date you accessed the Internet site (this indicates to readers that on this date the Internet document you are referring to was available at the given URL)

NOTE The Internet is a dynamic and rapidly changing environment. Information may be in one place today and either gone or in a new location tomorrow. New sites come up daily; others disappear. The use of an access date indicates when the information was available at the given URL.

Remember—the purpose of referencing items is to provide the necessary information so others can find your resources. It is therefore critical that you record this information accurately. When recording a URL, check and double-check the electronic address to be sure it is correct.

TIP . . .

*One way to be sure that you have copied the URL exactly is to have a word processing program open at the same time you are working within your Internet browser. Go to the **Address** location field in your browser, highlight the URL, then use the **Copy** command to copy the URL. Next, go to your word processing program and in an open file paste the URL. This ensures that you have the exact URL to record in your reference notes or bibliography.*

REFERENCING ELECTRONIC MEDIA

As with any published reference, the goal of an electronic reference is to credit the author and to enable the reader to find the material. The International Standards Organization (ISO) continues to modify a uniform system of citing electronic documents. The following guidelines and examples have been compiled from *The American Psychological Association (APA) Publication Manual, MLA-Style,* and *The Chicago Manual of Style.*

- Be consistent in your references to online documentation or information.

- Capitalization follows the "accepted practice for the language or script in which the information is given."

- Use your discretion for the choice of punctuation used to separate elements and in the use of variations in typeface or underscoring to distinguish or highlight elements.

- If a print form is available and the same as the electronic form, referencing of the print form is preferred.

Include the following in your reference:

- The author's name if it is available or important for identification.

- The most recent date of publication or a modification date if document undergoes revision.

- The date you accessed the document on the Internet.

- Title of the document, file, or World Wide Web site.

- Specific protocol: Telnet, Gopher, FTP, World Wide Web.

- Internet address or retrieval path for accessing the information including the file name, directory, and pathway.

- Subscription information, if the information is available via a listserv mailing list.

- Do not end a path statement with a period, because it is not part of the Internet address and may hinder retrieval if used.

 NOTE The examples provided in this section use APA style. Although the type of information required for referencing is similar, the format for the references varies between the APA, MLA, and the Chicago styles. Check with your professor to see which style to use. Refer to the style manual for the reference format.

The following is the format for referencing online information in the APA style.

Author, I. (date of work). *Title of full work* [online]. Available: Specify protocol and path (date document was accessed).

Author, I., & Author, I. (date). *Title of full work* [online]. Specify protocol and path (date document was accessed).

Examples of APA Style

WORLD WIDE WEB

The World Wide Web provides many types of information you may want to reference: text, images, video, or sound. To reference these information sources, include the following:

- author's name (if known)

- date of Web site information (if known or different from date you accessed)

- title of the page or article

- additional information such as version or edition

- the URL for the page you are referencing

- date you accessed this page

🦌 EXAMPLE 1

Referencing World Wide Web Site

The first reference is from CNET.COM, a computer network that integrates television programming with a network. CNET's Web site takes advantage of the Web's interactive capabilities to deliver valuable information on computer technology, the Internet, and the future of technology in a well-designed, creative, and rich multimedia environment (see Fig. 4.14).

FIGURE 4.14

World Wide Web page from CNET.COM to be referenced (Source: *Reprinted with permission from CNET, Inc. copyright 1995–1997 www.cnet.com.*)

World Wide Web Reference #1

Farell, C. (1997, February). Get animated: How to make your GIFs dance [Online]. Available: http://www.cnet.com/Content/Features/Howto/Webanim/index.html (March 1997).

EXAMPLE 2

World Wide Web Reference

The second example shown in Fig. 4.15 is an excellent Web site for helping students with career planning and finding a job. The Home Page for this site (**http://www.jobtrak.com/jobguide**) supplies much of the needed information for the reference.

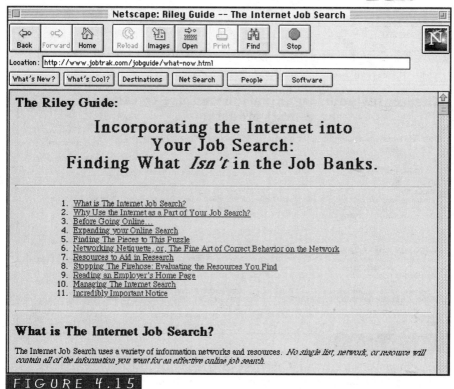

FIGURE 4.15

World Wide Web site for a reference

World Wide Web Reference #2

Riley, M. F. (1996). Incorporating the Internet into your job search [Online]. Available: http://www.dbm.com/jobguide/what-now.html (March 1997).

EXAMPLE 3

World Wide Web

Figure 4.16 references an article on Netscape World's site.

World Wide Web Reference #3

Bowen, B. D. (1997). Strategies your organization can use to tame the e-mail monster [Online]. Available: http://www.netscapeworld .com (March 1997).

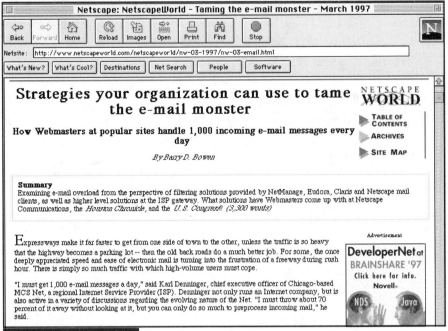

GOPHER

When referencing Gopher sites, include the following information:

- author's name (if known)
- date of publication
- title of the page, article, or file
- additional information such as version or edition
- the URL for the page you are referencing and the pathway to this information
- date you accessed this page

EXAMPLE 1

Gopher Reference

The Library of Congress (Fig. 4.17) has information on copyright. To reference this information visit their Gopher server.

```
Circular 1

                        COPYRIGHT BASICS


WHAT COPYRIGHT IS

Copyright is a form of protection provided by the laws of the
United States (title 17, U.S. Code) to the authors of "original
works of authorship" including literary, dramatic, musical,
artistic, and certain other intellectual works.  This protection
is available to both published and unpublished works.  Section 106
of the Copyright Act generally gives the owner of copyright the
exclusive right to do and to authorize others to do the following:

   --  To reproduce the copyrighted work in copies or phonorecords;

   --  To prepare derivative works  based upon the copyrighted work;
```

FIGURE 4.17

Library of Congress document at their Gopher site

Gopher Reference #1

Library of Congress. (updated 9/95). Copyright Basics [Online]. Available: gopher://marvel.loc.gov:70/00/.ftppub/copyright/circs/circ01 (March 1997).

EXAMPLE 2

Gopher Reference

The second example is a NASA Gopher site. Figure 4.18 shows the first page for this site (**gopher://naic.nasa.gov**). For this page numerous pathways (links) must be taken to find the information on the M.U.S.E report. It is essential that this information be provided for others to find this article.

NOTE   Gopher Reference #1 lists the server pathway as part of the URL. In Gopher Reference #2, the server pathway is very long and is therefore listed as a pathway separate from the URL. One factor to consider in determining whether to make the pathway part of the URL is its length. Remember that the location of information on a server may be moved and thus the pathway changes. If you list the server pathway separate from the URL it may be easier to find a site that has changed one part of its pathway links.

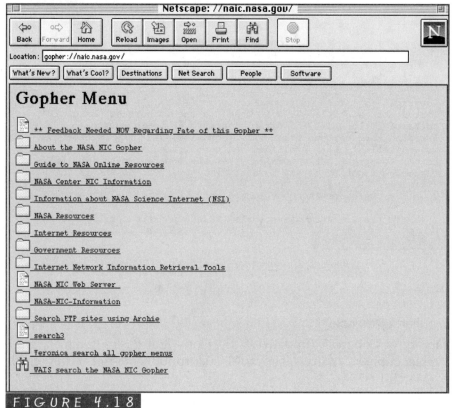

Back | Forward | Home | Reload | Images | Open | Print | Find | Stop

Location: gopher://naic.nasa.gov/

What's New? | What's Cool? | Destinations | Net Search | People | Software

Gopher Menu

** Feedback Needed NOW Regarding Fate of this Gopher **

About the NASA NIC Gopher

Guide to NASA Online Resources

NASA Center NIC Information

Information about NASA Science Internet (NSI)

NASA Resources

Internet Resources

Government Resources

Internet Network Information Retrieval Tools

NASA NIC Web Server

NASA-NIC-Information

Search FTP sites using Archie

search3

Veronica search all gopher menus

WAIS search the NASA NIC Gopher

FIGURE 4.18

The opening menu for NASA's Gopher server

Gopher Reference #2

Part I - M.U.S.E. Report (1993, December). [Online]. Available Gopher: gopher://naic.nasa.gov/ Pathway: /Guide to NASA Online Resources/ NASA Scientific, Educational, and Governmental Resources/ Government Resources/Americans Communicating Electronically/ Electronic Mail Issues for the Federal Government/ Unified Federal Government Electronic Mail Users Support Environment Report (November 1996).

FILE TRANSFER PROTOCOL

When referencing documents that you have accessed using FTP, include the following:

- author's name (if known)

- date of publication (if available)

- title of the document, article, or file

- the address for the FTP site, along with the pathway to this information

- date you accessed this site

 **EXAMPLE 1**

FTP Reference

Figure 4.19 is an article with information on how to use email to access Internet resources.

```
                Accessing The Internet By E-Mail
                    2nd Edition - August 1994


            Copyright (c) 1994, "Doctor Bob" Rankin

    All rights reserved.  Permission is granted to make and distribute
    verbatim copies of this document provided the copyright notice and
        this permission notice are preserved on all copies.


How to Access Internet Services by E-mail
------------------------------------------------

If your only access to the Internet is via e-mail, you don't have to
miss out on all the fun!  Maybe you've heard of FTP, Gopher, Archie,
Veronica, Finger, Whois, WAIS, World-Wide Web, and Usenet but thought
they were out of your reach because your online service does not provide
those tools.  Not so!  And even if you do have full Internet access,
using e-mail servers can save you time and money.
```

FIGURE 4.19

Internet By E-Mail document at NASA's FTP site

FTP Reference #1

Rankin, B. (1994, August). Accessing the Internet by e-mail, 2nd edition [Online]. Available: ftp://dftnic.gsfc.nasa.gov/general_info/internet .by-email (March 1997).

 EXAMPLE 2

FTP Reference

Figure 4.20 is from Project Gutenberg's FTP site. The article to be referenced is on the history and philosophy of Project Gutenberg.

FTP Reference #2

History and philosophy of Project Gutenberg (1992, August). In Gutenberg Archives [Online]. Available FTP: ftp://uiarchive.uiuc.edu Directory: /pub/etext/gutenberg/articles/history.gut (April 1997).

```
The History and Philosophy of Project Gutenberg (c)August 1992

Second edition prepared for August, 1992.    Updated regularly.
(margins are 62, about 10 pages, send only the complete file.)
(Includes answers to many Frequently Asked Questions (FAQ))

There is a lot of information in this little file. . .and your
requested information may be contained in a short portion.  It
is therefore recommended that you search for subjects.  It was
not feasible to break this file into smaller ones, but we have
been told that our audience responds best to quick, short, and
concise responses.  These are marked by subject headers and by
paragraphing.  Read fast, it is all quite simple.  If you find
something of great interest, you might want to read it again.

The purpose of this file is to answer questions. . .not create
flames.  We have long ago learned that flamers must be allowed
to burn themselves out.  However, we feel obliged to answer in
the forums in which the flames were posted. . .not to satisfy,
can't be done, the flamers, but to explain to the rest of that
audience what Project Gutenberg is and is not, however flamers
may have misstated the obvious.  Etext is certainly one of the
most obvious uses of computers, and the flamers can hardly put
a dent in that fact.  Plain Vanilla ASCII is also obviously an
important etext medium, but no one at Project Gutenberg states
that it is or should be the only etext medium.

"When you get something for free, you get what you pay for!!!"
That means if you don't use what you get for free, it won't do
you any good.  But sometimes it is nice to have a library your
friends and family can use, even if they don't always use it.
```

FIGURE 4.20

Article on an FTP site to be referenced

TELNET

When referencing Telnet sites, include the following:

- author's name (if known)
- date of publication (if available)
- title of the work or the name of the Telnet site
- the address for the Telnet site
- directions for accessing the publication when connected
- date you accessed this site

🐾 EXAMPLE 1

Telnet Reference

The first example shown in Fig. 4.21 is from the Smithsonian Institution's Telnet site.

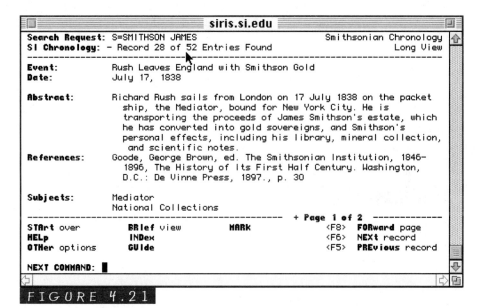

FIGURE 4.21

Abstract on the history of the Smithsonian founder, James Smithson

Telnet Reference #1

S1 Chronology (Record 28). Rush leaves England with Smithson gold [Online]. Available: telnet://siris.si.edu (March 1997).

🐾 EXAMPLE 2

Telnet Reference

Figure 4.22 is from the MOO, Diversity University.

Telnet Reference #2

Diversity University_Guest. Welcome to Diversity University MOO [Online]. Available: telnet://moo.du.org:8888 (March 1997).

EMAIL, LISTSERV MAILING LISTS, AND USENET NEWSGROUPS

Information from email, listservs, and newsgroups is both timely and personal, often representing an individual's point of view. This information must also be

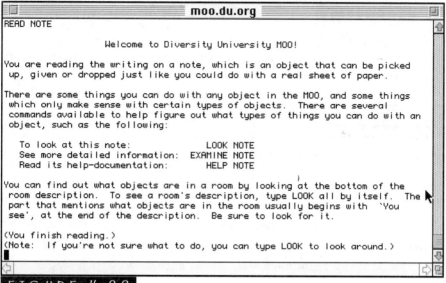

moo.du.org

```
READ NOTE

              Welcome to Diversity University MOO!

You are reading the writing on a note, which is an object that can be picked
up, given or dropped just like you could do with a real sheet of paper.

There are some things you can do with any object in the MOO, and some things
which only make sense with certain types of objects.  There are several
commands available to help figure out what types of things you can do with an
object, such as the following:

    To look at this note:              LOOK NOTE
    See more detailed information:  EXAMINE NOTE
    Read its help-documentation:       HELP NOTE

You can find out what objects are in a room by looking at the bottom of the
room description.  To see a room's description, type LOOK all by itself.  The
part that mentions what objects are in the room usually begins with `You
see', at the end of the description.  Be sure to look for it.

(You finish reading.)
(Note:  If you're not sure what to do, you can type LOOK to look around.)
```

FIGURE 4.22

Information on navigating within Diversity University's text-based virtual environment

referenced. *Do not reference personal email. Email references will mainly come from listservs and newsgroups. To reference these information sources, provide the following:*

- author's name (if known)

- date of the email message, listserv message, or Usenet posting

- subject

- name of the listserv or newsgroup

- address of the listserv or newsgroup

- information on how to find the group's archives, if available

- date accessed

EXAMPLE 1

Email Reference

The latest document on how to use email to access Internet resources is available by using email (see Fig. 4.19).

Email Reference #1

Rankin, B. (1994, August). Accessing the Internet by e-mail [Online].
  Available Email: LISTSERV @ubvm.cc.buffalo.edu: GET INTERNET
  BY-EMAIL NETTRAIN F=MAIL

🦎 EXAMPLE 2

Listserv Mailing List Reference

The example in Fig. 4.23 has been taken from a listserv for NASA's
Galileo expedition.

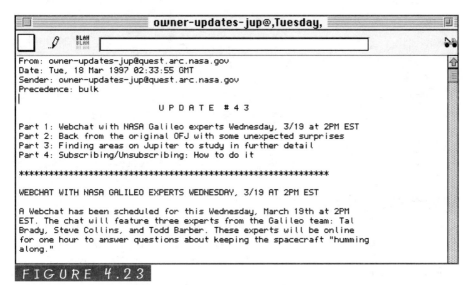

```
owner-updates-jup@,Tuesday,

From: owner-updates-jup@quest.arc.nasa.gov
Date: Tue, 18 Mar 1997 02:33:55 GMT
Sender: owner-updates-jup@quest.arc.nasa.gov
Precedence: bulk

              U P D A T E   # 4 3

Part 1: Webchat with NASA Galileo experts Wednesday, 3/19 at 2PM EST
Part 2: Back from the original OFJ with some unexpected surprises
Part 3: Finding areas on Jupiter to study in further detail
Part 4: Subscribing/Unsubscribing: How to do it

******************************************************************

WEBCHAT WITH NASA GALILEO EXPERTS WEDNESDAY, 3/19 AT 2PM EST

A Webchat has been scheduled for this Wednesday, March 19th at 2PM
EST. The chat will feature three experts from the Galileo team: Tal
Brady, Steve Collins, and Todd Barber. These experts will be online
for one hour to answer questions about keeping the spacecraft "humming
along."
```

FIGURE 4.23

NASA's listserv with updates on the Galileo mission

Listserv Reference #1

Orton, G. (1997, February). Back from the original OFJ with some unex-
  pected surprises [Online]. Available Email: listmanager@quest
  .arc.nasa.gov: subscribe updates-jup

Also available: http://quest.arc.nasa.gov/galileo/people.html

🦎 EXAMPLE 3

Usenet Newsgroup Reference

The example shown in Fig. 4.24 was taken from an environmental
newsgroup.

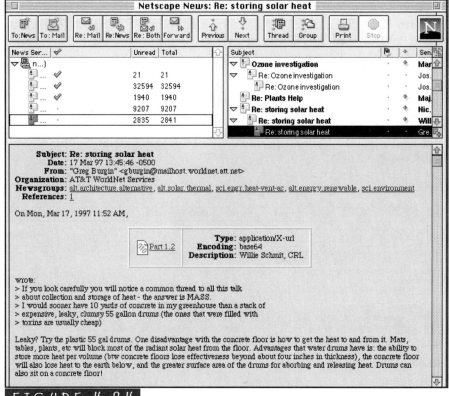

FIGURE 4.24

Newsgroup discussion on solar energy viewed from Netscape's news reader (Copyright 1996 Netscape Communications Corp. Used with permission. All rights reserved. This electronic file or page may not be reprinted or copied without the express written permission of Netscape.)

Newsgroup Reference #1

Burgin, G. (1997, March). Storing solar energy [Online]. Available Newsgroup: sci.environment (March 1997).

For more information on referencing Internet resources, visit the following Web sites for MLA:

MLA REFERENCE (http://www.cas.usf.edu/english/walker/mla.html)

(http://english.ttu.edu/kairos/1.2/inbox/mla_archive.html) An excellent online resource, "Beyond the MLA Handbook: Documenting Electronic Sources on the Internet."

(http://www.smpcollege.com/online-4styles~help) MLA's Home Page for discussions on problems that researchers encounter in cyberspace.

LEARNING ADVENTURES

Using the Internet for Research and Finding Cool Things

Select a topic of interest (i.e., a hobby, sport, country, a trip you plan to take, or a research topic.).

1. Use Yahoo, Excite, Infoseek, Galaxy, and Magellan to research your topic. Begin by investigating their subject directories. After you have explored the directories, do a keyword search.

2. How do Yahoo, Excite, Infoseek, Galaxy, and Magellan differ in the way they access information? Do you find one better or more useful than the other?

3. Explore the Advanced Options in Yahoo to refine and limit your search. Conduct a search using the Advanced Options. Did you get better returns?

4. Use each of the following search engines to research your topic: Infoseek Ultra, Excite, Alta Vista, Lycos, HotBot, Inktomi, Open Text, and Wired. Before you use these search engines, read how to use their advanced options for a more efficient search.

5. Compare and contrast the different search engines you used in number 4. Which one did you find most useful in providing the information you were searching for? What are the advantages of each? Disadvantages?

6. How do search tools such as Yahoo, Galaxy, and Magellan differ from search engines such as Infoseek, Excite, and Alta Vista? Do you think there would be times you would find one more useful than another?

7. Use Image Surfer and Lycos to research an image.

8. Find a subject category in Internet Collections and explore some of the online collections. How do collections compare to search directories in providing useful and valuable information? Would you use them as your only source for finding online information?

9. Explore the online reference resources.

10. Explore the online virtual libraries.

11. Begin a category or a file folder in your Internet browser for Internet research tools. Make bookmarks of search tools that you find helpful.

CHAPTER V

USING CYBERSPACE FOR CAREER PLANNING AND FINDING A JOB

The Internet provides an abundance of job resources including searchable databases, résumé postings and advertising, career planning information, and job-search strategies. There are several databases and newsgroups that allow you to post your résumé at no cost. Many companies post job listings on their Web pages.

The Internet also encourages networking with people around the country and around the world. People that you meet on the Internet can be important resources for helping you to find a job and learn more about the business or career you are interested in.

Each day, the number of job openings increases as new services become available. Many believe that the real changes and opportunities are still to come. The question is no longer whether the Internet should be used to find a job or an employee, but rather, how to use it.

In this chapter, you will

- take a self-awareness journey to learn more about yourself and your personal and professional needs;
- research jobs that fit you as a person;
- learn how to use the Internet for career exploration: communication with people, electronic publications, career resources, and professional services.
- find companies with job opportunities;
- use the Internet as a tool for learning about job resources;
- develop résumés to showcase talent and skill;
- find Internet sites to post your résumé with;
- use the Internet as a tool to maximize your potential for finding a job; and
- prepare for a job interview by researching prospective companies.

In this chapter you will also find Guided Tours for using the Internet for finding and obtaining information about four different types of jobs.

JOB SEARCH 1 uses Internet resources for finding a job in management training. You will also learn how to research companies with posted jobs to learn more about their corporate culture and work environment.

JOB SEARCH 2 uses different Internet resources for finding information on job opportunities for accounting.

JOB SEARCH 3 introduces you to Internet sites where you will find environmental job opportunities. You will also learn how to research the city where they are located.

JOB SEARCH 4 uses different Internet resources for finding information on job opportunities in environmental technology.

SELF-AWARENESS JOURNEY

Self-assessment is the first step in career planning. Self-assessment is an important process that requires inner reflection. The goal of this reflective process is to help you develop a better understanding of your interests, talents, values, goals, aptitudes, abilities, personal traits, and desired lifestyle. You will use this information to help find a job that fits you as a person. This personal survey is very important in helping you become aware of the interrelationship between your personal needs and your occupational choices.

Start by identifying:

- your interests and what is important to you;
- what you enjoy doing in your free time;
- skills you learned in the classroom or from an internship that are related to your career interests;
- your accomplishments;
- abilities and capabilities;
- work experience related to your career interests;
- personal traits and characteristics;
- your strengths and weaknesses; and
- physical and psychological needs.

Ask these questions regarding career considerations:

- Where would you like to live? In a city, the suburbs, the country, the seashore, or the mountains?

- Is there a specific geographic location where you would like to live?

- How do you feel about commuting to work? Would you drive a long distance to work for the advantage of living outside of a city?

- Is the community that you live in important? For example, do you value a community that is outdoor oriented or family oriented?

- What type of work environment is important to you? Do you want to wear a power suit every day or be casual?

- Is making a lot of money important to you?

- How do you feel about benefits and promotion options?

- Are flexible hours and free weekends important? For example, do you value free time to exercise and participate in outdoor activities? Are you willing to sacrifice this part of your life for a job? Would you be satisfied with making enough money to live on and have more free time?

- Do you mind working long hours each day, or weekends? How do you feel about taking vacation time?

- Do you want to work for a large or small company? Would you rather work for a small company where everyone knows each other and the atmosphere is perhaps a little more casual? Or is it more important to be with a large company with many career advancement opportunities?

- Where would you like to be in your professional life in 5 years? 10 years? Does this company offer advancement opportunities that fit your goals?

- How do you feel about work-related travel? Do you mind traveling if a job requires you to do so? Do you mind giving up portions of your weekend to travel? How many days a month are you willing to be away from home?

- How do you feel about being a member of a work team?

After you have completed your self-awareness journey, you are ready to use this information to explore career options.

CAREER EXPLORATION

The goal of career exploration is to help you to find job opportunities that match your personal and professional needs. Career exploration involves gathering information about the world of work. You will eliminate or select jobs based on what you learned in your self-assessment. For example, if you determine that location is an important factor when selecting a job, you would use this criteria to select or eliminate job opportunities based on where a particular company is located. Information about the work environment and corporate culture will be more difficult to obtain.

There are many ways to learn about the world of work. In this section we will explore several options involving the use of the Internet to acquire information.

People as Information Resources

Internships and work experience provide excellent opportunities to learn about companies and their world of work. For example, if you are doing an internship for a company, observe the work ethic and corporate environment. Ask someone doing a job that interests you what it is like to work for the company. How many hours do they work per day? Are they expected to work weekends? How does their department, boss, and other employees view vacations? Do they have free time during a day for personal interests such as running, cycling, or working out at the gym? What are the company's expectations of its employees? If a job position requires the employee to travel, how many days per month do they travel? When do they leave to travel; when do they return? How are they compensated for overtime?

Other sources for obtaining information from people include

- talking with career counselors;

- attending seminars and workshops where you can interact with professionals and ask questions;

- attending conventions and job fairs;

- joining a professional organization; and

- NETWORK, NETWORK, NETWORK!

Publications as Information Resources

Professional publications have valuable information about the world of work. Check with your career counselor or professors for publications that will provide useful information. One Web site with links to electronic publications is the Electronic Newsstand at **http://www .enews.com.**

The Internet as an Information Resource

The Internet has many valuable resources for learning about the world of work. Resources include:

- World Wide Web sites of companies
- Usenet newsgroups
- listserv mailing lists
- job and career resources

WORLD WIDE WEB

Many companies have World Wide Web sites. You will find their Web sites useful in learning about the company's products and services and, in some instances, about their work environment. Use search engines described in Chapter 4 to help you find the home page of companies you are interested in. Listed below are Web sites to visit that have links to companies on the Internet.

COMMERCIAL SITES INDEX (http://www.directory.net) lists businesses that have set up home pages on the Web.

INTERESTING BUSINESS SITES ON THE WEB (http://www.owi.com/ netvalue/index.html) is a relatively small list of sites (less than 50) that covers most of the exciting business uses of the Web.

THE LIST (http://www.sirius.com/~bam/jul.html) is an excellent Web site with links to online businesses.

USENET NEWSGROUPS

Listed below are several Usenet newsgroups that are relevant to job searching and career planning:

```
misc.jobs.contract
misc.jobs.misc
misc.jobs.offered
misc.jobs.offered.entry
misc.jobs.resumes
```

Visit this Web site for a listing of Usenet newsgroups: **http://ibd.ar .com/ger**

Visit this Web site and use a simple search tool to locate Usenet newsgroups of interest: **http://www.cen.uiuc.edu/cgi-bin/find-news**
You can also find newsgroups on topics of interest by using search engines such as Excite, Infoseek, and Lycos.

LISTSERV MAILING LISTS

There are several Web sites to help you to find a listserv mailing list for jobs or career planning.

http://www.yahoo.com/Business_and_Economy/Employment/ Mailing_Lists

http://www.liszt.com

http://www.tile.net/tile/listserv/index.html

You can also use electronic mail to request information on listserv mailing lists on a particular topic. Send an email message to **LISTSERV@ vm1.nodak.edu**. In the message body, type: **LIST GLOBAL/**keyword. For example, if you were looking for a mailing list on jobs you would type in the message body: **LIST GLOBAL/jobs**

Professional Services as Information Resources

One valuable service to job seekers who want to learn what it's really like to work at a specific company or within a specific industry is Wet Feet Press. This service provides comprehensive in-depth analyses of companies at a cost of $25 per report. If you are currently enrolled as a Bachelor's or Master's student at a Wet Feet Press "Information Partnership" university, your cost is only $15 per report. As an alumnus of these universities, the cost is $20 per report. For more information call 1-800-926-4JOB. Visit the career center at your university or college to see if it belongs to Information Partners. For information on becoming an Information Partners member, call 415-826-1750.

THE NATIONAL BUSINESS EMPLOYMENT WEEKLY published by Dow Jones & Company, Inc., is the nation's preeminent career guidance and job-search publication. It offers all regional recruitment advertising from its parent publication, *The Wall Street Journal,* as well as timely editorials on how to find a new job, manage the one you have, or start a business. You will find information on a wide range of careers. You will also get the latest on business and franchising opportunities, and special reports on workplace diversity. To view additional *NBEW* articles, subscription information, and job hunters' résumés, go to **http://www.nbew.com.**

CAREERMAGAZINE also publishes articles from National Business Employment Weekly. **http://www.careermag.com/db/ cmag_index**

USING CYBERSPACE TO FIND A JOB

The Internet provides new opportunities for job-seekers and companies to find good employment matches. Many companies are turning to the Internet believing that the people who keep up with the most current information and technological advances in their field are the best candidates for positions. The growing perception among employers is that they may be able to find better candidates if they search online.

The types of jobs offered on the Internet have changed dramatically over the last ten years. In the past, job announcements were primarily academic or in the field of science and technology. Now, thousands of positions in all fields from graphic artists to business and marketing professionals, from medical professionals to Internet surfers and Web programmers, are being advertised.

Many companies realize the impact of the digital revolution on business and are searching for professionals who are already online cybersurfing, networking with peers, researching information, asking questions, and learning collaboratively from others around the world. A number of companies report difficulty finding such qualified individuals.

How Do I Begin?

Listed below are a few ways to use the Internet in your job search:

- Visit Web sites with business resources or links to employment opportunities.

- Research companies that you are interested in by finding and exploring their Web pages. Many of these companies post job openings.

- Learn more about job resources, electronic résumés, and employment opportunities available on the Internet.

- Create an electronic résumé.

- Use the Internet to give yourself and your résumé maximum visibility.

- Participate in Usenet newsgroups and listserv mailing lists to network and learn about companies you are interested in working for.

- Learn as much as possible about a prospective company before going for a job interview.

SEVEN STEPS TO INTERNET JOB SEARCHING

STEP 1

Research companies or organizations that you are interested in by finding and exploring their Web pages. There are many ways to find companies to match your personal and professional needs. Use the information from your self-assessment to refine and define your search for companies. Use both online and off-line resources. Listed below are sources to assist you with finding companies related to your field of study.

   Go to your library and review publications in your field of study. Look for classified ads in these publications. Find names of companies that interest you. Research these companies using the search tools you learned in Chapter 4.

   Search the classified section in newspapers in the cities or regions where you would like to live. Use the Internet to research these companies.

   Use Internet search tools described in Chapter 4 to find companies and employment opportunities. Begin by using broad terms. For example, if you are looking for environmental jobs use keywords such as *employment* or *employment and environment*. If you are looking for employment opportunities at a company, you might enter keywords that describe a job position, such as *environmental manager, environmental health scientist, hazardous waste system operator,* or if you know the name of the company, do a search entering the company name as your keyword.

   Visit Web sites related to your field of study. You will find that some have links to job opportunities.

STEP 2

Explore job resources and employment opportunities available on the Internet. Many Web sites have job postings and information on how to write résumés and effectively use the Internet to find a job. Listed below are several excellent Internet resources to help you begin.

BEST BETS FOR EXTENDING YOUR SEARCH: OTHER INTERNET JOB GUIDES
http://www.lib.umich.edu/chdocs/employment This guide

pulls together the Net's best sources of job openings and career development information, along with a description and evaluation of each resource.

EMPLOYMENT OPPORTUNITIES AND JOB RESOURCES ON THE INTERNET
http://www.jobtrak.com/jobguide Margaret F. Riley's Web site has excellent job resources. A MUST VISIT Internet stop.

JOB SEARCH AND EMPLOYMENT OPPORTUNITIES: BEST BETS FROM THE NET, Phil Ray and Brad Taylor, University of Michigan SILS.
http://asa.ugl.lib.umich.edu/chdocs/employment

JOBHUNT: http://rescomp.stanford.edu/jobs.html A meta-list of online job-search resources and services.

JOBTRAK http://www.jobtrak.com In partnership with over 500 college and university career centers across the nation, JOB-TRAK provides the information that students and recent graduates need most—more than 2,100 new full- and part-time job openings each day. Search their databases for jobs, view company profiles, or read job search tips.

SURVIVAL GUIDE FOR COLLEGE GRADUATES
http://www.mongen.com/getgo This award-winning Web site featured in Fig. 5.1 has valuable information for college graduates seeking employment.

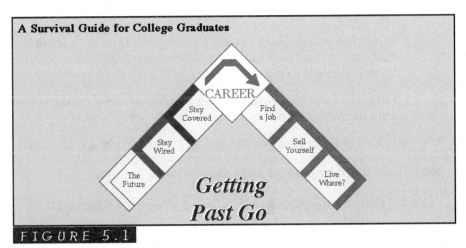

FIGURE 5.1

Web page for A Survival Guide for College Graduates

TRIPOD http://www.tripod.com/tripod Jobs don't last. Careers don't last. Health is a struggle rather than a natural fact. Skill lets you travel farther than money—a lot farther. Saving money? You know you have to, but how? Too often, community is found in places other than where we live. Tripod is for people trying to live well in a world of constant shift and transition. It also is designed to help prepare college students for the real world. Tripod offers practical advice via real-life stories, humor, and other members who share their answers to life's hard questions.

YAHOO EMPLOYMENT RESOURCES http://www.yahoo.com/ Business_and_Economy/Employment

STEP 3

Learn about electronic résumés. The World Wide Web has created opportunities for new types of résumés and business cards. Those who take advantage of the power of this new medium stand out as being technologically advanced and in touch with the future.

Listed below are Web sites to visit to examine online résumés. The individuals who have created these résumés understand how to use this medium to sell themselves. At the same time, they are stating that they have special skills that set them apart from other candidates.

Visit these Web sites and study their online résumés. Ask yourself the following questions as you look at them:

- How are online résumés different from traditional résumés?

- How do online résumés have an advantage over traditional résumés?

- What are some characteristics of the Internet as a medium that can be used to your advantage when designing a résumé to sell yourself to a company?

- How are these individuals taking advantage of the Internet as a medium to communicate?

- What do you view as advantages of using online résumés?

MIKE SWARTZBECK http://myhouse.com/mikesite/resume

JOHN LOCKWOOD http://ipoint.vlsi.uiuc.edu/people/lockwood/ lockwood.html

ALLAN TRAUTMAN http://www.smartlink.net/~trautman

To view additional online résumés visit Yahoo's résumé site at Follow the Link Individual Résumés **http://www.yahoo.com/Business_and_ Economy/Employment/Resumes**

STEP 4

Visit online sites for job seekers. The next step is to visit Web sites that post résumés. Identify sites where you would like to post your résumé. There are many services available for job-seekers and for companies looking for employees. Companies usually pay to be listed; job-seekers may be allowed to post their résumés at no cost.

AMERICA'S JOB BANK http://www.ajb.dni.us/index.html The Department of Labor's Internet job bank offers information on over 500,000 employment opportunities. It is the largest online job bank and a wonderful resource for finding job opportunities.

AT&T COLLEGE NETWORK http://www.att.com/college This site has job resources for college graduates as well as career tips and information on how to use technology to your advantage in today's competitive market. You will also find links to academic sites— researched and categorized by subject—and links to shareware.

CAREER CITY http://www.careercity.com Career City offers some basic guidelines for job searching as well as services to help you find a job. Over 125,00 job openings, tips on how to post résumés that get interviews, how to turn interviews into job offers, information on cover letters, and a free résumé posting.

CAREER CONNECTION http://iccweb.com Internet Career Connection (ICC) is a full-service, professional career and employment guidance agency operating exclusively online. The central mission of the ICC is to help you advance your career development and to achieve a higher level of career satisfaction and success. A variety of services has been designed to help you achieve these ends. Visit their site to learn more.

CAREER MAGAZINE http://www.careermag.com/db/cmag_index Online publication with news and articles for career planning and finding a job. This site also has job openings, employer profiles, and a résumé bank.

CAREER PATH http://www.careerpath.com Review employment opportunities from a number of the nation's leading daily newspapers such as *The New York Times, Los Angeles Times, The Boston Globe, Chicago Tribune, San Jose Mercury News,* and *The Washington Post.*

CAREER RESOURCES HOME PAGE http://www.rpi.edu/dept/cdc/ homepage.html This Web site has links to online employment services including professional and university-based services.

CAREERMOSAIC http://www.careermosaic.com Begin your Career-Mosaic tour by visiting the J.O.B.S. database, with thousands of up-to-date opportunities from hundreds of employers. Then stop by their USENET "jobs.offered" page to perform a full-text search of jobs listed in regional and occupational newsgroups in the U.S. and abroad. If you would also like to make your résumé accessible to interested employers from all corners of the globe, key into ResumeCM and post your résumé online.

CAREERSITE http://www.careersite.com CareerSite uses state of the art technology to match job seekers with employers. Interactive features include the ability to respond electronically to job opportunities as well as to have employers match confidential profiles. CareerSite's Virtual Agent automatically notifies job seekers via email of new jobs matching their profile. CareerSite attracts both experienced job seekers and new graduates. Sign up for free and try this highly rated job service.

CAREERWEB http://www.cweb.com Search by job, location, employment, or keyword to find the perfect job. You can also browse employer profiles and search the library's list of related publications.

COLLEGE GRAD JOB HUNTER http://www.collegegrad.com Figure 5.2 gives your link to life after college.

E-SPAN http://www.espan.com E-Span, one of the country's foremost online recruitment services, provides tools designed to meet the needs of an increasingly competitive career market. Recently added to their services in Résumé ProKeyword Database that is available to more than 60,000 individually registered career service consumers. Select Job Tools.

HELPWANTED.COM http://helpwanted.com This site offers a searchable index of job openings for companies that have paid to be listed.

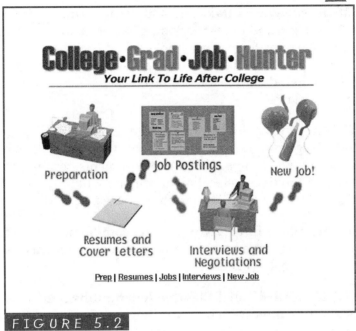

FIGURE 5.2

Home Page for College·Grad·Job·Hunter

INTELLIMATCH http://www.intellimatch.com Connect to Intelli-Match and fill out a résumé; hundreds of employers will have access to your profile via the Holmes search software. Review other services such as job-related sites and products, participating companies, and descriptions of available jobs.

INTERNET CAREER CONNECTION http://www.iccweb.com This site has many excellent resources including links to employment opportunities, their résumé talent bank, and resources for college students (select the link to Other Career and Employment Web sites).

THE INTERNET ONLINE CAREER CENTER http://www.occ.com This career center and employment database is one of the highest-volume job centers with a long list of employment opportunities and resources. Post your résumé in HTML format. Use multimedia (images, photographs, audio, and video) to enrich your résumé.

JOBHUNT http://rescomp.stanford.edu/jobs An award-winning Web site with a meta-list of online job-search resources and services.

JOBTRAK http://www.jobtrak.com JOBTRAK partners with more than 500 colleges and university career centers across the nation providing the information that students and recent graduates need most. Over 2,100 new full- and part-time job openings each day. Search their database for jobs postings, company profiles, and job search tips.

JOBWEB http://www.jobweb.org JobWeb is a resource designed for students, graduates, and professionals with valuable information about internships, diversity recruitments, resources for those with disabilities, relocation information, links to career libraries, and many other job search resources.

THE MONSTER BOARD http://www.monster.com/home.html This unusual ad agency is a service for recruitment and furnishes information for job seekers.

NATIONAL EMPLOYMENT JOB BANK http://www.nlbbs.com/ ~najoban/ Executive Search of New England is pleased to post current career opportunities on its newest service, The National Employment Job Bank. These positions are current and represent some of the finest employers and employment services in the country. There is never a fee charged to any applicant. These positions will be from nearly all states in the United States.

SALUDOS WEB http://www.hooked.net/saludos The Saludos Web site is devoted exclusively to promoting Hispanic careers and education.

STANFORD UNIVERSITY http://rescomp.stanford.edu Stanford University's site provides listings of online job services such as Medsearch and the Chronicle of Higher Education. They also have links to other agencies.

STUDENTCENTER http://www.studentcenter.com If you are just beginning to job search you may want to visit the StudentCenter. The StudentCenter helps college students, graduate students, and recent graduates identify their personal strengths, define their career goals, and learn about the companies that best match their interests. By providing career-planning and research information, they help job seekers develop the sophisticated job search skills they need in today's competitive environment.

Another service, The Career Doctor, matches your interests with school majors and jobs, clarifies your marketable skills, and more. Career Doctor is located in Who Am I?

SUMMER JOBS http://www.summerjobs.com Summer Jobs is a database of seasonal and part-time job opportunities. Jobs are organized by country, state or province, region, and city or town. While the primary focus is summer employment, other jobs may be posted here as well.

YAHOO JOBS http://www.yahoo.com/yahoo/Business/Employment/ Jobs Many excellent links to help you find a job.

STEP 5

Create an online résumé to showcase your talents. In Steps 1–4, you learned about

- companies that fit your career interests;
- job and career resources on the Internet;
- electronic résumés and how they can showcase talents; and
- Web sites for job seekers.

You are now ready to use this information to create your own electronic résumé to showcase your talents and skills. Well-designed and interesting online résumés set creative job seekers apart from others. When many individuals are competing for the same job, it is essential to stand apart and showcase your talents as to how they will benefit a company, especially in a time when businesses realize the importance of being networked to the world.

Creating an exceptional online résumé takes planning and careful thought. Online résumés take different forms. Some may be an electronic version of a text-based résumé. Others may be home pages with links to resources that showcase a person's work and expertise.

Preparing Your Résumé for the Internet

Before you begin, think about your goals and what you would like to accomplish with an online résumé. Your primary goal is hopefully to find a job and not just to impress friends with a cool Home Page.

You will need to determine whether to create your online résumé yourself or hire a résumé service. If you are creating an electronic résumé on your own, consider whether you want to develop your own

Home Page for your résumé or use an online database service to post your résumé. If you plan to create a Home Page you will need to learn HTML programming or use a software application program that creates an HTML code from your text. There are many software programs to assist you with this, as well as word processing programs that convert text to HTML.

If you are using an online résumé service, find out what type of text file they want. Usually, you will be asked for ASCII text. Most word processors and résumé writing programs have options for saving a file as ASCII or plaintext.

Investigate Résumé Services

Consider using a résumé service to create an online résumé. One advantage of using a service is that you may be able to get your résumé online quickly with instant exposure to many job opportunities. One disadvantage of using a service is that you do not have as much control over how your résumé will look. You may not be able to use complex graphics or other multimedia effects when using a service.

Cost is another limiting factor. Some companies charge a monthly fee to post your résumé, in addition to a set-up and sign-on fee. Look for companies that charge a reasonable fee to write a résumé ($35–$50) and no fee to post it on their Web site. Investigate what other services they provide. How many visitors does this site have each day, each week? Will this site give you maximum exposure to potential employers?

Visit Web sites with résumé services. Evaluate their services: How many online résumés are posted? Are the résumés well done, creative, interesting? How well do they promote the job seeker?

Visit Tripod's résumé builder at **http://www.tripod.com/work/resume** Tripod's Resume Builder will automatically generate the best choice from six different résumé formats based upon your personal job history and search criteria. The Resume Builder then allows you to easily circulate your résumé to other online résumé sites.

THE SEVEN ESSENTIAL ELEMENTS OF ELECTRONIC RÉSUMÉS

Whether you choose to use a résumé service or to create your own online résumé, there are seven essential elements to follow.

1. **Text must be properly formatted as an ASCII text file.**

   Using ASCII ensures that your résumé can be read universally by everyone and that readers will be able to scroll through your text. Additionally, an ASCII document can be emailed to anyone in the world and read.

2. **Showcase your experience and education.**

At the top of your résumé, provide links to your experience and education. Experience is usually the first thing employers look for. A fancy résumé will not help you get a job if you do not have the right qualifications. Notice that many online résumés provide examples of their work.

3. **Provide an email hyperlink.**

An email hyperlink provides an easy way for prospective employers to contact you by email. By clicking on the link, they can send you a message, ask questions, or request additional information. Anything that makes it easier for recruiters improves your chances of being called for an interview.

4. **Use nouns as keywords to describe your experience.**

When employers use the Internet to search for qualified individuals, they will frequently use search engines that require keywords. The keywords used by employers are descriptors of the essential characteristics required to do a job, such as education, experience, skills, knowledge, and abilities. The more keywords that your résumé contains, the better your chances of being found in an electronic database.

Action words such as *created, arbitrated, managed, designed,* and *administered* are out. Therefore, use words such as *manager, law enforcement, accountant, MBA.* The use of nouns will tend to produce better results.

5. **Use white space.**

An electronic résumé does not need to be one page long and single spaced. The use of white space makes reading easier and is visually more appealing. Use space to indicate that one topic has ended and another has begun.

If you are a new graduate, a résumé equivalent of one page is appropriate. For most individuals with experience, the equivalent of two pages is the norm. Individuals who have worked in a field for many years may use two to three pages.

6. **Keep track of the number of visitors to your page.**

A counter will keep track of the number of visitors that view your page. A counter is important when paying for a résumé service, to monitor how successful the service is with getting exposure for your résumé.

7. **Be sure your page gets maximum exposure to potential employers.**

One way that employers look for prospective employees is to do a keyword search using search engines such as Yahoo, Excite, and Alta Vista. Each search engine uses a different criteria for selection of Internet resources that are available in their database. Be sure that your page is listed with search engines. Visit search engine Web sites and learn how to submit your page. Additionally, investigate the selection criteria for these search engines.

Other Points to Consider

- Think of creative ways to show your talents, abilities, and skills. World Wide Web pages are excellent for linking to examples of your work.

- REMEMBER that experience is perhaps the most critical element for recruiters. Be sure your résumé showcases your experience and skills in as many ways as possible.

- Visit the top 10–15 companies that you are interested in working for. Research their World Wide Web home pages. Learn as much as possible about the companies. Use this information when designing and creating your résumé to include information and skills that they are looking for in employees. Use this information before an interview to show your knowledge and interest in them.

- Investigate whether you will be able to submit your résumé electronically to the company.

- Are you concerned about confidentiality? Inquire about who will have access to the database you are posting your résumé with. Will you be notified if your résumé is forwarded to an employer? If the answers to these questions are not satisfactory to you, reconsider posting with this database.

- Once you post your résumé, anyone can look at it and find your address and phone number. You may want to omit your home address and just list your phone number and an email hyperlink.

Many recruiters and employers prefer to contact individuals by phone; if you decide not to post your phone number, you may be overlooked.

- Can your résumé be updated at no cost? You may want to add something to your résumé or correct a typo. Look for services that do not charge for updates.

- How long will your résumé be posted with the service? A good service will delete résumés after 3 to 6 months if they have not been updated.

🐦 STEP 6

Use the Internet to give yourself and your résumé maximum visibility. Successful job searches using the Internet require an aggressive approach. A résumé should be filed with many job-listing databases as well as with companies that you are interested in working for. Listed below are additional guidelines for giving yourself maximum exposure using the Internet.

- File your résumé with as many databases as possible. Visit the Net Sites for Job Seekers and find as many sites as possible to submit your résumé to.

- Use search engines and their indexes to locate resources specific to your occupation of interest.

- Visit the Home Pages of companies that you are interested in and explore their pages to find job listings. Find out if you can submit your résumé to them electronically.

- Use Usenet newsgroups and listserv mailing lists for information on finding jobs and posting your résumé.

Listed below are several Usenet newsgroups to investigate for posting résumés.

```
biz.jobs.offered
misc.jobs.contract
misc.jobs.misc
misc.jobs.offered
misc.jobs.offered.entry
misc.jobs.resume
```

STEP 7

Learn as much as possible about a prospective company before going for a job interview. Before going for a job interview, it is important to learn as much as possible about the prospective company.

The Internet is an excellent tool to assist you with finding up-to-date information about a company. Annual reports and information found in journals, books, or in the library will not be as current as what you will find on the Internet. World Wide Web sites are being constantly changed and updated.

The information that you should be investigating about a prospective company includes:

- What are the company's products and services?

- Who are the company's customers?

- What is the size of the company? Has the company grown over the last five years?

- Is the company profitable?

- Has the company laid off employees?

- How do customers and competitors view the company's products and services?

- Who are the company's major competitors?

- What is the corporate culture like?

- Is the employee turnover rate low, high, or average?

- Are work schedules flexible?

- How many hours a day do employees work?

- What is the typical hiring process?

- Is the organization nonprofit or for-profit? (There are differences in how these types of organizations operate.)

Listed below are Internet business collections and directories to assist you with finding information on a company.

ALL BUSINESS NETWORK http://www.all-biz.com This site would like to be your one-stop shopping site for business resources. A pull-down menu offers an excellent selection of business topics to connect to for Internet resources. Winner of the "Top Business Site" award.

APOLLO http://apollo.co.uk This Web site offers options for searching for a company by country and keyword.

COMMERCIAL SITES INDEX http://www.directory.net The Commercial Sites Index lists businesses that have set up home pages on the Web. Make this a scheduled visit to see how companies are using the Net for business.

GALAXY http://galaxy.einet.net/galaxy/Business-and-Commerce/ Business-General-Resources.html This search directory has links to business resources.

GTE SUPERPAGES http://superpages.gte.net This useful Web site will help you find information about businesses in their Yellow Pages or their Business Web Site Directory. In their nationwide Interactive Yellow Pages, you'll find comprehensive and accurate business information derived from more than 11 million listings found in over 5,000 Yellow Pages directories from virtually every city in the United States. The Business Web Site Directory features links to over 60,000 Web sites owned and operated by businesses throughout the world.

HIP, HOT, 'N' HAPPENING http://pathfinder.com/ @@7PcvogYAweyjsu6N/fortune/index.html Fortune has identified 25 very cool companies that are HIP, HOT, 'N' HAPPENING. Visit this site to learn about "being cool on the Internet."

HOT BUSINESS SITES http://www.hbs.harvard.edu/applegate/ hot_business Links to good examples of businesses using the Internet.

INTERESTING BUSINESS SITES ON THE WEB http://www.owi.com/ netvalue/v1i1l1.html Since its inception, the Interesting Business Sites on the Web page has listed over 220 innovative and interesting sites for those interested in business on the Net. Sites included are not just glitz, but appear to provide a significant business value.

THE LIST http://www.sirius.com/~bam/jul.html Links to businesses online.

NEW RIDER'S WWW YELLOW PAGES http://www.mcp.com/ newriders/wwwyp New Rider's World Wide Web Yellow Pages

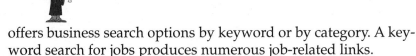

offers business search options by keyword or by category. A keyword search for jobs produces numerous job-related links.

NYNEX INTERACTIVE YELLOW PAGES http://www.niyp.com The largest of the business directories has options for searching for companies by business location, category, or business name.

WORLD WIDE YELLOW PAGES http://www.yellow.com World Wide Yellow Pages has a link to assist you with finding information on businesses.

Finding Employment Opportunities on the Net

JOB SEARCH 1

Management

There are many excellent Internet resources for assisting you with your career exploration. This guided tour takes you on a journey to Web sites with career and business resources for employment opportunities in management training. The same resources can be used for finding other business jobs for which you are qualified.

NOTE There are many ways to find employment opportunities and information about businesses. The more knowledgeable you are about using Internet resources for finding information, the more options you will have open to you. This example merely serves as one pathway you might take.

STEP 1

Explore job opportunities. Visit Internet's Online Career Center (**http://www.occ.com/occ**) to search for management training jobs by keyword search. See its Home Page in Fig. 5.3.

This resource has links to Frequently Asked Questions, Jobs, Résumés, Career Fairs and Events, Career Assistance, and much more. Before you begin, you may want to explore some of these links. Visit the Career Assistance Center for information on writing electronic résumés and how to submit a résumé to the Online Career Center.

STEP 2

Search for a job. Use the search tool at this site to search for management training employment opportunities. In the **Keyword Search** field,

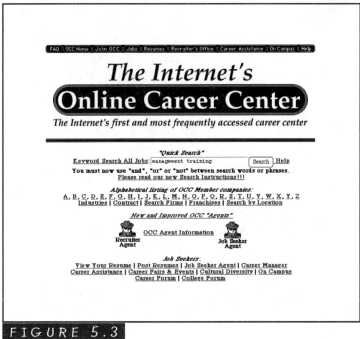

FIGURE 5.3

Online Career Center's Home Page to find job opportunities

type in the job description; in this case, *management training*. Click on the **Search** button. See Fig. 5.4 for the results of this search.

When you click on the link to *Manager-Customer Service Training OMNI-POINT* you are given this information about the job.

1. [Jun 25] US AR Positions in Managed Health Care & HMO - Sales Consultants
2. [Jun 24] US-NY-Financial Professionals- First Investors Corporation
3. [Jun 24] US-MARKETING and SALES PROFESSIONALS- RCI NATIONAL SEARCH
4. [Jun 24] US-MARKETING and SALES PROFESSIONALS- RCI National Search
5. [Jun 24] US-MARKETING and SALES PROFESSIONALS- RCI National Search
6. [Jun 24] US-MARKETING and SALES PROFESSIONALS- RCI National Search
7. [Jun 24] US-MARKETING and SALES PROFESSIONALS- RCI National Search
8. [Jun 24] US-CTI Market Manager- Fujitsu Business Communication Systems Inc
9. [Jun 24] US-Management Consultants- M. F. Smith & Associates Inc
10. [Jun 24] US-NJ-Business Systems Analysts- M. F. Smith & Associates Inc
11. [Jun 24] US-NJ-Documentation Specialists- M. F. Smith & Associates Inc
12. [Jun 24] US-NJ-Technology Consultants- M. F. Smith & Associates Inc
13. [Jun 24] US-NJ-Programmers/Systems Analysts- M. F. Smith & Associates Inc
14. [Jun 24] US-PA-Network Administrator- AAA Mid-Atlantic
15. [Jun 24] US-MARKETING and SALES PROFESSIONALS- RCI NATIONAL SEARCH
16. [Jun 24] US-MARKETING and SALES PROFESSIONALS- RCI NATIONAL SEARCH
17. [Jun 24] US- MARKETING and SALES PROFESSIONALS- RCI NATIONAL SEARCH
18. [Jun 24] US-MARKETING and SALES PROFESSIONALS- RCI NATIONAL SEARCH
19. [Jun 24] US-MARKETING and SALES PROFESSIONALS- RCI NATIONAL SEARCH
20. [Jun 24] US-MARKETING and SALES PROFESSIONALS- RCI NATIONAL SEARCH
21. [Jun 24] US-NY-Director of Corporate Sales - OMNIPOINT
22. [Jun 24] US-NY-Customer Service Team Leader - OMNIPOINT
23. [Jun 24] US-NY-Manager - Customer Service Training - OMNIPOINT
24. [Jun 24] US-PA-Customer Support Specialists- Delta Health Systems

FIGURE 5.4

Search results from the Online Career Center using keywords, management training

STEP 3

Note companies of interest. List companies of interest from your search. You will use the Internet to research these companies to learn more about them. For example, in the search results for management training opportunities, the company OMNIPOINT, profiled in Fig. 5.5, may have interested you. Note the name to research on the Internet.

```
Later this year, OMNIPOINT will be the first provider of PCS
services in the greater New York area,
bringing on a new era of advanced DIGITAL WIRELESS
COMMUNICATIONS and innovative services.
We are seeking a few highly accomplished individuals, from
both inside and outside the wireless industry,
to fill out a senior management team that is already unrivaled
in the industry.

Develop and customize customer service, billing, P/C training
programs. Facilitate programs developed
internally and monitor their effectiveness through analysis.
You must possess 3-5 years of training
experience including demonstrated skills in platform
techniques, training methodology, curriculum
development, training/development needs analysis.
Experience in computer based training and its related
technologies will be preferred. Bachelor's Degree or
equivalent and a very thorough knowledge of wireless
applications preferred. Respond to MCST.

Openings are also available in the following areas:
Network Technicians
RF Engineers
Field Technicians
Finance & Accounting
Real Estate Site Acquisition Associate
Please send, fax, or e-mail your resume with salary requirements
indicating position applied for to:

Omnipoint Communications, Inc.
16 Wing Drive
Cedar Knolls, NJ 07927
Fax: (201) 257-2425  ð  e-mail#: hr@omnipoint_pcs.com
# ad number 3124022
(c) Copyright Recourse Communications, Inc.
All rights svd
Agency Account Code xrcix
```

FIGURE 5.5

Description of job at OMNIPOINT

STEP 4

Learn about companies where jobs are offered. There are many ways to learn more about companies. In this instance, we will use the search engine Excite, displayed in Fig. 5.6, to research OMNIPOINT to learn more about the company, its products, and services. The search produces a link to the OMNIPOINT Home Page shown in Fig. 5.7.

NOTE When trying to find the Home Page of a company online, try entering the name of the company as your URL. For example, enter only **omnipoint** or **www.omnipoint.com**.

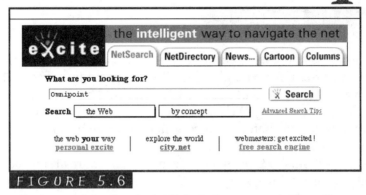

FIGURE 5.6

Excite search for Omnipoint links to the company's Home Page

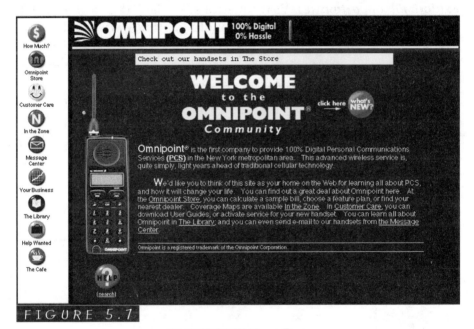

FIGURE 5.7

OMNIPOINT Home Page

The job search information indicated that OMNIPOINT was located in Cedar Knolls, New Jersey. You may want to research this city or town to learn more about it. In Job Search 3, you will learn how to find information on a city.

JOB SEARCH 2

Accounting

As you explore and use career- and job-related Internet resources, you will find that there is no single Web site that provides all the information and tools that you will need to help you find a job.

You will find that many Web sites have a search tool to help you locate jobs and companies. Before you conduct a search, be sure you understand how the search engine can be used most effectively to find information. Select links to **Options** or **Help** to learn more about the search tool. Other pages will equip you with information on how to conduct a search.

🎓 STEP 1

Explore job opportunities. Visit America's Job Bank (Fig. 5.8) to search for employment opportunities in accounting. **http://www.ajb.dni.us**

FIGURE 5.8

Home Page for America's Job Bank

🎓 STEP 2

Select the link to the Job Search Index. Select Keyword Search (Fig. 5.9). The Keyword Search option links you to this page.

🎓 STEP 3

Select keyword search by job titles. Notice the difference in searching criteria used by the America's Job Bank (Fig. 5.10) in comparison to the Online Career Center (Fig. 5.4).

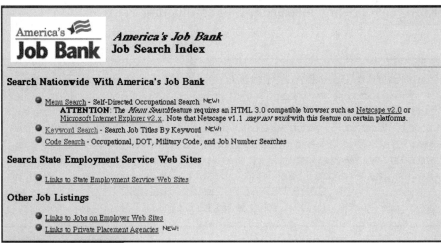

FIGURE 5.9

*Clicking on the **Job Search Index** link takes you to the Job Search Index Web page*

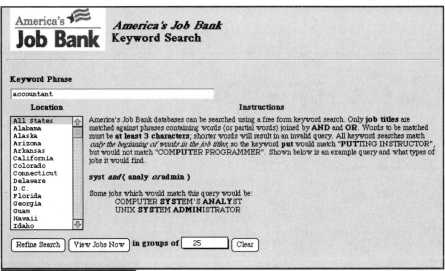

FIGURE 5.10

America's Job Bank page for finding a job by location and job title

Read the following instructions for conducting a search:

America's Job Bank databases can be searched using a free form keyword search. Only job titles are matched against phrases containing words (or partial words) joined by AND and OR. Words to be matched must be at least three characters; shorter words will result in an invalid query. Listed below are examples of job titles.

COMPUTER SYSTEMS ANALYST

UNIX SYSTEM ADMINISTRATOR

Notice that this search engine will sort jobs in an order that you select: city, state, job title, or salary (see Fig. 5.11). For this search, jobs were sorted first by state, city, job title, and salary.

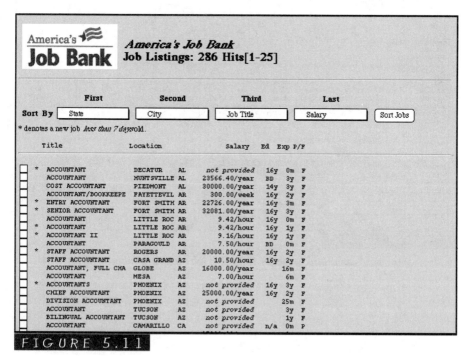

Search results produced 286 leads for jobs under the keyword accountant

To learn about each job, click once in the box next to each of the job postings you are interested in reading about. Then click on the button, **View Jobs.**

Click on the **Next** button for a job description of the second job you are interested in.

At the bottom of each page is a button to apply for the job if you feel you are interested and qualify (Fig. 5.12). By selecting this option, you may learn more about the company or the recruiter posting the job.

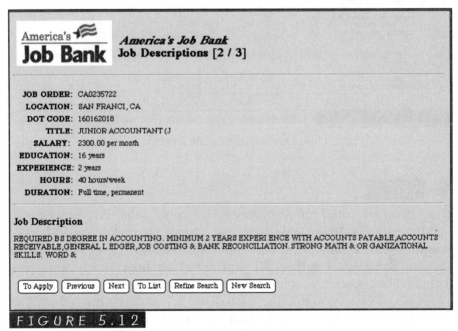

America's
Job Bank

America's Job Bank
Job Descriptions [2 / 3]

JOB ORDER:	CA0235722
LOCATION:	SAN FRANCI, CA
DOT CODE:	160162018
TITLE:	JUNIOR ACCOUNTANT (J
SALARY:	2300.00 per month
EDUCATION:	16 years
EXPERIENCE:	2 years
HOURS:	40 hours/week
DURATION:	Full time, permanent

Job Description

REQUIRED B S DEGREE IN ACCOUNTING. MINIMUM 2 YEARS EXPERI ENCE WITH ACCOUNTS PAYABLE, ACCOUNTS RECEIVABLE, GENERAL L EDGER, JOB COSTING & BANK RECONCILIATION. STRONG MATH & OR GANIZATIONAL SKILLS. WORD &

[To Apply] [Previous] [Next] [To List] [Refine Search] [New Search]

FIGURE 5.12

Job description for an accountant in San Francisco, California

✱ STEP 4

Learn more about the cities where these jobs are located. After reading the job description you may be interested in applying for the job (see Fig. 5.13), but would first like to learn more about the city where the job is located.

To learn about the cities for the jobs you selected, visit City Net at **http://www.city.net.** (You will learn more about finding information on a city in Job Search 3.)

America's
Job Bank

America's Job Bank
Internet Referral

If you meet the employer's requirements and wish to apply for this job, please enter your name below. To apply you must be a U.S. Citizen or an individual authorized to work in the United States.

    Job Number: CA0235722

           Name:

   Social Security #:

Once entered, you should print this panel and attach it to your resume/statement of qualifications and either fax or mail them both to the employment service order holding office at:

        CALIF. EMPLOYMENT DEV. DEPT.
        P.O. BOX 491929
        REDDING, CA, 96049
        FAX: (916)-225-2458

Please do not call this office. They will review your information and send it to the employer. If the employer is interested, you will be contacted directly.

[Enter Information] [Previous] [Next] [To List] [Refine Search] [New Search]

FIGURE 5.13

Example of online application form for a job

STEP 5

Use other career and job resources to search for jobs. Two other excellent Internet sites to assist with finding jobs are CareerWeb and Monster Board. Their job searches differ from Online Career Center and America's Job Bank. Enter in this URL for CareerWeb: **http://www.careerweb .com** and begin your search using the tools available in Fig. 5.14.

This job site asks you to select a job discipline and a state or country of your preference. Scroll down through the job disciplines to find one that best matches the job you are searching for. For your first search you may want to select Any State/Country to see what is available. Later you can refine your search.

STEP 6

Visit Monster Board to investigate its job search resources. **http://www .monster.com** is its URL. When you connect to Monster Board, sign in as a first-time visitor. There is no charge for using and visiting this site.

After clicking on the two links, job opportunities and career search, you are at the page shown in Fig. 5.15.

This job site presents job locations and job disciplines for you to select. For more information on each job discipline, click on the link for more information. After you select a location and discipline and conduct a

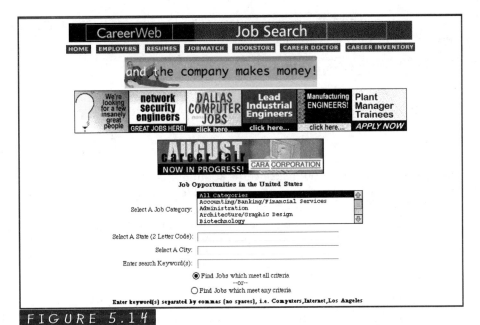

FIGURE 5.14

CareerWeb's search tool for finding a job by discipline and state/country

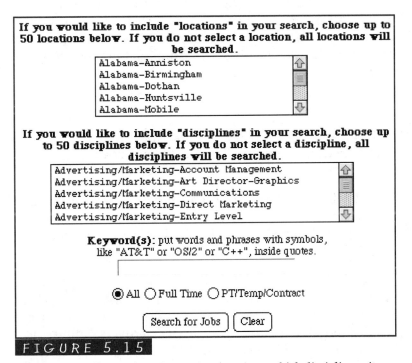

FIGURE 5.15

Monster Board's search options using location and job discipline crit search, you may be asked to refine your search. Monster Board also has options for keyword searches.

JOB SEARCH 3

Environmental Technology

This guided tour takes you on a journey to Web sites with career and employment opportunities in environmental technology.

NOTE With increasing public concerns about our environment, jobs and career opportunities in environmental technology continue to grow. The field is still very young and while there are many jobs available, many of the online job and career centers do not have postings for environmental positions at this time.

 ## STEP 1

Visit environmental Web sites to explore job opportunities and/or internships. Listed below are sites with many environmental postings.

ENVIRONMENTAL CAREERS ORGANIZATION http://www.eco.org The Environmental Careers Organization (ECO) is a national, non-profit, educational organization dedicated to the development of individuals' environmental careers. Through four basic services (placement, career planning, products, and research), ECO supports the development of environmental professionals and citizens who will make effective, balanced, and responsible decisions.

ENVIRONMENTAL HEALTH PERSPECTIVE BULLETIN BOARD http:// ehpnet1.niehs.nih.gov/docs/bboard/bboard.html Global environmental job opportunities can be found at this site.

ENVIROWORLD http://www.enviroworld.com/classifieds.html Enviroworld is one of the best online sources for environmental jobs. Select the link to national Environmental Classifieds (see Fig. 5.16).

NATIONAL WILDLIFE FOUNDATION http://www.nwf.org/nwf/about/ jobopp.html The National Wildlife Foundation posts environmental jobs on their Web site. Their mission is to educate, inspire, and assist individuals and organizations of diverse cultures to conserve wildlife and other natural resources and to protect the

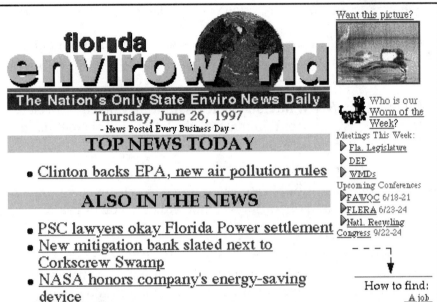

FIGURE 5.16

Enviroworld's page for environmental job links (Source: Reprinted by permission of Florida Environments Publishing, Inc.)

earth's environment in order to achieve a peaceful, equitable, and sustainable future. You can also receive a complete list of job vacancies by calling 703-790-4522.

TEXAS PARKS AND WILDLIFE http://www.tpwd.state.tx.us/involved/ jobvac/job.htm The Texas Parks and Wildlife department posts available jobs in the following areas: human resources, wildlife, coastal fisheries, inland fisheries, public lands, law enforcement, communications, and resource protection.

WATER RESOURCE EMPLOYMENT OPPORTUNITIES http://www.uwin .siu.edu/announce/jobs The Employment Opportunities Directory at this site is designed to serve as a clearinghouse for jobs and related opportunities in various water resources fields. These positions are categorized into academic, nonacademic (government, private, nonprofit), and student (assistantships, fellowships, internships, etc.) opportunities.

Other Sites to Visit for Job Opportunities in Environmental Technology

CAREER MAGAZINE http://www.webdirectory.com/Employment
Links to environmental employers, job opportunities, and résumés.

CORSAIR http://www.interstat.net/corsair.html Corsair is an electronic publishing firm bringing you the latest bid solicitations for environmental contracting work in the Northeast.

ECO VIRTUAL RESOURCE LIBRARY http://www.eco.org/eps_virt.html
This page contains publications, resources, job listings, volunteer opportunities, and organizations that will help you develop your environmental career.

GREENBEAT http://earth.tec.org/greenbeat/mar96 GreenBeat is a monthly Internet magazine profiling environmental endeavors and related subject matter, and Internet resources and career opportunities in the nation. Its goal is to show the starting points and strategies of successful environmental efforts.

NEW SCIENTIST http://www.newscientist.com *New Scientist* is a weekly news magazine originating in England in 1956, and is devoted to science and technology and their impact on the world and the way we live. *New Scientist* has achieved a high reputation for its news on humankind's effects on the environment. Registered users receive a listing of jobs.

THE SUNSHINE COAST http://www.sunshine.net The Sunshine Coast of British Columbia is a well-kept secret. Twenty miles from downtown Vancouver, the Coast is separated from the rest of the mainland by a deep inlet and is reached by a 40-minute ferry ride across Howe Sound from Horseshoe Bay. Use their search tool to learn more about their work with the Endangered Spaces Campaign to protect wilderness in British Columbia.

STEP 2

Investigate and research environmental companies. Another resource for finding jobs are the companies themselves. Many times a business will have links to job opportunities on its Web pages. This site has a list of environmental employers. **http://www.webdirectory.com/Employment/Employers**

🏃 STEP 3

Learn about the companies where the jobs are being offered. One environmentally active company that can be found on this list is Ben & Jerry's ice cream. To research information on Ben & Jerry's use your favorite search engine. For this example, we will be using Infoseek Ultra (**http://.ultra.infoseek.com**).

When you connect to Infoseek Ultra, notice the suggestion for doing a search on a phrase (see Fig. 5.17). Ultra recommends using quotes around the phrase or multiple words.

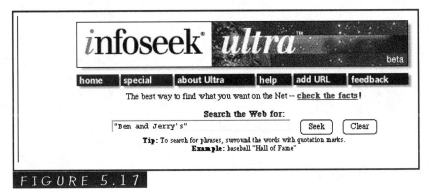

FIGURE 5.17

Infoseek Ultra's Home Page with a keyword search for Ben & Jerry's

The Infoseek Ultra search provided over 500 hits for the words *Ben & Jerry's*. From this list the Home Page was found (Fig. 5.18).

🏃 STEP 4

Learn more about the cities where these jobs are located. After reading a job description, you may be interested in applying for the job but would first like to learn more about the city where the job is located. An environmental job posting from Enviroworld was in Brunswick, Georgia. We will use City.Net (**http://www.city.net**) to research this city.

The City.Net Web site (Fig. 5.19) provides options for learning about cities by visiting its Most Popular U.S. City Destinations; selecting the link to the United States, Country, or Region where the city is located; or by conducting a keyword search. City.Net also has built-in links to interactive maps for any U.S. city.

In this example, we will do a keyword search for Brunswick, Georgia. Notice that City.Net uses Excite as its search tool.

FIGURE 5.18

Ben & Jerry's Home Page

The search results in Fig. 5.20 display several links to information on Brunswick, Georgia.

Select the link to Brunswick and the Golden Isles of Georgia to visit their Home Page (Fig. 5.21) or click on the Interactive Map to see where Brunswick is located (Fig. 5.22).

JOB SEARCH 4

Finding Environmental Employment Opportunities

Many Web sites have a search tool to help you locate jobs and companies. Before you conduct a search, be sure you understand how the search engine can be used most effectively to find information. Select links to **Options** or **Help** to learn more about the search tool. Other pages will give you information on how to conduct a search.

STEP 1

Explore job opportunities. Visit America's Job Bank (AJB) (Fig. 5.23) to search for environmental employment opportunities. **http://www.ajb .dni.us/index.html**

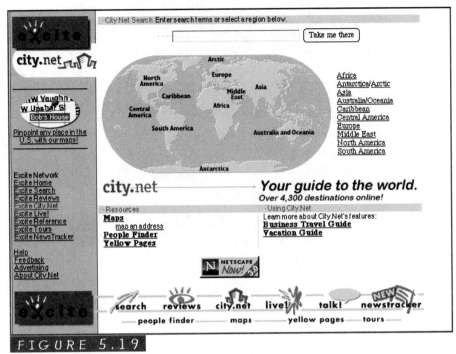

Web site for City.Net

Excite City.Net Search found documents about: **Brunswick, Georgia**

100% Brunswick, Georgia, United States

80% **Maps of United States, Georgia, Brunswick** [More like this]

80% Interactive Map of Brunswick [More like this]

78% United States, Georgia, Brunswick [More like this]

74% **United States, Georgia** [More like this]

Search results

FIGURE 5.21

Home Page for Brunswick, Georgia and the Golden Isles of Georgia (St. Simons Island, Sea Island, Little St. Simons Island, and Jekyll Islands.)

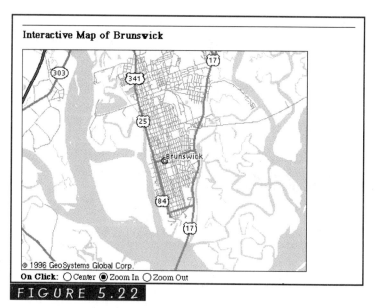

FIGURE 5.22

Interactive map for Brunswick, Georgia

FIGURE 5.23

Home Page for America's Job Bank

STEP 2

Select the link to the Job Search Index. From this Index you have many resources. If you select *Menu Search* you will find that there is no category for environmental jobs. Therefore, review the *Occupational Outlook Handbook* to search for environmental jobs and how they are listed with AJB. This *Handbook* contains long-term employment prospects in 250 occupations that account for 7 out of 8 jobs in the United States. The *Handbook,* developed by the Bureau of Labor Statistics, also includes information about each occupation, such as usual work activities, earnings and education, and training requirements.

STEP 3

Select Keyword Search by job titles or Menu Search for categories of jobs. The *Occupational Outlook Handbook* provided a listing for jobs in wastewater treatment. Therefore, do a keyword search for *wastewater treatment.* Refer to Job Search 2 in Accounting for America's Job Bank search resources.

STEP 4

Use other career and job resources to search for jobs. Listed below are several Web sites that link to online career and job centers.

(http://www.interbiznet.com/ibn/top25.html) Links to the top 25 electronic recruiters. As a part of the 1996 Electronic Recruiting Index, over 500 recruiting Web sites were evaluated, scored and ranked against a set of criteria. The result is this list of the Top 25.

(**http://www.jwtworks.com:80/hrlive/topmark/index.html**) Top Markets for jobs—an AWESOME collection of online sources for jobs organized categorically.

(**http://www.att.com/college/jobs.html**) The AT&T College Network has researched the best sites for college students to use to find a job.

For additional career and job opportunities, refer to pages 135–139. We will visit two other excellent Internet sites to assist with finding jobs—E-Span and Monster Board.

1. *Visit E-Span to investigate its job resources.* Enter this URL for E-Span: **http://www.espan.com** and connect to its Home Page shown in Fig. 5.24.

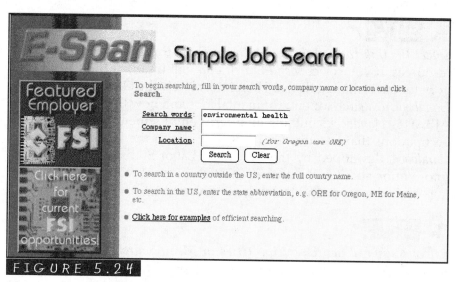

E-Span's page for conducting a simple job search

Click on the position title to obtain more information about the job (Fig. 5.25). Note the companies you are interested in.

2. *Visit JobTrak—a service for college students and graduates to help with job searches. http://www.jobtrak.com.* JOBTRAK is a leading job listing service used by college students, graduates, and alumni. JOBTRAK partners with hundreds of college and university career centers and is used by more than 200,000 employers posting over 2,000 new job openings each day (Fig. 5.26). Search their job database, view company profiles, and read job search tips.

E-Span   **Keyword Search**

Click on the job title listed below for detailed information about the job listing.

Displaying 1 - 6 of 6 records.

# Position title	Company Name	Job Location
1. SAFETY ENGINEER	Intel Corporation	Israel
2. TECHNICAL FIELD SALES ENGR.	efector, inc.	US
3. SAFETY & ENVIRONMENTAL HEALTH ADMINISTRATOR	Flexfab Horizons Intermtnl.	MI
4. QUALITY ASSURANCE GLP AUDITOR	Dow Corning Corporation	MI
5. RESEARCH SCIENTIST: TOXICOLOGIST/CHEMIST	Brown & Williamson Tobacco	GA
6. Environmental Health Specialist	Dynamic Technology Systems, Inc.	VA

FIGURE 5.25

Results of E-Span's search for environmental health jobs

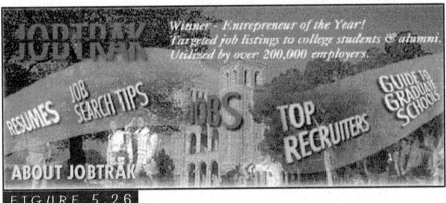

FIGURE 5.26

JOBTRAK Home Page

LEARNING ADVENTURES

Career Planning and Finding a Job

1. Write 25 things you love to do.

2. What do you do best?

3. What are your greatest achievements?

4. What do you find most rewarding when you work?

5. List and prioritize the 10 things that are most important to you. Which of these could you live without? Which of these are an essential part of your life that you cannot live without?

6. When you were a child, what did you want to be when you grew up?

7. What is your dream job now? Describe the perfect work environment. The perfect boss.

8. What is most important to you when evaluating a job?

9. List 5 jobs that incorporate the things you enjoy doing.

10. List 5 things that you would like to do at work.

11. List 5 ways that you will use people as a resource for learning about jobs and careers.

12. Subscribe to a Usenet newsgroup and learn more about job opportunities.

13. After you have read the newsgroup postings, list 10 things you learned about job opportunities on the Internet.

14. Find a listserv mailing list related to jobs in your field of study.

15. If you have participated in a Usenet newsgroup or a listserv mailing list, describe your experiences. What have you learned? What are the advantages/disadvantages of a newsgroup? A listserv?

16. Visit job and career resources on the Internet (pages 135–139). Describe information that you found useful.

17. Research five companies you are interested in working for. Use the search tools described in Chapter 4. Visit and explore their Web pages. List the products and services of these companies. What have you learned about their work environment? Do they post job openings? How do you apply for a job?

18. Explore job resources and employment opportunities available on the Internet. List 5 jobs that you find from Internet resources that are of interest to you.

19. Research the city/state where these jobs are located.

20. Learn about electronic résumés by visiting the Web sites with online résumés. How are online résumés different from traditional résumés?

21. What characteristics of the Internet as a medium for communication and information-sharing can be used to showcase your talents and skills with an online résumé?

22. What are the advantages/disadvantages of online résumés?

23. Design an online résumé that showcases your talents and skills.

24. Visit online sites for job seekers. Explore their online résumés. Identify the sites where you would like to post your résumé. What features do you like about each site? What do you have to do to post your résumé? Is there a cost? How long will it be posted? How will you learn if your résumé is seen by prospective employers?

25. List 5–10 jobs you found on the Internet that you are interested in. Research the city and state where they are located. Does the information on the Internet help you determine which of these jobs interest you most?

26. You are preparing for an interview with a company that you are interested in working for. You know that it is important to have as much knowledge as possible about this company before the interview. How will you obtain this information? Select one company that you would like to interview with. Research information on this company using the Internet.

CHAPTER VI

COOL WEB SITES

In this chapter, you will find many valuable Internet resources for your educational journey. Categories include:

Preparing for College

- Associations
- Applying for College
- Financial Aid
- Financial Aid—Banks and Loan Information
- Finding a College
- Publications for College and College-Bound Students
- Tests—Standardized

Improving Your Grades

- Communication—Using the Internet as a Communication Tool
- Composition and Grammar
- Learning Lab
- Libraries
- Reference Desk
- Speeches and Speech Writing
- Writing Resources

Extra Credit

- Books and Literary Resources
- Government
- History of the Internet and Computers
- Maps
- News Publications
- Study Abroad
- Substance Abuse
- Weather
- Virtual Universities

Surfing Adventures—Cool Web Sites
Shareware and Software
Some Useful Internet Services

The World Wide Web sites in this chapter have been assigned the following rating based on quality of the information, presentation, use of graphics, creativity, ease of use, organization, and use of the medium's capabilities. Commercial sites generally receive lower ratings unless they offer valuable information and services to Web visitors at no charge.

☑ ☑ ☑ ☑   an exemplary site—a DEFINITELY MUST VISIT. Go to the top of the bookmark list.

☑ ☑ ☑   well-done site, DEFINITELY worth a visit—outstanding content.

☑ ☑   useful information, could improve presentation and ease of use.

☑   information may be useful. The page appears as if it is merely a cut-and-paste of a text document. No interactivity or use of the medium's capabilities.

PREPARING FOR COLLEGE

ASSOCIATIONS

UNITED STATES STUDENT ASSOCIATION ☑ ☑ **http://www.essential. org/ussa** The United States Student Association (USSA) is committed to increasing access to higher education. As the country's oldest and largest national student organization, it has been a continuous voice for students on Capitol Hill, in the White House, and in the Department of Education since 1947.

APPLYING FOR COLLEGE

CB NET (COLLEGE BOUND NET) ☑ ☑ ☑ **http://www.cbnet.com** A student interactive guide to college life from Ramholtz Publishing. Its *College Bound Magazine* provides information about the college application process.

COLLEGE LINK ☑ ☑ **http://www.collegelink.com** Apply to college using your computer. CollegeLink's award-winning software simplifies the application process by making it easy to apply to multiple colleges at once. Visit this site to learn more about customized applications to match the regular forms for hundreds of colleges.

COLLEGEAPPS.COM ☑ **http://www.collegeapps.com** Sharon Barth and Sue Berescik claim to be able to help motivate students to get started in the college application process. The site advertises their book and consulting services for taking the fears out of applying to college, showing how to self-assess and find one's unique qualities and experiences, and giving a sure-fire method of writing essays that LEAP OFF THE PAGE!

U.S. NEWS COLLEGE AND CAREER CENTER ☑ ☑ ☑ ☑ **http://www .usnews.com/usnews/edu-** U.S. News provides services to assist high school seniors as they finalize their list of colleges and prepare the applications that will determine the next four years of their lives.

USENET newsgroup for college admissions at **soc.college .admissions**.

FINANCIAL AID

When browsing Web sites for financial aid, it is useful to know the difference between scholarships and fellowships. The term scholarship refers to awards intended primarily for undergraduate students. The term fellowship refers to awards intended primarily for graduate and postgraduate students.

COLLEGEVIEW ☑ ☑ ☑ **http://www.collegeview.com/finaid** CollegeView has a number of resources to help you through the financial aid process: determining funds, loans, financial aid glossary, estimating expenses, sample financial aid packages, applying for aid, filing the FAFSA, financial aid calendar, managing money, free money, and more.

FASTWEB ☑ ☑ ☑ **http://www.fastweb.com** FastWEB (Financial Aid Search Through the WEB) is a searchable database of more than 180,000 private sector scholarships, fellowships, grants, and loans from more than 3,000 sources. Used by colleges across the United States, fastWEB is now available free through the World Wide Web, courtesy of the Financial Aid Information Page and fastWEB.com.

FELLOWSHIPS FOR MINORITY STUDENTS ☑ **http://www-college .uchicago.edu/GMF/MF.html** This noninteractive Web site has information on CIC (Committee on Institutional Cooperation) fellowships for minority students.

FINANCIAL AID INFORMATION PAGE ☑ ☑ ☑ ☑ **http://www .finaid.org** This AWESOME comprehensive site maintained by Mark Kantrowitz may have all the links to every online financial aid resource you are looking for. A go to the top of the bookmark list site.

This supplemental site links to information on scholarships and fellowships worldwide at **http://www.finaid.org/finaid/awards .html**

FINANCIAL AID SEARCH ☑ ☑ **http://www.finaid.org/finaid/ database/search.html** This Web site created by Mark Kantrowitz is a search form for finding financial aid awards. This is a free service.

FULBRIGHT SENIOR SCHOLAR PROGRAM ☑ **http://www.cies.org** This site has information that pertains to the Fulbright Senior Scholar Program and is made available to Fulbright alumni, grantees, prospective applicants, and the public at large. Although this site has useful information about Fulbright programs, it is difficult to find—often buried many links deep. One feels as if much of this information has been cut and pasted from a print publication. It would be helpful if this site used more of the interactive capabilities of the Internet for applying for awards.

GRANT INFORMATION ✓ ✓ ✓ **http://www.finaid.org/finaid/ awards/grants.html** This link to grant information is from the Financial Aid Home Page. Here you will find a listing of grant databases and funding opportunities.

MACH25 ✓ ✓ ✓ ✓ **http://www.collegenet.com/mach25** This excellent tool finds college scholarships for which you qualify. If you are a new user, you must first create a MACH25 account for which there is no charge.

MOLIS SCHOLARSHIP AWARD ✓ ✓ **http://www.fie.com/molis/ scholar.htm** Minority Online Information Service (MOLIS) helps you to find information about scholarship opportunities for qualified minority applicants.

PETERSONS'S FINANCING EDUCATION ✓ ✓ **http://www.petersons .com/resources/finance.html** Petersons's Financing Education page has links to the following resources: college financial aid information, the financial aid story, help in paying for college, questions and answers on financial aid, glossary of financial aid terms, and financial planning tools.

SCHOLARSHIP RESOURCE NETWORK (SRN) ✓ ✓ ✓ **http://www .rams.com/srn** SRN is an online database resource for finding college financial aid and scholarship information as well as student loan forgiveness programs with a focus on portable scholarship information. SRN offers programs for eligible students for their undergraduate studies through their postgraduate work.

U.S. GOVERNMENT FINANCIAL AID INFORMATION ✓ ✓ **http://www .finaid.org/finaid/gov.html** This page contains a listing of government financial aid resources.

USENET newsgroup for financial aid is **soc.college.financial-aid**

FINANCIAL AID—BANKS AND LOAN INFORMATION

The resources in this section are commercial loan companies.

CRESTAR STUDENT LOANS ✓ ✓ **http://www.student-loans.com** Information on Crestar's student loans includes a number of interactive services such as the Crestar Student Lending Calculator that allows parents to compare two or three savings strategies for more than one student at the same time.

FIRST BANK COLLEGE FUNDING ☑ ☑ **http://www.fbs.com/ student/index.html** First Bank provides online services to help you locate the lending program to solve your tuition quandary.

KAPLOAN ☑ ☑ ☑ **http://www.kaploan.com** This Web site has excellent information for preparing for college, grad school, and a career. They also have financial aid for parents and students.

SALLIE MAE ☑ ☑ ☑ **http://www.salliemae.com** Sallie Mae is a company whose goal is to make paying for college easier and less expensive for all involved. As one of the nation's largest financial services companies, they provide funds for education loans. In addition to business services, they have some useful financial calculators and tools.

SIGNET BANK ☑ ☑ **http://www.signet.com/collegemoney** SIGNET's site has information on educational funding for college expenses, including an interactive tool for college budgeting and cash flow management.

U.S. BANK'S STUDENT LOANS ☑ ☑ ☑ **http://www1.usbank.com/ personal/loans/student_loans/student_index.html** Online resources to help you determine if you qualify for a student loan, as well as other financial aid resources.

WELLS FARGO ☑ ☑ **http://wellsfargo.com/per/perstu/stulon/** This Wells Fargo site helps students find the information they need for borrowing money for education.

FINDING A COLLEGE

Resources for finding colleges, universities, community colleges, and technical schools.

AMERICAN UNIVERSITIES ☑ ☑ **http://www.clas.ufl.edu/CLAS/ american-universities.html** This site is a collection of home pages for American universities granting bachelor or advanced degrees.

COLLEGE AND UNIVERSITY HOME PAGES ☑ ☑ ☑ **http://www.mit .edu:8001/people/cdemello/univ.html** Links to more than 3,000 colleges and universities.

COLLEGE GUIDE SEARCH FORM ☑ ☑ ☑ **http://www.jayi.com/ jayi/ACG/search.html** Use this search form to find the perfect college for you. Use the pull-down menus and keyword to choose the variables of your preference. Or, if you'd prefer, you may simply view regional and alphabetical lists of colleges.

COLLEGE LINK ☑ ☑ ☑ **http://www.collegelink.com** Apply to college using your computer. CollegeLink's award-winning software simplifies the application process by making it easy to apply to multiple colleges at once. Visit this site to learn more about customized applications to match the regular forms for hundreds of colleges.

COLLEGE LOCATOR ☑ ☑ **http://www.ecola.com/college** A tool to help you locate a college or university by city and state.

COLLEGE VIEW ☑ ☑ ☑ **http://www.collegeview.com** A free online database of 3,500 colleges and universities, with virtual tours, financial aid information, career planning tools, and electronic applications. Visit the Coffee Shop to find others with similar interests and chat interactively.

COLLEGENET ☑ ☑ ☑ ☑ **http://www.collegenet.com/ cnmain.html** CollegeNET is an AWESOME guide to colleges and universities. CollegeNET lets you browse institutions by various criteria including geography, tuition, and enrollment. Other resources include a search tool to assist you with finding a college, information on financial aid and scholarships, featured schools, online application forms, graduate programs, and academic resources.

COMMUNITY COLLEGES ☑ ☑ The following Web sites have links to community colleges and technical schools.

http://www.utexas.edu/world/comcol/alpha

http://www.sp.utoledo.edu/twoyrcol.html

http://www.yahoo.com/Education/Higher_Education/ Community_Colleges

KAPLAN ☑ ☑ ☑ **http://www.kaplan.com/library/precoll/ listing.html** The Kaplan site has links to over 420 online colleges, as well as a featured college of the week and detailed information about what they feel are some of the best colleges.

PLANET EARTH HOME PAGE ☑ ☑ ☑ **http://www.nosc.mil/ planet_earth/uni.html** Planet Earth has an excellent collection of college resources including: university phone directories; an alphabetical listing of academies, colleges, and universities; other college and university sources; faculty and student body home pages; departments of education, scholarships; career centers; job opportunities; and links to other educational resources.

SELECTING A SCHOOL—A GUIDED TOUR ☑ ☑ ☑ ☑ **http://www .tgslc.org/adventur/selectng.htm** On this virtual tour you'll learn what to look for when choosing a college or training program and how to find the best school for you. This well-done site has many links to information, from career planning to financing your education to finding a job.

U.S. NEWS COLLEGE AND CAREER CENTER ☑ ☑ ☑ ☑ **http://www .usnews.com/usnews/edu/college/cosearch.htm** This excellent site has an interactive tool to help you find a college using personal selection criteria. They also have an online college rating taken from their publication—*America's Best Colleges*—that shakes up the college world.

PLANNING FOR YOUR COLLEGE EDUCATION

The Net sites in this section are for high school and college students. There are resources to help make the transititon smooth from high school to college, information on the fastest-growing careers, student success, internships, and career programs.

CAREER PLANNING GUIDED TOUR ☑ ☑ ☑ **http://www.tgslc.org/ adventur/planning.htm** On this tour, you can find out how to choose a career and how to reach your career goal. You can also pick up useful tips on job hunting, résumé writing, and job interviewing techniques.

COLLEGE BOARD ONLINE ☑ ☑ ☑ ☑ **http://www.collegeboard.org** This impressive site brings the authoritative educational and information resources of the College Board to your desktop. Here students and parents will find the Web's most comprehensive menu of information to aid in the transition from school to college. Services include online SAT test dates, online SAT registration, a test question of the day, a college search tool, a financial aid calculator, and much more.

COLLEGEEDGE ☑ ☑ ☑ ☑ **http://www.CollegeEdge.com** This award-winning site offers a powerful college search tool, useful links, advice, and guidance from an expert college panel. Explore careers and majors. In the CollegeEdge Forums, talk with other students about careers and majors. Career Advice provides information on the fastest-growing careers as well as advice and information on choosing the right career for you.

EASI ☑ ☑ ☑ **http://easi.ed.gov** EASI (Easy Access for Students and Institutions) is made available from the U.S. Education Department as a resource for families of college-bound students. This site (Fig. 6.1) provides links to information on financial aid resources by state, standardized tests for postsecondary schoool admission, student's rights, and loan repayment responsibilities.

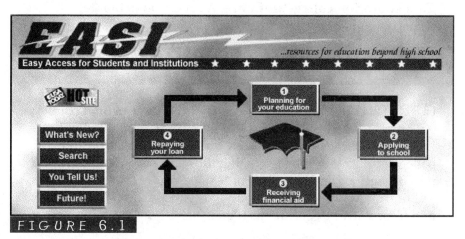

Home Page—EASI

KAPLAN EDUCATIONAL CENTER ☑ ☑ ☑ **http://www.kaplan.com** Kaplan helps prepare students for tests and success. Their online resources include links to many fun sites to test yourself—I.Q. tests, personality games, career inventories—an online SAT course, SAT vocabulary flash cards, and a college simulator to help determine if you are a scholar or a party animal. You will also find college sites of the week, links to over 460 online colleges, and information for student success.

THE PRINCETON REVIEW ☑ ☑ ☑ ☑ **http://www.review.com/ index.shtml** The Princeton Review offers students a wealth of free and unique resources. Through special student programs and an informative and comprehensive Web site, students can gather information about tests, admissions, internships, and career programs. The focus is on helping students.

U.S. NEWS COLLEGE AND CAREER CENTER ☑ ☑ ☑ ☑ **http://www .usnews.com/usnews/edu** U.S. News provides services to assist high school seniors as they finalize their list of colleges and prepare the applications that will determine the next four years of their lives. Get Into College takes you step-by-step through the process, from choosing schools to filling out the applications to planning the campus visit. They also have an exclusive college rankings published in their *America's Best Colleges,* now online.

YAHOO COLLEGE ENTRANCE COLLECTION ☑ ☑ **http://www.yahoo .com/education/college_entrance** A collection of online resources to help prepare for college.

PUBLICATIONS FOR COLLEGE AND COLLEGE-BOUND STUDENTS

CB NET (COLLEGE BOUND NET) ☑ ☑ ☑ **http://www.cbnet.com** A student interactive guide to college life from Ramholtz Publishing. Their *College Bound Magazine* provides information about the college application process, taking those BIG exams, getting you into college, and making the grade once you're there! Now their publication is wired and surrounded with all sorts of interactive and informative departments (Fig. 6.2).

TOP ONLINE ☑ ☑ ☑ **http://www.product.com/top** TOP Online is a service bringing educational and informational resources into the home. Here students and parents will find a wide array of information geared toward helping students make the transition from high school to college a smooth one.

21ST CENTURY NEWS ☑ ☑ A monthly magazine and newspaper written entirely by teens for teenagers since 1989, with over one million copies mailed yearly to 1,800 middle schools and high schools nationwide. The paper is published for young adults by The Young Authors Foundation which feels that teenagers have

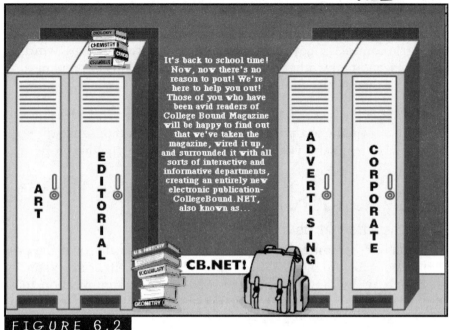

It's back to school time! Now, now there's no reason to pout! We're here to help you out! Those of you who have been avid readers of College Bound Magazine will be happy to find out that we've taken the magazine, wired it up, and surrounded it with all sorts of interactive and informative departments, creating an entirely new electronic publication—CollegeBound.NET, also known as...

CB.NET!

A R T

E D I T O R I A L

A D V E R T I S I N G

C O R P O R A T E

FIGURE 6.2

Home Page for CB NET

a great deal to say if they are given a chance. The monthly publication has become a print version of "talk radio" for teenagers, offering opportunities for teens to express a tremendous range of issues, feelings, and talents.

TESTS—STANDARDIZED

COLLEGE BOARD ONLINE ☑ ☑ ☑ ☑ **http://www.collegeboard.org**
The College Board site provides online SAT test dates, online SAT registration, a test question of the day, a college search tool, a financial aid calculator, and much more.

KAPLAN ☑ ☑ ☑ **http://www.kaplan.com/library/precoll/ listing.html** Testing services include the opportunity to take a sample SAT or GRE online at no cost. Visit their site to learn more about their test preparation services.

PRINCETON REVIEW ☑ ☑ ☑ **http://www.review.com/undergr/ college_homepage.shtml** Visit this site to learn about standardized tests and how to prepare for them. Included is information on SAT, SATII, The ACT, and The PSAT.

SYNDICATE ☑ ☑ ☑ **http://syndicate.com** Learning vocabulary can be fun for everyone! Compete for prizes in monthly word puzzle contests. Enjoy grade specific puzzles, comic strips, word games, and many other ways to sharpen your skills in preparation for the SAT(R), SSAT, GRE, or LSAT tests.

TESTPREP.COM ☑ ☑ ☑ **http://www.testprep.com** This Web site offers free online test preparation solutions with thousands of screens of math and verbal lessons and over 700 practice problems.

IMPROVING YOUR GRADES

Using the Internet as a Communication Tool

Methods of communication have changed dramatically over the past two decades. Before the 1970s, communication was either in person, by telephone, or by U.S. mail. In the 1980s, new communication tools began to emerge with the introduction of fax machines, personal computers, computer networks, electronic mail, express mail, cellular phones, and telecommunication technologies. In the 1990s the Internet emerged as the fastest-growing communication medium of all times. Some have called the World Wide Web the fourth media, positioned to take a place with print, radio, and television as a mass market means of communication.

ANALYSIS FOR INTERNET COMMUNICATION ☑ ☑ ☑ **http://shum .huji.ac.il/jcmc/vol1/issue4/december.html** This very interesting site offers thought-provoking discussion and analysis on using the Internet for communication.

THE BUSINESS OF THE INTERNET ☑ ☑ ☑ **http://www.rtd.com/ people/rawn/business.html** An introduction to the Internet for commercial organizations with a focus on what the Internet can do for businesses: product analysis, market analysis, expert advice and help, recruitment of new employees, rapid information access, wide-scale information dissemination, rapid communication, cost-effective document transfer, peer communication, and new business opportunities.

DIGITAL PLANET ☑ ☑ ☑ ☑ **http://www.digiplanet.com/index .html** For anyone who wants to communicate a message, the most important issue is engaging and retaining one's audience. Whether conveying a corporate message or providing entertain-

ing consumer content, Digital Planet explores the interactive medium's power to communicate a message that is entertaining, enlightening, and informative. Visit this site to learn how the Internet is being used to communicate with customers.

GLOBAL VILLAGE COMMUNICATION ☑ ☑ **http://www.info .globalvillag.com/index.html#NewsStand** Global Village develops and markets communication products and services for personal computer users. Visit the different areas in The Village to learn more about communicating from your computer, including faxing, accessing online services and the Internet, and connecting to remote networks.

THE INTERNET, A REVOLUTION IN COMMUNICATION ☑ ☑ ☑ **http://www.nih.gov:80/dcrt/expo/talks/overview/index.html** This site has information on the Internet as a communication medium and links to information on the Internet revolution as reported in the media.

SANDBOX ☑ ☑ ☑ **http://www.sandbox.net** Sandbox is entertainment with a clue—a free online network that explores how to use the Internet for entertainment.

Composition and Grammar

ELEMENTS OF STYLE ☑ ☑ ☑ **http://www.columbia.edu/acis/ bartleby/strunk** *The Elements of Style* by William Strunk is a book intended for use in English courses in which the practice of composition is combined with the study of literature.

GRAMMAR AND STYLE NOTES ☑ ☑ ☑ ☑ **http://www.english .upenn.edu/~jlynch/grammar.html** This award-winning Web site has articles on grammatical rules and explanations, and comments on style.

Learning Lab

U.S. News and World Report ranks the top U.S. colleges. Its selection of the Top 10 for 1996 includes Yale as number 1 (see Fig. 6.3), followed by Princeton, Harvard, Duke, Massachusetts Institute of Technology, Stanford, Dartmouth, Brown, California Institute of Technology, and Northwestern University. Visit the home pages of these leading academic institutions. Explore their online educational resources for teaching and learning.

FIGURE 6.3

Home Page—Yale University (Reprinted with permission *from* Yale University.)

BROWN UNIVERSITY http://www.brown.edu

CALIFORNIA INSTITUTE OF TECHNOLOGY http://www.caltech.edu

DARTMOUTH COLLEGE http://www.dartmouth.edu

DUKE UNIVERSITY http://www.duke.edu

HARVARD http://www.harvard.edu

MASSACHUSETTS INSTITUTE OF TECHNOLOGY (MIT) http://web.mit.edu

NORTHWESTERN UNIVERSITY http://www.nwu.edu

PRINCETON http://www.princeton.edu

STANFORD UNIVERSITY http://www.stanford.edu

YALE UNIVERSITY http://www.yale.edu

Libraries

Libraries from around the world can be accessed for research. Some libraries require a Telnet connection and the use of commands to find and retrieve information. Some libraries provide Help menus to assist you; others do not. Many libraries now have World Wide Web access, thus eliminating the need for commands to find information. Listed below are library resources on the Web.

ELECTRIC LIBRARY ☑ ☑ ☑ ☑ **http://www.elibrary.com** The Electric Library is a virtual library where you can conduct research online. Submit a question and a comprehensive search is launched of over 150 full-text newspapers, 800 full-text magazines, two international newswires, 2,000 classic books, hundreds of maps, thousands of photographs, as well as major works of literature and art.

LIBCAT ☑ ☑ ☑ ☑ **http://www.metronet.lib.mn.us/lc/lc1.html** An AWESOME guide to library resources on the Internet.

LIBRARY OF CONGRESS ☑ ☑ ☑ ☑ **http://www.loc.gov** Access the Library of Congress databases, historical collections, exhibitions, publications, links to other electronic libraries, information on copyright, and much more.

LIBWEB ☑ ☑ ☑ **http://sunsite.Berkeley.EDU/Libweb** A collection of online libraries worldwide.

SMITHSONIAN INSTITUTION ☑ ☑ ☑ ☑ **http://www.si.edu/ newstart.htm** A valuable online research service, the Smithsonian Institution provides over one million resources. Click on the link to Resources and Tours to begin your journey.

WEBCHATS ☑ ☑ **http://library.usask.ca/hywebcat/** Library catalogs on the Web.

Reference Desk

The Internet is the newest and perhaps largest reference library. This rich source of information is available to Net users. Listed below are a few reference resources that you will find useful.

BRITANNICA ONLINE ☑ ☑ ☑ ☑ **http://www.eb.com** For a minimal fee you can subscribe to Britannica Online and Merriam-Webster's Collegiate Dictionary. Some of the encyclopedia text is linked to Internet sites.

CIA WORLD FACT BOOK ☑ ☑ ☑ ☑ **http://www.odci.gov/cia/ publications/95fact/index.html** Published by the Central Intelligence Agency (CIA), The World Fact Book has a subject index for researching facts about countries.

COPYRIGHT HOME PAGE ☑ ☑ ☑ ☑ **http://www.benedict.com**
This award-winning Web site has everything you will ever want
to know about copyright.

DICTIONARIES & THESAURI ☑ ☑ ☑ ☑ **http://www.arts.cuhk.hk/**
Ref.html#dt A GOLDMINE collection of cyberdictionaries, thesauri, and other subject-oriented references.

ENCYBERPEDIA ☑ ☑ ☑ ☑ **http://www.encyberpedia.com/**
ency.htm The HOTTEST encyclopedia from cyberspace
designed to help you find good stuff in the jungle of over two
million Web sites.

MLA STYLE SHEET FOR DOCUMENTING ONLINE RESOURCES ☑ ☑ ☑
http://www.cas.usf.edu/english/walker/mla.html Information
on how to document online research.

MY VIRTUAL REFERENCE DESK ☑ ☑ ☑ ☑ **http://www.refdesk**
.com/main.html Links to many excellent reference resources
including a link to a subject directory of resources—My Encyclopedia link.

NOBLE CITIZENS OF PLANET EARTH ☑ ☑ ☑ **http://www.tiac.net/**
users/parallax This dictionary contains biographical information on more than 18,000 people who have shaped our world
from ancient times to the present day. Information contained in
the dictionary includes birth and death years, professions, positions held, literary and artistic works, and other achievements.

ONELOOK DICTIONARIES ☑ ☑ ☑ **http://www.onelook.com** Type
in a word and this search tool will look for multiple definitions
from a variety of online dictionaries: computer/Internet dictionaries, science, medical, technological, medical, business, sports,
religion, acronym, and general.

ONLINE REFERENCE WORKS ☑ ☑ ☑ ☑ **http://www.cs.cmu.edu/**
Web/references.html This site has a collection of online reference works such as English, foreign, and computing dictionaries;
acronym guides; thesauri; quotation resources; encyclopedias;
and more.

REFERENCE CENTER ☑ ☑ ☑ ☑ **http://www.ipl.org/ref** This virtual library helps to make finding valuable information online
easy. Click on a reference shelf and be linked to resources.

REFERENCE DESK ☑ ☑ ☑ ☑ **http://www-sci.lib.uci.edu/ ~martindale/Ref.html** This GOLDMINE site has won multiple awards for its SUPERB resource collection. A go to the top of the bookmark list site.

REFERENCE INDEXES ☑ ☑ ☑ **http://www.lib.lsu.edu/weblio .html** Links to online references such as dictionaries, library catalogs, newsstand, and subject collections.

REFERENCE SHELF ☑ ☑ ☑ **http://gort.ucsd.edu/ek/refshelf/ refshelf.html** The University of California, San Diego, sponsors this collection of online reference resources.

THE VIRTUAL REFERENCE DESK ☑ ☑ ☑ ☑ **http://thorplus.lib .purdue.edu/reference/index.html** Purdue University's links to an AWESOME list of valuable online resources.

WIRED SOURCE ☑ ☑ ☑ **http://www.wiredsource.com/ wiredsource** A collection of search engines to use for your research.

Speeches and Speech Writing

HOW TO WRITE YOUR SPEECH ☑ ☑ **http://www.coffingco.com/ doc/tjwrite.html** Tips for writing a speech for a particular audience.

PUBLIC SPEAKING ANXIETY ☑ ☑ **http://www.mwc.edu/~bchirico/ psanxinf.html** Symptoms of public speaking anxiety (PSA) and how to overcome PSA.

RESEARCHPAPER.COM ☑ ☑ ☑ ☑ **http://www.researchpaper .com/directory.html** This award-winning online research tool offers an archive of thousands of magazines, newspapers, books, and photographs.

SPEECH WRITING ☑ ☑ ☑ ☑ **http://speeches.com/index.shtml** This award-winning site has excellent resources for writing speeches. You're just a click away from everything you need to help you in your speech preparation. There's a speech archive: links to thousands of other speeches on the Web, free help with your speech writing, and the one and only Automatic Wedding Speech Writer.

SPIN DOCTOR'S CLINIC ☑ ☑ **http://speeches.com/writer.html** Get help with your speech draft from the Spin Doctor.

VISUAL PRESENTATION ASSISTANT ☑ ☑ ☑ **http://www.ukans.edu/ cwis/units/coms2/vpa/vpa.htm** An online tutorial for improving public speaking skills.

WORDS OF MOUTH ☑ ☑ ☑ **http://www.cohums.ohio-state.edu/ english/facstf/kol/diverse.htm** The Words of Mouth Home Page has been created to meet two distinct needs of editors and others interested in learning more about communication skills.

Writing Resources

BARTLETT'S FAMILIAR QUOTATIONS ☑ ☑ ☑ **http://www.ccc .columbia.edu/acis/bartleby/bartlett/index.html** Looking for a quote for your class presentation or paper? Connect to this Web site and search by keyword or choose from a list of people.

EDITORIAL EYE ☑ ☑ ☑ **http://www.eei-alex.com/eye** The Eye is a resource for writers, editors, designers, project managers, communications specialists, and everyone else who cares about excellence in publishing practices. Any aspect of effective written communication is likely to appear as a topic in the Eye.

RHETNET—A CYBERJOURNAL FOR RHETORIC AND WRITING ☑ ☑ ☑ **http://www.missouri.edu/~rhetnet** RhetNet is a concerted effort to see what publishing on the Net might be in its "natural" form without merely adapting Net publishing to print-based convention. However, print heritage should not be left behind entirely. This site explores the creative possibilities that Net publishing offers. Here you will find links to many electronic publications—essays, Net journals, and other written resources.

SUPERQUOTES ☑ ☑ ☑ **http://www.columbia.edu/acis/bartleby/ bartlett** Bartlett's familiar quotations, passages, phrases, and proverbs traced to their sources.

UNIVERSITY WRITING RESOURCES ☑ ☑ ☑ **http://www.interlog .com/~ohi/inkspot/university.html** Links to many writing resources.

WRITER'S BLOCK ☑ ☑ ☑ http://www.magi.com/~niva/
writblok/index.html *Writer's Block* is a quarterly newsletter that deals with technical writing and the business of documentation. It contains material of interest to communications specialists including writers, editors, graphic designers, and desktop publishing operators.

WRITER'S RESOURCE CENTER ☑ ☑ ☑ http://www.azstarnet.com/
~poewar/writer/writer.html John Hewitt is the writer and curator of the Writer's Resource Center. Here you will find links to writing tips such as 14 Tips for Sending Effective Press Releases; How to Become an Expert Writer in Any Industry; Technical Writing: Books and Reference Sources; The Art of Networking; and much more.

WRITING LAB ☑ ☑ ☑ http://owl.english.purdue.edu At Purdue, students go to the Writing Lab to talk with tutors about planning and writing their papers. Online, the Writing Lab offers other services as well, including materials on writing and useful links to other sources of information.

WRITING PAGE ☑ ☑ ☑ http://www.stetson.edu/~hansen/
writguid.html This page is designed to provide as much information and resources as possible for writers. While this site has all types of resources and links, its main focus is helping college students improve their writing skills. This page is a companion page to the Write Your Way to a High GPA page.

WRITING RESOURCES ☑ ☑ ☑ http://www.public.iastate.edu/
~psisler/resources.html Writing resources from the University of Iowa for writing instructors, professional communicators, technical writers, and rhetoric and composition scholars.

WRITING RESOURCES ON THE NET ☑ ☑ ☑ http://owl.trc.purdue
.edu/resources.html Purdue University has compiled many excellent writing resources on the Internet. If you're looking for good indexes and directories, also check out their extensive collection of Writing Labs on the Internet.

EXTRA CREDIT
Books and Literary Resources

THE COMPLETE WORKS OF WILLIAM SHAKESPEARE ☑ ☑ ☑ ☑ **http://
the-tech.mit.edu/Shakespeare/works.html** An online collection
of Shakespeare's work from MIT including resources for discussion, Shakespearean quotations, and links to other related online
resources.

IBIC GUIDE TO BOOK-RELATED RESOURCES ON THE INTERNET
☑ ☑ ☑ ☑ **http://sunsite.unc.edu/ibic/guide.html** IBIC
(Internet Book Information Center) has an extensive collection
of book-related resources that can be found on the Internet:
authors, publishers, booksellers, online books and magazines,
poetry, short stories, rare books, and more.

LABYRINTH ☑ ☑ ☑ **http://www.georgetown.edu/labyrinth/
labyrinth-home.html** The Labyrinth is a global information network providing free, organized access to electronic resources in
medieval studies through a World Wide Web server at George-
town University. The Labyrinth's easy-to-use menus and hypertext links provide automatic connections to databases, services,
and electronic texts on other servers around the world.

LITERARY RESOURCES ON THE NET ☑ ☑ ☑ ☑ **http://www.english
.upenn.edu/~jlynch/Lit** This award-winning site is a collection
of links to sites on the Internet dealing especially with English
and American literature, excluding single electronic texts.

MODERN ENGLISH COLLECTION ☑ ☑ ☑ **http://etext.lib.virginia
.edu/modeng.browse.html** An extensive collection from the
University of Virginia.

ONLINE BOOKS PAGE ☑ ☑ ☑ **http://www.cs.cmu.edu/books
.html** Look here for an index of thousands of online books and
for common repositories of online books and other documents.

SCIENCE FICTION RESOURCE GUIDE ☑ ☑ ☑ **http://sflovers
.rutgers.edu/Web/SFRG** A MUST VISIT site for sci-fi enthusiasts.

VOICE OF THE SHUTTLE ☑ ☑ ☑ ☑ **http://humanitas.ucsb.edu**
An AWESOME collection of Humanities resources. An important research site.

Government

FEDERAL GOVERNMENT AGENCIES ✓ ✓ ✓ **http://www.lib.lsu.edu/ gov/fedgov.html** A collection of over 200 government sites.

GOVERNMENT AGENCY LINKS ✓ ✓ ✓ **http://www.fjc.gov/ govlinks.html** Links to the federal courts and other government agencies.

GOVERNMENT DOCUMENT LINKS ✓ ✓ ✓ **http://thorplus.lib .purdue.edu/reference/gov.html** Purdue University has an impressive collection of online U.S. Government documents.

LIBRARY OF CONGRESS ✓ ✓ ✓ ✓ **http://www.loc.gov** Access the Library of Congress databases, historical collections, exhibitions, publications, links to other electronic libraries, information on copyright, and much more.

PRESIDENT ✓ ✓ ✓ **http://sunsite.unc.edu/lia/president** A Web site with a collection of presidential resources and an exhibit on the First Ladies of the United States.

TEXAS A&MS WHITE HOUSE ARCHIVES ✓ ✓ ✓ **http://www.tamu .edu/whitehouse** A collection of information about the White House and those who have resided there dating back to 1992.

THE WHITE HOUSE ✓ ✓ ✓ ✓ **http://www1.whitehouse.gov/ WH/Welcome.html** Visit this site and explore the virtual library for a collection of Presidential documents, speeches, and photos.

History of Internet and Computers

THE ABACUS ✓ ✓ ✓ **http://www.ee.ryerson.ca:8080/~elf/ abacus.html**

CALCULATING MACHINES ✓ ✓ ✓ **http://www.webcom.com/calc/ mult_maps.html**

COMPUTER HISTORY WEB SITE ✓ ✓ ✓ **http://granite.sentex.net/ ~ccmuseum/hist_sites.html**

HISTORY OF COMPUTERS AND THE INTERNET ✓ ✓ ✓ **http://www .yahoo.com/Computers_and_Internet/History/**

HOBBES INTERNET TIMELINE ☑ ☑ ☑ http://info.isoc.org/guest/zakon/Internet/History/HIT.html

HOBBES INTERNET WORLD ☑ ☑ ☑ http://info.isoc.org/guest/zakon/Internet/

LIBRARY OF CONGRESS—HISTORY OF THE INTERNET ☑ ☑ ☑ http://www.loc.gov/global/internet/history.html

PUBLIC BROADCASTING SYSTEM—HISTORY OF THE INTERNET ☑ ☑ ☑ http://www.pbs.org/internet/history/

TRIUMPH OF THE NERDS—PBS ☑ ☑ ☑ ☑ http://www.pbs.org/nerds/

VIRTUAL MUSEUM OF COMPUTING ☑ ☑ ☑ http://www.comlab.ox.ac.uk/archive/other/museums/computing.html

Maps

BIG BOOK ☑ ☑ ☑ ☑ http://www.bigbook.com Big Book has an interactive map service—enter the street name, city, and state and Big Book will generate a map for you. Big Book has street-level locations of 11 million U.S. businesses. Zoom in or pan out on maps for more detailed information.

MAGELLAN MAPS ☑ ☑ ☑ http://pathfinder.com/@@RUvpagcAJhE*G*3i/Travel/maps Magellan Maps (Fig. 6.4) is a Time Warner Pathfinder site with links to maps worldwide.

MAPQUEST ☑ ☑ ☑ ☑ http://www.mapquest.com This site features Interactive Atlas with a street guide for access to maps anywhere in the world. Trip Quest is a driving travel aid that provides city-to-city driving directions in the continental United States, Canada, and Mexico.

MICROSOFT AUTOMAP ROAD ATLAS ☑ ☑ ☑ http://www.microsoft.com/automap/default.htm Try this interactive route planner with detailed driving instructions between any two of 6,700 places in the United States.

NATIONAL PARKS MAPS ☑ ☑ ☑ http://www.lib.utexas.edu/Libs/PCL/Map_collection/National_parks/National_parks.html

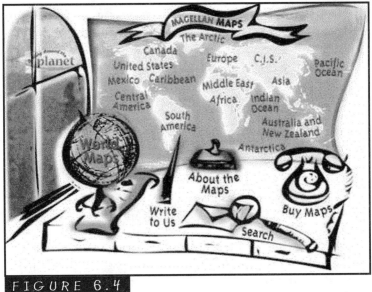

FIGURE 6.4

Home Page—Magellan Maps

This site has links to maps of United States national parks and monuments.

News Publications

CNET.COM ☑ ☑ ☑ ☑ **http://www.cnet.com/Content/Reviews/ Bestofweb/cat.html** CNET.COM offers a well-done, high-quality, and timely news site. This outstanding site offers daily up-to-the-minute technology and computer news for which there is no print counterpart. This site offers more than news. You will find reviews of software and hardware, links to interesting stories found in other online publications, news sections on major topics, collections of programs and games to download, and much more. It also produces several TV shows that air on the Sci Fi channel on Sunday: Web, Edge, and CNET. A must visit site to stay up-to-date on the latest technology news.

HOT WIRED ☑ ☑ ☑ ☑ **http://www.hotwired.com** Visit this innovative digital storefront that contains services, advertising, opportunities for advertising, special guest appearances, chat rooms, and much more. This site is an excellent example of the Internet's capabilities to deliver services and products.

NATIONAL PUBLIC RADIO ☑ ☑ ☑ ☑ **http://www.realaudio.com/ contentp/npr.html** Stop by NPR online to see how audio is being used on the Internet. Visit the NPR archive to find your favorite programs.

NEW YORK TIMES ☑ ☑ ☑ ☑ **http://nytimesfax.com/index.html** This site delivers highlights from the daily newspaper as well as articles on technology. You will need to download a copy of Adobe Acrobat reader (free) before you can read the *Times* online.

NEWSLINK ☑ ☑ ☑ ☑ **http://www.newslink.org/** This excellent site provides links to over 2,000 news sites.

NEWSPAGE ☑ ☑ ☑ ☑ **http://www.newspage.com** With 500 information sources and 25,000 pages refreshed daily, NewsPage is the most comprehensive news site on the Web. To use News-Page, simply select an industry and drill your way through cate-gories and topics to today's news, hot off the virtual presses.

THE OTIS INDEX ☑ ☑ ☑ **http://www.interlog.com/~gordo/ otis_pubpubs.html** This site helps you search the Internet to find software, online books, commercial sites, newsgroups, and electronic publications.

PBS ONLINE ☑ ☑ ☑ ☑ **http://www.pbs.org** The latest news from Public Broadcasting Station as well as links to programs from popular PBS series and other news-related resources.

POINTCAST NETWORK ☑ ☑ ☑ ☑ **http://www.pointcast.com/ products/index.html** Voted one of the best Internet applications, the PointCast Network (PCN) broadcasts news, financial news, stock quotes, weather, sports, and more to your desktop 24 hours a day. The PointCast Network is the first news network to use the Internet to broadcast news and information to a viewer's computer screen (Fig. 6.5). The software and the service are free, financed by advertising. You can customize PointCast to receive only the news that interests you.

SAN JOSE "MERCURY NEWS" ☑ ☑ ☑ **http://www.sjmercury.com/ main.htm** The Mercury Center Web is the first complete daily newspaper on the World Wide Web. This service offers continu-ally updated news coverage, the complete text of each day's final

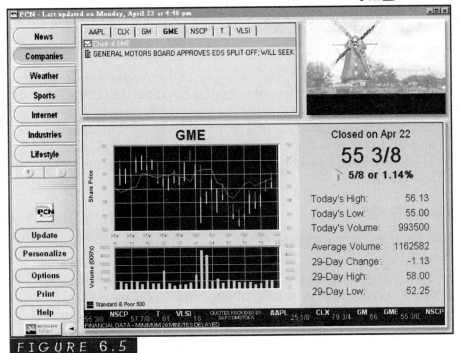

FIGURE 6.5

PointCast Network application

edition of the *San Jose Mercury News* including classified ads, and a variety of special features.

TIME WARNER ☑ ☑ ☑ ☑ **http://www.pathfinder.com**
Pathfinder from Time Warner is an excellent Web site for discovering how an information-providing company pushes the capabilities of the new Internet medium.

THE WALL STREET JOURNAL ☑ ☑ ☑ ☑ **http://www.wsj.com** This online version of *The Wall Street Journal* has hyperlinks to money and investing updates, a variety of *Journal* offerings including headlines from today's paper, and *The Wall Street Journal* Classroom Edition—the *Journal's* award-winning educational program for secondary school students and teachers.

WALL STREET NEWS ☑ ☑ ☑ ☑ **http://wall-street-news.com/**
forecasts Stop by WALL STREET - U.S.A. and drop in on the Internet Broadcasting Super-Station. Meet the News Director, Dr. Paul B. Farrell, who has a unique approach to financial news— the forecasting business. The news comes directly from financial

newsletters published by Wall Street's leading forecasters. WSTN goes beyond reporting the news; it forecasts tomorrow's news today.

WALL STREET RESEARCH NET ☑ ☑ ☑ ☑ **http://www.wsrn.com**
Wall Street Research Net consists of more than 110,000 links to help professional and private investors perform fundamental research on actively traded companies and mutual funds, and to locate important economic data that moves markets. A MUST VISIT site for those who want to find information on companies.

Study Abroad

COUNCIL ON INTERNATIONAL EDUCATIONAL EXCHANGE ☑ ☑
http://www.ciee.org The Council on International Educational Exchange is a nonprofit, nongovernmental organization dedicated to helping people gain understanding, acquire knowledge, and develop skills for living in a globally interdependent and culturally diverse world. Founded in 1947, Council has developed a wide variety of programs and services for students and teachers at secondary through university levels and related constituencies. Services include college and university programs, secondary programs, English-language development, work exchanges, voluntary services, and travel services.

WORLDWIDE CLASSROOM ☑ ☑ **http://www.worldwide.edu/**
WorldWide Classroom is a compilation of intercultural and educational programs around the world that welcome international visitors. They include: university study; adult enrichment; foreign language immersion; teen camps; volunteerism; internships; and cultural, craft, and heritage programs.

Substance Abuse

ADDICTION RESEARCH FOUNDATION ☑ ☑ ☑ **http://www.arf.org**
The Addiction Research Foundation develops and makes available knowledge and programs that can be used to reduce the problems caused by the abuse of alcohol and other drugs in Ontario. This site has information on community-based planning and development services, health promotion activities, treatment programs, research, and more.

ALCOHOL & DRUG INFORMATION (FROM NCADI) ☑ ☑ ☑ ☑

http://www.health.org/ NCADI sponsors PREVLINE—Prevention Online. This site has links to information on what to do if someone you love has a problem—resources and referrals, publications, latest press releases, research, surveys, statistics, drug and alcohol databases, online discussion forums, and links to related Internet resources.

CANADIAN CENTRE ON SUBSTANCE ABUSE ☑ ☑ ☑ **http://www**

.ccsa.ca Canadian Centre on Substance Abuse is a nonprofit organization working to minimize the harm associated with the use of alcohol, tobacco, and other drugs. This site has links to substance abuse statistics, publications, and activities. You can also search their database for general information on substance abuse.

CENTER FOR EDUCATION AND DRUG ABUSE RESEARCH (CEDAR)

☑ ☑ ☑ **http://www.pitt.edu/~mmv/cedar.html** CEDAR's mission is to elucidate the factors contributing to the variation in the liability to drug abuse and determine the developmental pathways culminating in drug abuse outcome, normal outcome, and psychiatric/behavioral disorder outcome. Their Internet site supports this mission by providing information on drug and alcohol abuse projects and links to drug-related sites.

CENTER FOR SUBSTANCE ABUSE RESEARCH (CESAR) ☑ ☑ ☑

http://www.bsos.umd.edu/cesar/cesar.html CESAR is a research center within the College of Behavioral and Social Sciences, University of Maryland–College Park. A primary mission of CESAR is to collect, analyze, and disseminate information on the nature and extent of substance abuse and related problems. Second, CESAR conducts policy-relevant research on specific initiatives to prevent, treat, and control substance abuse and evaluates prevention and treatment programs. Visit this site and learn more about their services and online support information.

DRUG ENFORCEMENT ADMINISTRATION ☑ ☑ **http://www.usdoj.gov/**

dea/deahome.html Visit this site to learn more about what DEA is doing to combat the war against drugs.

DRUG INFORMATION ☑ ☑ ☑ **http://www.paranoia.com:80/drugs**

This Web site has a place to submit and read drug users' stories;

cold, hard information on substances such as alcohol, marijuana, MDMA, nontropics, opiates, psychedelics, and stimulants; information on the war on drugs; and better living through the use of drug prevention links.

DRUGS AND CRIME ☑ ☑ ☑ http://www.ncjrs.org/drgshome.htm
Links to information on community efforts and prevention, corrections, courts, drug testing, drug treatment, drug use indicators, enforcement, policy and law, research, and evaluation.

DRUGS IN THE MEDIA ☑ ☑ ☑ http://www.he.net/~storm/drugs/
media.html Links to articles and special reports about drugs including the MacNeil/Lehrer News Hour, an article by William F. Buckley, and *New York Times* and *Los Angeles Times* stories.

NATIONAL INSTITUTE ON DRUG ABUSE (NIDA) ☑ ☑ ☑ http://www
.nida.nih.gov The mission of the National Institute on Drug Abuse (NIDA) is to lead the nation in bringing the power of science to bear on drug abuse and addiction. To accomplish this mission, NIDA conducts research across a broad range of disciplines and provides rapid and effective dissemination and use of the results of that research to significantly improve drug abuse and addiction prevention, treatment, and policy. This site has links to NIDA's research and programs.

RAND DRUG POLICY RESEARCH CENTER (DPRC) ☑ ☑ ☑ http://www
.rand.org/centers/dprc DPRC was established in 1989 to conduct the empirical research, policy analysis, and outreach needed to help community leaders and public officials develop more effective strategies for dealing with drug problems. The center is strongly committed to ensuring that its findings reach those who can make a difference. Visit this Web site to learn more about their work.

SUBSTANCE ABUSE AND MENTAL HEALTH SERVICES ADMINISTRATION
(SAMHSA) ☑ ☑ ☑ http://www.samhsa.gov SAMHSA's mission is to assure that quality substance abuse and mental health services are available to the people who need them and to ensure that prevention and treatment knowledge is used more effectively in the general health care system. This site provides information on SAMHSA's programs and services, statistical information on drug abuse, funding opportunities, events and conferences, and other related Internet resources.

UNITED NATIONS INTERNATIONAL DRUG CONTROL PROGRAMME ☑ ☑
http://www.undcp.org The United Nations International Drug Control Programme is the United Nations agency responsible for coordinating activities relating to the international control of narcotic drugs and psychotropic substances. Visit this site to learn more about its programs and services as well as links to national drug information.

WEB OF ADDICTIONS ☑ ☑ ☑ **http://www.well.com:80/user/woa**
The Web of Addictions is dedicated to providing accurate information about alcohol and other drug addictions. The Web of Addictions was developed due to concerns about the extent of misinformation about abused drugs on the Internet.

Weather

USA TODAY WEATHER UPDATES ☑ ☑ ☑ ☑ **http://www.usatoday.com/weather/wfront.htm** Find current weather and 5-day forecasts for the United States and locations worldwide (Fig. 6.6).

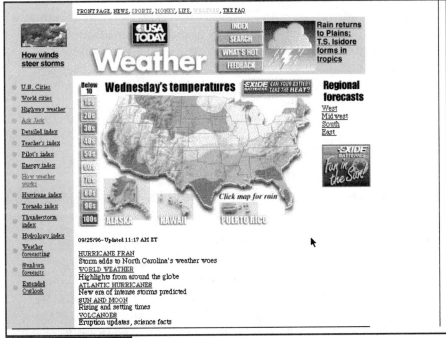

FIGURE 6.6

USA Today Home Page

INTELLICAST ☑ ☑ ☑ **http://www.intellicast.com** Microsoft's NBC Web site has links to U.S. and worldwide weather, as well as ski conditions and general news.

THE WEATHER CHANNEL ☑ ☑ ☑ ☑ **http://www.weather.com** The Weather Channel is a 24-hour television network devoted entirely to weather. Each day The Weather Channel broadcasts local forecasts for more than 4,000 National Weather Service zones across the country.

WEATHERNET ☑ ☑ ☑ ☑ **http://cirrus.sprl.umich.edu/wxnet** WeatherNet, sponsored by The Weather Underground at the University of Michigan, connects you to the world of weather. This site accesses thousands of forecasts, images, and the Net's largest collection of weather links. WeatherNet is perhaps the most comprehensive and up-to-date source of weather data on the Web.

Virtual Universities

INTERNET UNIVERSITIES ☑ ☑ ☑ **http://www.caso.com/iuhome .html** This site has almost 300 individual pages of info. It is one of the most comprehensive sources of information about online college courses available on the Internet today. You will find information on courses—a listing of more than 700 courses that you can take via the Internet; providers—contacts for over 30 online course-providing colleges and universities; research— educational mailing lists, newsgroups, FTP, Telnet, and WWW links; and articles from those who teach online.

SURFING ADVENTURES

This section features some of the coolest Web sites that present valuable information in visually well-designed interactive environments.

AIRLINES ON THE WEB ☑ ☑ ☑ **http://w2.itn.net/airlines** The Airlines on the Web page is maintained by a graduate student at the University of California—Berkeley Haas School of Business studying the rapid changes in the airline industry for a dissertation. At this site you will find links to most of the passenger carriers worldwide, frequent flyer programs, airline stock quotes, medical airline transports, cargo airlines, manufacturers and suppliers, aviation organizations, airline 800-numbers, related Internet sites, and Airlines on the Web statistics.

ALCATRAZ ✓ ✓ ✓ ✓ **http://www.nps.gov/alcatraz** Out in the middle of the San Francisco Bay, the island of Alcatraz is a world unto itself. Isolation, one of the constants of island life for any inhabitant—soldier, prisoner, bird, or plant—is a recurrent theme in the unfolding history of Alcatraz. Follow its pelican for a complete tour of the island. Learn about the military and penitentiary history, Native American Occupation, Natural History, or visit the bookstore.

ALTERNATIVE ENTERTAINMENT NETWORK ✓ ✓ ✓ ✓ **http://www .cummingsvideo.com** Eleven great channels. Check it out.

AMAZING ENVIRONMENTAL WEB DIRECTORY ✓ ✓ ✓ ✓ **http://www .webdirectory.com** The directory is another GOLDMINE of online environmental resources.

ART CRIMES—THE WRITING ON THE WALL ✓ ✓ ✓ ✓ **http://www .gatech.edu:/desoto/graf/Index.Art_Crimes.html** Graffiti art from all over the world. Visit this fascinating Web site and answer this question, "Is graffiti a crime?"

ARTIST UNDERGROUND ✓ ✓ ✓ ✓ **http://www.aumusic.com** The award-winning site is the place to discover artists and their music.

AUDIONET ✓ ✓ ✓ ✓ **http://www.audionet.com** The broadcast network on the Internet.

CYBERTOWN ✓ ✓ ✓ ✓ **http://www.cybertown.com/ cybertown/index.html** The purpose of Cybertown is to create a virtual community where people can have fun, be entertained, learn things, and explore the best of the Earth Internet. Cybertown is set in the latter half of the 21st century and is not far from this galaxy. It is populated mostly by people originally from Earth. Many of them left Earth after the Great War in the hopes that a new start would lead to more peaceful times. Visit Cybertown to continue the journey.

CYBORGANIC GARDENS ✓ ✓ ✓ **http://www.cyborganic.com** Kick off your shoes and wander around the Cyborganic Gardens. A creative, interesting, and fun site.

DEAD MAN TALKIN' ☑ ☑ ☑ **http://monkey.hooked.net/m/hut/ deadman/deadman.html** Dean is currently an inmate at San Quentin Prison in California and is awaiting his fate on "Death Row." His desire in these columns is to give you an idea of what it is like as you wait to die. This Web site has been recognized by *USA Today* as a HOT site.

DIGITAL PASSPORT ☑ ☑ ☑ ☑ **http://www.rubicon.com/ passport.html** This hot Web site is worth a visit. Valuable and useful information is provided for those interested in international travel: an excellent world exchange rate tool, time zone information, international holidays, embassies, air travel information, and information on international deliveries.

DISCOVERY CHANNEL ☑ ☑ ☑ ☑ **http://www.discovery.com** This well-done interactive environment is a place to learn about the world and interesting phenomena on planet Earth. Here you will find that learning can be FUN!

EARTHSHIP ☑ ☑ ☑ **http://www.slip.net/~ckent/earthship** If you're looking for UFOs, aliens, and other such things, this is not the place. Earthships are a new approach to sustainable living. Imagine building a house out of discarded tires and aluminum cans. Imagine using environmentally friendly materials and techniques to create a truly self-sufficient home. Imagine interfacing and harnessing nature to create a dwelling that lives with the land, not on top of it.

ECOMALL ☑ ☑ ☑ ☑ **http://www.ecomall.com** A place for businesses and individuals to shop their preferred method to help save the Earth (Fig. 6.7).

EDWARD ABBEY WEB ☑ ☑ ☑ **http://www.utsidan.se/abbey/ abbey.html** Meet Edward Paul Abbey, twentieth-century polemicist and desert anarchist, a character of elaborate contradictions and eccentricities whose words either infuriated or delighted his readers. In a career spanning four decades, he wrote passionately in defense of the Southwest and its inhabitants, often mocking the mindless bureaucratic forces hell-bent on destroying it. "Resist much, obey little," from Walt Whitman, was this warrior's motto. His Home Page appears in Fig. 6.8.

—from *Epitaph for a Desert Anarchist*

FIGURE 6.7

EcoMall Home Page

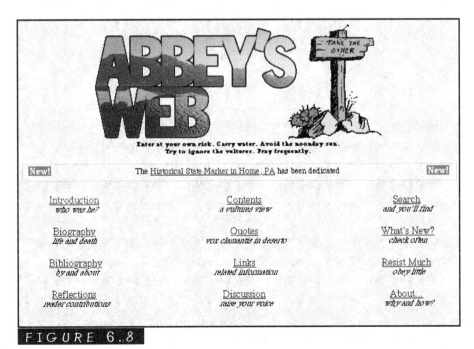

FIGURE 6.8

Edward Abbey's Home Page

ELECTRONIC ZOO ☑ ☑ ☑ ☑ **http://netvet.wustl.edu/e-zoo.htm**
Back in the spring of 1993, a veterinarian started a (then) very
manageable project of organizing and categorizing veterinary
medical information available on the Internet. The project grew
and today has become one of the best Web sites with "everything animal."

ESPNET SPORTSZONE ☑ ☑ ☑ ☑ **http://ESPNET.SportsZone.com**
The latest sports news can be found at ESPNET.

EXPLORATORIUM ☑ ☑ ☑ ☑ **http://www.exploratorium.edu**
Stop by San Francisco's Exploratorium—a museum of science,
art, and human perception with over 650 interactive "hands-on"
exhibits. This virtual museum has something of interest for
everyone, so plan to spend some time exploring.

FODOR'S TRAVEL ☑ ☑ ☑ ☑ **http://www.fodors.com**
http://www.ypn.com/travel Use Fodor's Trip Planner (Fig. 6.9)
to prepare for your next vacation. Build a customized miniguide
to scores of destinations around the world. The Trip Planner
leads you through a series of checklists where you tell Fodor's
your destination and exactly what you want in the way of hotels,
restaurants, travel info, and more. When you're finished, it uses
your choices to build a personalized guide that you can print out
for easy reading or to take with you on your trip. The Know
Before You Go section links to information on travel advisories,
world weather, currency conversion, government health advisories, and more.

THE HEART—AN ONLINE EXPLORATION ☑ ☑ ☑ **http://sln.fi.edu/**
biosci/heart.html Explore the heart. Discover the complexities
of its development and structure. Follow the blood through the
blood vessels. Wander through the weblike body systems. Learn
how to have a healthy heart and how to monitor your heart's
health. Look back at the history of heart science.

INDIGENOUS PEOPLES RESOURCES ☑ ☑ ☑ ☑ **http://www.halcyon**
.com/FWDP/othernet.html The Internet has many other sources
of information regarding indigenous peoples. This is an AWE-
SOME list of resources.

MAINE SOLAR HOUSE ☑ ☑ ☑ ☑ **http://solstice.crest.org/**
renewables/wlord This award-winning site is a MUST VISIT
stop even if you have no interest in solar power.

FIGURE 6.9

Fodor's travel Home Page

MEDIADOME ☑ ☑ ☑ ☑ **http://www.mediadome.com/About/ index.html** CNET and Intel collaborate to bring the best cutting-edge multimedia Web entertainment to your desktop. A new interactive program debuts every two weeks providing the ultimate Web experience, where you become a participant rather than just an observer.

NASA ☑ ☑ ☑ ☑ **http://www.nasa.gov** Learn more about what lies beyond planet Earth by visiting the NASA site. Stop by the Gallery where you will find video, audio clips, and still images to download. In the Aeronautics section you will find aeronautics research and links to related Webs. In Space Science there is information on NASA's planetary exploration, astronomy, and research into the origins of life. Mission to Planet Earth is dedicated to understanding the many ways the Earth is constantly changing and how humans influence those changes. Human Space Flight provides links to the space shuttle research.

RAIN FOREST ACTION NETWORK ☑ ☑ ☑ ☑ **http://www.igc.apc .org/ran** This graphic and well-designed site has information on global rain forests as well as educational information on how to protect them.

SONY ☑ ☑ ☑ ☑ **http://www.sony.com** The Sony site is an excellent example of how interactivity can be used on the Internet. It contains links to music, film, and electronics. Information can be found on musicians, their tour schedules, sound clips, record cover art, music videos, and special promotions, as well as information on Sony products.

THE SPOT ☑ ☑ ☑
http://www.thespot.com
By day, the beach.
Sand. Surf.
A cigarette.
Melrose to shop. Grunge. Prep. Pop.
Whatever.
Walk the walk.
Just survive until tomorrow.
Be cool . . .
Jeff. Carrie. Lon. Michelle. Jordan.
Twentysomethings.
Living the scene.
Exposing their lives on the net.
First, a grad project.
Now, a big time venture.
Everyone's readin' it.
On the edge . . .
Groovin', man.
This is their world. This is their Spot.

TELEGARDEN ☑ ☑ ☑ ☑ **http://www.usc.edu/dept/garden** *For the experienced gardener, the TeleGarden offers a search for the soul of*

gardening. Sowing a single, unseen and untouched seed thousands of miles away might seem mechanical, but it engenders a Zen-like appreciation for the fundamental act of growing. Though drained of sensory cues, planting that distant seed still stirs anticipation, protectiveness, and nurturing. The unmistakable vibration of the garden pulses and pulls, even through a modem. —Warren Schultz

Visit the TeleGarden and interact with a remote garden filled with living plants. At no cost, become a member—plant, water, and monitor the progress of seedlings via the movements of a robotic arm.

THOREAU CYBERSAUNTER ☑ ☑ ☑ **http://umsa.umd.edu/thoreau** This growing site is the home of a wealth of knowledge about the life and works of Henry David Thoreau. Coming in the near future, an interactive tour of Concord and Walden.

THE TREE OF LIFE ☑ ☑ ☑ **http://phylogeny.arizona.edu/tree/ phylogeny.html** The Tree of Life is a collection of World Wide Web pages that presents information about the world's organisms. This site is designed to illustrate the diversity and unity of living organisms. Each page presents information about a particular group.

VOYAGER ☑ ☑ ☑ ☑ **http://www.voyagerco.com** Visit this ever-changing Voyager site to experience how one successful company uses art and technology.

SHAREWARE AND SOFTWARE

FREEWARE CENTRAL ☑ ☑ **http://www.ptf.com/free** Freeware Central is an exploratory news and information resource for the free software community. Topic areas include: archives of free software, calendar of upcoming events related to free software, legal issues related to free software, news about free software, organizations involved with free software, and services related to free software.

JUMBO ☑ ☑ ☑ ☑ **http://www.jumbo.com** The Biggest, Most Mind-Boggling, Most Eye-Popping, Most Death-Defying Conglomeration of Freeware and Shareware Programs on the Web: 24,582 PROGRAMs at this time!

MIT'S HYPERARCHIVE ☑ ☑ ☑ ☑ **http://hyperarchive.lcs.mit .edu/HyperArchive/HyperArchive.html** Search MIT's archive for software or browse by categories.

SHAREWARE.COM ☑ ☑ ☑ ☑ **http://www.shareware.com** An extensive collection of shareware with an online search engine for finding what you are looking for.

TUCOWS (THE ULTIMATE COLLECTION OF WINSOCK SOFTWARE)
☑ ☑ ☑ ☑ **http://www.tucows.com/** This site has an excellent selection of Internet software for Windows 95. TUCOWS provides Windows 3.x and '95 winsock programs to facilitate PC access to the Internet.

USEFUL INTERNET SERVICES

AT&T TOLL FREE ☑ ☑ ☑ **http://www.tollfree.att.net/dir800** This Web site is one example of how a company has used the Internet to provide a useful service. The site helps you find 800-numbers of companies.

CAR RENTAL 800 NUMBERS ☑ ☑ ☑ **http://www.travlang.com/ carrental.800.html** Toll-free numbers for car rental agencies.

FEDEX ☑ ☑ ☑ ☑ **http://www.fedex.com/cgi-bin/track_it** Wondering where your FedEx package is, when it got delivered, or who signed for it? Visit FedEx's Package Tracking interactive and fascinating Web site.

HOTEL TOLL FREE NUMBERS ☑ ☑ ☑ **http://www.go-explore.com/ CONTENT/USA/hotel800.htm** Click on the first letter of the hotel's name, or scroll through the list to find the toll-free number of a hotel in the United States or Canada.

INTERNATIONAL DIALING CODES ☑ ☑ ☑ **http://www.cris.com/ ~Kropla/dialcode.htm** This site has a listing of Country Codes and IDD (International Direct Dialing) prefixes.

UNITED PARCEL SERVICE ☑ ☑ ☑ ☑ **http://www.ups.com** Learn more about how businesses provide useful services by visiting the United Parcel Service's interactive site. This site also helps you track your packages, calculate approximate costs for sending a package, and provides a form to help estimate how long it will take for your package to reach its destination.

ZIP+4 CODE LOOKUP ☑ ☑ ☑ **http://www.usps.gov/ncsc/ lookups/lookup_zip+4.html** Have you ever been frustrated trying to find a zip code? This Web site by the United States Postal System provides a useful Internet resource. Enter an address and, if found in their database, this lookup will standardize the address, return the ZIP+4 code, and provide the county name.

GEEK SPEAK

ACTIVEX: Microsoft's response to Java was the *ActiveX* development platform. This technology makes it possible for Web programmers to create and for Web surfers to view moving and animated objects, live audio, scrolling banners, and interactivity. The *ActiveX* technology—available in Microsoft Internet Explorer—allows viewing of many plug-in applications without first downloading and installing the required plug-in. *ActiveX* lets desktop applications be linked to the World Wide Web, for example, programs such as Word can be viewed directly from Explorer.

administrative address: The email address used for sending requests to listservs for either text documents or subscriptions to a mailing list.

anonymous FTP: The method used in file transfer protocol that allows Internet users to log into an FTP server as an unregistered user. Before browsers were used for FTP, users connecting to an FTP server would have to log in by entering a login name and password. The login name was anonymous; the password, your email address.

applets: Mini-applications that a software program such as Netscape downloads and executes.

ASCII (text) files: One of the file transfer modes (binary is another mode) used when transferring files on the Internet. ASCII treats the file as a set of characters that can be read by the computer receiving the ASCII text. ASCII does not recognize text formatting such as boldface, underline, tab stops, or fonts.

avatar: In online chat environments, users create nicknames that they are known by online. In 3D chat worlds, an avatar is the graphical representation that a user creates for himself. Avatars can look like a person, an animal, or an object.

binary file: Another transfer mode available for transferring Internet files. In the binary mode, files are transferred which are identical in appearance to the original document.

Binhex (BINary HEXadecimal): A method for converting non-text files (non-ASCII) into ASCII. Used in email programs that can handle only ASCII.

bit: A single-digit number, either a 1 or a 0, that represents the smallest unit of computerized data.

bookmarks: A feature providing the user with the opportunity to mark favorite pages for fast and easy access. Netscape's bookmarks can be organized hierarchically and customized by the user through the Bookmark List dialog box.

Boolean operators: Phrases or words such as "AND," "OR," and "NOT" that limit a search using Internet search engines.

browser: A client program that interprets and displays HTML documents.

client: A software program assisting in contacting a server somewhere on the Net for information. Examples of client software programs are Gopher, Netscape, Veronica, and Archie. An Archie client runs on a system configured to contact a specific Archie database to query for information.

compression: A process by which a file or a folder is made smaller. The three primary purposes of compression are to save disk space, to save space when doing a backup, and to speed the transmission of a file when transferring via a modem or network.

cookie: Cookie technology allows the storage of personal preferences for use with Internet information and communication tools. A text file is created of a user's preferences, saved in their browser's folder, and stored in RAM while the browser is running. For example, a popular Web audio site, Timecast, allows users to select their personal audio preferences to be played with RealAudio. These personal preferences are saved in a browser folder called a *cookie file.* When the user connects to the site, the server at that site looks for the cookie file on the user's computer to find their specifications.

delayed-response media: Internet communication tools that require time for an end-user to respond (e.g., electronic mail, listservs, and newsgroups).

digerati: A community of diverse professionals—computer scientists, film makers, designers, engineers, architects, artists, writers, musicians—who are becoming increasingly wealthy through their creative and innovative use and exploration of digital technology. Louis Rossetto and Jane Metcalfe (*Wired* magazine) were the first to give a name to these digital elite whom they believed were becoming the most powerful people on earth.

domain name: The unique name that identifies an Internet site. Names have two or more parts separated by a dot such as **xplora.com.**

finger: An Internet software tool for locating people on the Internet. The most common use is to see if an individual has an account at a particular Internet site.

fire wall: A combination of hardware and software that separates a local area network into two parts for security purposes.

flame: Flaming is the word used in Internet communication (email and news-groups) to personally attack another person. A flame war occurs when the flamer is flamed back.

frames: A new feature of Netscape Navigator 2.0 makes it possible to create multiple windows on a Netscape page. To navigate within frames and to save bookmarks, you will use your mouse. To move forward and back within frames, position your cursor within the frame and hold down the mouse button (Macintosh users); Windows users hold down the right mouse button. A pop-up menu appears. Choose **Back in Frame** or **Forward in Frame.** To book-mark a frame, place your cursor over the link to the frame and hold down the mouse button. A different pop-up menu appears. Select **Add Bookmark for this Link.** To print a frame, click the desired frame and select **Print Frame** from the **File** menu.

FTP (file transfer protocol): Protocol for transferring files between computers on the Internet.

GIF (Graphic Interface Format): A format developed by CompuServe, Inc. for storing complex graphics. This format is one of two used for storing graphics in HTML documents.

Helper Applications: Programs used by Netscape to read files retrieved from the Internet. Different server protocols are used by Netscape to transfer files: HTTP, NNTP, SMTP, and FTP. Each protocol supports different file formats for text, images, video, and sound. When these files are received by Netscape, the external helper applications read, interpret, and display the file.

History List: Netscape keeps track of your Internet journeys. Sites that you visit are listed in the History List found under the **Go** pull-down menu. Click on an Internet site on your list, and you will be linked to that destination.

Home Page: The starting point for World Wide Web exploration. The Home Page contains highlighted words and icons that link to text, graphics, video, and sound files. Home Pages can be developed by anyone: Internet providers, universities, businesses, and individuals. Netscape allows you to select which Home Page is displayed when you launch the program.

HTML (HyperText Markup Language): A programming language used to create a Web page. This includes the text of the document, its structure, and links to other documents. HTML also includes the programming for accessing and displaying media such as images, video, and sound.

HTTP (HyperText Transfer Protocol): One protocol used by the World Wide Web to transfer information. Web documents begin with **http://**

hyperlinks: Links to other Web information such as a link to another page, an image, or a video or sound file.

Hypermedia: The combined use of multimedia (text, images, video, and sound) in a Web presentation page.

hypertext: A document containing links to another document. The linked document is displayed by clicking on a highlighted word or icon in the hypertext.

intranet: An intranet is usually owned by a company or corporation for communication within the organizattion. It is referred as a restricted-access network.

IP address: Every computer on the Internet has a unique IP address. This number consists of four parts separated by dots such as 198.68.32.1

ISDN: Normal telephone lines are low-bandwidth analog lines. ISDN lines are digital lines that can handle large amounts of information very quickly—up to four times as fast as the standard 28.8Kbps modem. An ISDN line is a single phone wire that makes it possible to download Web pages, send and receive faxes, and talk on the phone—all at the same time. An ISDN line is divided into three channels: two B channels and one D channel, thus making it possible to surf the Internet with one B channel and have the other two channels available for phone calls or faxes.

ISP: Internet Service Provider

JavaScript: A new programming language developed by Sun Microsystems that makes it possible to incorporate mini-applications called *applets* onto a Web page.

JPEG (Joint Photographic Experts Group): A file format for graphics (photographs, complex images, and video stills) that uses compression.

listserv mailing list: A listserv is the automated system that distributes electronic mail. Listservs perform two functions: distributing text documents stored on them to those who request them, and managing interactive mailing lists.

live objects: Java brings life and interaction to Web pages by making it possible to create live objects. Move your mouse over an image of a house and see the lights go on. Move your mouse to a picture of a woman and hear her welcome you to her Home Page.

MIME (Multimedia Internet Mail Extension): Most multimedia files on the Internet are MIME. The MIME type refers to the type of file: text, HTML, images, video, or sound. When a browser such as Netscape retrieves a file from a server, the server provides the MIME type to establish whether the file format can be read by the software's built-in capabilities or, if it cannot, whether a suitable helper application is available to read the file.

Mozilla: Users of Netscape may run into a little cartoon dragon that pops up on Netscape screens. This character is called Mozilla—the Netscape mascot. The name originated in the early days of Netscape. The creators of the first Web browser—NCSA Mosaic—formed a company and created what we now know as Netscape. The developers code-named the first beta version of Netscape "mozilla" for Mosaic mated with Godzilla—a mutant or monstrous version.

multimedia: The term used when referring to the use of more than one medium—such as text supplemented with animation, video, or sound.

news reader: A software program required to read Usenet newsgroups. Netscape has a news reader built in. Explorer requires the downloading and installing of the news reader, Internet Mail and News.

newsgroups: Large, distributed bulletin board systems that consist of several thousand specialized discussion groups. Messages are posted to a bulletin board by email for others to read.

NNTP (News Server): A server protocol used by Netscape for transferring Usenet news. Before you can read Usenet news, you must enter the name of your news server to interact with Usenet newsgroups. The news server name is entered in the Mail and News dialog box (**Options** pull-down menu; **Preferences;** Mail and News).

page: A file or document in Netscape that contains hypertext links to multimedia resources.

PKZIP: A popular compression program for Windows computers.

platform: Netscape Navigator 2.0 is referred to as a platform rather than a browser. A platform program makes it possible for developers to build applications onto it.

plug-in: Software programs designed to play multimedia files from your browser window or page, running as a system resource as long as they are needed.

pop-up menu: Menus that activate software features and navigational aids.

PPP (Point-to-Point Protocol): A method by which a computer may use a high-speed modem and a standard telephone line to have full Internet access. A PPP or SLIP connection is required to use graphical interfaces with the Internet such as Netscape Navigator and Explorer. Using a PPP or SLIP connection enables you to point and click your way around the Internet.

quick links: Microsoft Internet Explorer provides an option for creating toolbar buttons of your favorite sites. This feature is called quick links.

real-time media: Internet communication tools where interaction occurs in real-time (i.e., chats, MOOs, MUDs, Internet telephone, and Internet video-conferencing).

.sea (self-extracting archives): A file name extension indicating a compression method used by Macintosh computers. Files whose names end in .sea are compressed archives that can be decompressed by double-clicking on the program icon.

search directory: Descriptive subject indexes of Web sites.

search engine: Software programs designed for seeking information on the Internet. Some of these programs search by keyword within a document, title, index, or directory.

server: A computer running software that allows another computer (a client) to communicate with it for information exchange.

shell account: The most basic type of Internet connection. A shell account allows you to dial into the Internet at your provider's site. Your Internet software is run on the computer at that site. On a shell account your Internet interface is text-based. There are no pull-down menus, icons, or graphics. Some Internet providers offer a menu system of Internet options; others merely provide a Unix system prompt, usually a percent sign or a dollar sign. You must know which commands to enter at the prompt to access the Internet.

SLIP (Serial Line Internet Protocol): A method by which a computer with a high-speed modem may connect directly to the Internet through a standard telephone line. A SLIP account is needed to use Netscape. SLIP is currently being replaced with PPP (Point-to-Point Protocol).

SMTP (Simple Mail Transport Protocol): A protocol used by the Internet for electronic mail. Before using Netscape email, the host name of the Internet provider's mail server must be designated. The mail server name is entered in the Mail and News dialog box (**Options** pull-down menu; **Preferences;** Mail and News).

source file: When saved as "source," the document is preserved with its embedded HTML instructions that format the Internet page.

status bar: A horizontal bar found at the bottom of some browser windows that indicates the status of the document or file that is being transferred to the computer from an Internet site.

streaming audio and video: Audio or video files that flow continuously over the Internet to your computer, immediately playing the video or sound file as it arrives at the desktop. RealAudio is an example of one of the more popular streaming audio programs.

submission address: The email address used to send a message to subscribers of a listserv mailing list.

TCP/IP (Transmission Control Protocol/Internet Protocol): The protocol upon which the Internet is based and which supports transmission of data.

Telnet: One of the oldest Internet tools that allows users to log onto another computer and run resident programs.

toolbar: Navigational buttons used in graphical interface applications.

URL (Uniform Resource Locator): URLs are a standard for locating Internet documents. They use an addressing system for other Internet protocols such as access to Gopher menus, FTP file retrieval, and Usenet newsgroups. The format for a URL is **protocol://server-name:/path.**

URL object: Any resource accessible on the World Wide Web: text documents, sound files, movies, and images.

Usenet: Developed in the 1970s for communication among computers at various universities. In the early 1980s, Usenet was being used for electronic discussions on a wide variety of topics and soon became a tool for communication. Today, Usenet groups are analogous to a café where people from everywhere in the world gather to discuss and share ideas on topics of common interest.

viewer: Programs needed to display graphics, sound, and video. For example, pictures stored as a GIF image have the file name extension ".gif" and need a gif helper application to display the image. Netscape has the required viewers (external helper applications) built into the software. A list of programs required to view files can be found in the Helper Application menu of Netscape. Open the **Options** pull-down menu, select **Preferences,** then **Helper Applications.**

VRML (Virtual Reality Modeling Language): A programming language that makes 3-dimensional virtual reality experiences possible on Web pages.

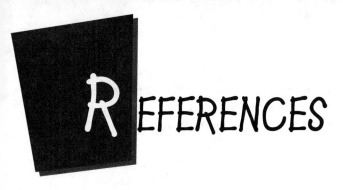

REFERENCES

Angell, D. (1996, March). The ins and outs of ISDN. *Internet World*, 78–82.

Bennahum, D. S. (1995, May). Domain street, U.S.A. *NetGuide*, 51–56.

Butler, M. (1994). *How to Use the Internet*. Emeryville, CA: Ziff-Davis Press.

Career Center (1996). [Online]. Available: http://www.monster.com/home.html or http://199.94.216.77:80/jobseek/center/cclinks.htm

CareerMosaic Career Resource Center (1996). [Online]. Available: http://www.careermosaic.com/cm/crc/

Conte, R. (1996, May). Guiding lights. *Internet World*, 41–44.

Dixon, P. (1995, May). Jobs on the web. *SKY*, 130–138.

Ellsworth, J. H., & Ellsworth, M. V. (1994). *The Internet Business Book*. New York: John Wiley & Sons, Inc.

Grusky, S. (1996, February). Winning résumés. *Internet World*, 58–68.

Harnack, A. & Kleppinger, E. (1997). *Online—A Reference Guide to Using Internet Sources*. New York: St. Martin's Press, Inc.

Leibs, S. (1995, June). Doing business on the net. *NetGuide*, 48–53.

Leshin, C. (1996). *Internet Adventures—Step-by-Step Guide to Finding and Using Educational Resources*. Boston: Allyn and Bacon.

Leshin, C. (1997). *Netscape Adventures—Step-by-Step Guide to Netscape Navigator and the World Wide Web*. Upper Saddle River, NJ: Prentice Hall.

Lewis, P. H. (1996, June 13). Judges turn back law to regulate Internet decency. *The New York Times*, pp. A1, A18.

Life on the Internet: Net history from PBS. [Online]. Available: http://www.pbs.org/internet/history.html (October 1996).

Miller, D. (1994, October). The many faces of the Internet. *Internet World*, 34–38.

Netscape Communications Corporation. (1996, January/February). *Netscape Handbook*. [Online]. Currently available by calling 1-415-528-2555 or online by selecting the Handbook button from within Netscape.

O'Connell, G. M. (1995, May). A new pitch: Advertising on the World Wide Web is a whole new ball game. *Internet World*, 54–56.

Reichard, K., & King, N. (1996, June). The Internet phone craze. *Net-Guide*, 52–58.

Resnick, R., & Taylor, D. (1994). *The Internet Business*. Indianapolis, IN: Sams Publishing.

Richard, E. (1995, April). Anatomy of the World Wide Web. *Internet World*, 28–30.

Riley, Margaret F. (1996). Employment Opportunities and Job Resources on the Internet [Online]. Available: http://www.jobtrak.com./job guide/

Sachs, D., & Stair, H. (1996). *Hands-on Netscape, a Tutorial for Windows Users*. Upper Saddle River, NJ: Prentice Hall.

Sanchez, R. (1994, November/December). Usenet culture. *Internet World*, 38–41.

Schwartz, E. I. (1996, February). Advertising webonomics 101. *Wired*, 74–82.

Signell, K. (1995, March). Upping the ante: The ins and outs of SLIP/PPP. *Internet World*, 58–60.

Strangelove, M. (1995, May). The walls come down. *Internet World*, 40–44.

Taylor, D. (1994, November/December). Usenet: Past, present, future. *Internet World*, 27–30.

Venditto, G. (1996, March). Online services—how does their net access stack-up? *Internet World*, 55–65.

Venditto, G. (1996, May). Search engine showdown. *Internet World*, 79–86.

Venditto, G. (1996, June). Internet phones—the future is calling. *Internet World*, 40–52.

Weiss, A. (1994, December). Gabfest—Internet relay chat. *Internet World*, 58–62.

Weiss, A. (1997, January). Activating activex. *Internet World*, 108–112.

Welz, G. (1995, May). A tour of ads online. *Internet World*, 48–50.

Welz, G. (1997, February). Multimedia comes of age. *Internet World*, 44–49.

Wiggins, R. W. (1994, March). Files come in flavors. *Internet World*, 52–56.

Wiggins, R. W. (1994, April). Webolution: The evolution of the revolutionary World Wide Web. *Internet World*, 33–38.

Wilson, S. (1995). *World Wide Web Design Guide*. Indianapolis, IN: Hayden Books.

Zakon, R. H. (1996). Hobbes' Internet timeline v2.4a [Online]. Available: http://info.isoc.org/guest/zakon?internet/History.html (December 1996).

APPENDIX

FINDING WEB SITES THAT HAVE MOVED

The Internet is a dynamic and rapidly changing environment. Information may be in one place today and either gone or in a new location tomorrow. New sites appear daily; others disappear. Some sites provide forwarding address information; others will not. As you travel in cyberspace and find that a resource you are looking for can no longer be found at a given Internet address, there are several steps you can take to find if the site has a new address.

- Check for a new Internet address or link, often provided on the site of the old address.

- Shorten the URL.

  The format for a URL is: **protocol//server-name/path**

  Try deleting the last section of the URL (path), so that the URL ends with the domain name or server name (com, edu, net, org). For example, you may be looking for NASA's links to astronomy sites. Take the original URL provided for the site, in this case **http://quest.arc.nasa.gov/lfs/other_sites.html,** and delete the last part of the address. **lfs/other_sites.html** leaving **http://quest.arc.nasa.gov.** You will most likely get to NASA's Home Page and can navigate to the specific topic or category you are looking for.

- Type in a company name for the URL.

  Companies usually use either their name, some part of their name, or an abbreviation as their domain name that becomes their URL. Netscape 2.02 and 3.0 accept abbreviated Net addresses, without the **http://www.** prefix. If you type a single word as your URL, Netscape adds the prefix **http://www.** and the suffix **.com.** For example, to connect to Netscape's Home

Page, type **Netscape.** Microsoft Internet Explorer, however, requires the **http://www.** prefix.

- Identify a domain name or server name.

  If you are trying to find an educational institution (edu), nonprofit organization (org), networking organization (net), government (gov), or military agency (mil), identify a portion of the name that they may have chosen for their domain name. For example, Rainforest Action Network (RAN) is a nonprofit organization (org) that has changed the location of its Web site several times. Typing an old address **http://gaia1 .ies.wisc.edu/research/pngfores/welcome** gives this message: **HTTP/1.0 404 Object Not Found**

  To find the Rainforest Action Network, look at their name and try to identify what they may have chosen for their domain name. Since Rainforest Action Network is long, perhaps they chose their acronym, RAN. Try entering a URL using **RAN** and **org.** In this instance type **http://www.ran.org.** This URL connects to the Rainforest Action Network's Home Page.

- Do a keyword search using search engines.

EXAMPLE 1

Finding a new URL for the Rainforest Action Network. When researching the new URL for the Rainforest Action Network, a search engine such as Infoseek Ultra, Alta Vista, or Excite can be used. For this example, we will use Infoseek Ultra. Type in the keywords *rainforest action network* and enclose the keywords with quotation marks as suggested by this search tool. Otherwise all instances of the words *rainforest, action,* and *network* will be found and returned in the search results.

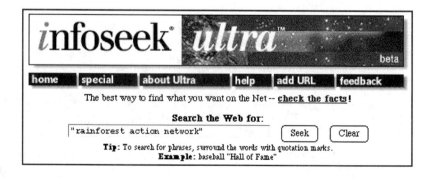

Entering "rainforest action network" in Infoseek Ultra produced the link to RAN's Home Page.
Infoseek Ultra seems to provide the highest relevant returns for keyword searches at this time.

NOTE When the same search was done using Infoseek Ultra, and the word *rainforest* was made into two words *rain forest*, the search did not immediately provide the Home Page for RAN. It is important to use the same keywords that the organization or company uses. In this case, *Rainforest Action Network*, not *Rain Forest Action Network*. Although the Web site will eventually be found, it may take longer to review an extensive list of returns.

EXAMPLE 2

Finding a new URL for the Bucknell Engineering Beast project. When the URL **http://www.eg.bucknel.edu/~beast96** for Bucknell Engineering's Beast 96 project was entered, Netscape returned this message.

> ⚠ **Netscape is unable to locate the server: www.eg.bucknel.edu The server does not have a DNS entry.**
> **Check the server name in the Location (URL) and try again.**
>
> [OK]

Since no forwarding URL was given, the Infoseek Ultra search engine was used. To identify keywords for the search, refer to the Web site information in your book (in this case, *Internet Investigations in Electronics*, p. 77).

Beast96 is a project with Bucknell Engineering Animatronics Systems Technology. The keywords selected for the search were *Bucknell Engineering*. Since two words are being entered in the search, use Infoseek's suggestions to place keywords in quotation marks, limiting the search to returns that contain both words *Bucknell* and *Engineering*.

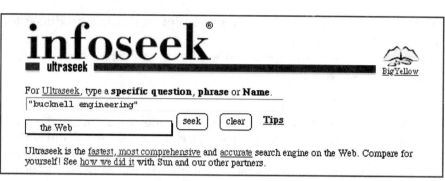

The search produced the following results:

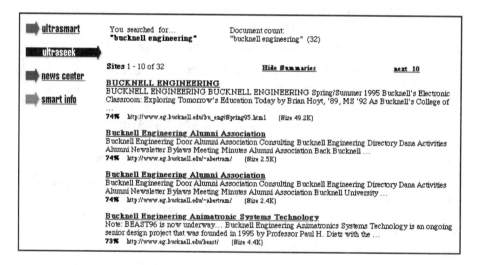

Review the search engine returns for the Web site you are looking for. In this case, the fourth return indicated that the Beast project could be found at the given site **http://www.eg.bucknell.edu/beast/**.

Finding information on the Internet is often a Treasure Hunt. Become an Explorer and your Journey will become an Adventure.

BUYER'S GUIDE

WHAT TO LOOK FOR WHEN PURCHASING A COMPUTER–PERFORMANCE AND PRICING

If you are interested in surfing the Web and experiencing cool graphics, animation, sound, video, virtual reality, Internet phones, and the latest multimedia environment, you will need a powerful personal computer (PC). If on the other hand you are interested only in desktop applications such as database, spreadsheet, financial, or word processing applications, you will not need as powerful a PC.

The information listed on this page assumes that you are interested in purchasing a PC for multimedia-oriented environments alive with action and interaction.

Hardware

Whether you decide to purchase a Macintosh or a Windows personal computer, use the following guidelines for selecting hardware:

- **CPU** (central processing unit)

  Windows PC: a Pentium unit with a minimum of 133MHz processor. Do not purchase a computer with a 486 processor unless you are interested only in desktop applications (word processing etc.). Processor speeds of 200 MHz or above are best.

  Macintosh: a Power PC with a minimum of 100 MHz processor.

- **Memory:** minimum of 32 MB to 64 MB of RAM.

- **Hard Drive:** 1–2 GB (gigabyte)

- **Modem:** Minimum 28.8 Kbps (kilobits)

  Your modem is very important since it affects the speed at which Web pages download to your computer. A computer's processor and RAM affect computing performance but have little to do with the speed at which data can be transferred from a Web site. Your modem is the variable affecting fast Net access; therefore, a 28.8 Kbps modem is essential. Do not buy a 14.4 modem or a computer with a built-in 14.4.

A new class of modems was introduced in 1997 that permits users to download material from the Internet at speeds of 56 Kbps—twice as fast as today's standard models. U.S. Robotics—a leading modem company—offers these new high-speed modems. Visit their Web site to learn more: **http://www.usr.com.**

Top modems include:

U.S. ROBOTICS SPORTSTER (800) 342-5877 **http://www.usr.com**

CARDINAL MVP288IS (800) 755-0899 **http://www.cardtech.com**

ZOOM V.341 PLUS MODEL 2805 (800) 631-3116 **http://zoomtel.com**

LOGICODE QUICKTELL 28800 V.34 DSVD (800) 735-6442 **http://www .logicode.com**

HAYES TOTAL INTERNET SOLUTION (770) 840-9200 **http://www .hayes.com**

MOTOROLA ISG ONLINE SURFR (800) 426-6336 **http://www.mot .com/modems**

MICROCOM DESKPORTE 28.8S (800) 822-8224 **http://www .microcom.com**

NOTE For really fast Net access, consider ISDN. **MAKE THIS A LINK TO ISDN INFO.** (More about ISDN on page 228.)

- **Audio:** A sound board is necessary and does not usually come with many computers. If you are purchasing a Windows PC, consider the following highly recommended sound boards:

Sound Blaster (Creative Labs) AWE32 PnP	(800) 998-1000
Sound Blaster (Creative Labs) 32	(800) 998-1000
Aztech Waverider Pro32-3D PnP	(800) 222-2603
CrystaLake Model 110	(800) 222-2603
CrystaLake Model 140	

- **Upgradable:** One frustrating thing about computers is that they very quickly become obsolete. Every few months new models are released with more powerful features and often at lower prices. Additionally, much of the new multimedia software requires the powerful features of the latest PCs. It is therefore imperative that you purchase a computer that is fully upgradable. This translates into making sure your unit has 3–4 expansion slots.

NOTE: Many less expensive computers DO NOT have upgrade capabilities. This is frequently the reason for the lower pricing.

- **CD-ROM:** Most computers come with a CD-ROM. Be sure the CD-ROM is at least quad speed (4X). A flood of high-speed CD-ROM players is hitting the market offering 12X and most recently 16X CD players. Do not begin out-of-date, with limited capabilities to use new CDs.

- **Monitor:** A 15-inch monitor with a viewable screen of at least 13.7 inches is highly recommended.

- **Microphone** (optional): If you plan to use Internet phones, you will need a microphone.

- **Backup for data files** (optional): Although you will not need data backup hardware if you are only surfing the Net, this hardware is a must to avoid DATA DISASTER if you are using your computer for other applications. A backup device prevents the loss of hours of work that you have invested in working with computer applications such as desktop publishing, word processing, databases, spreadsheets, graphics etc. The two backup storage units highly recommended are Zip and Syquest drives with 100MG storage disks.

NOTES Variations in pricing can be attributed to the use of cheaper internal components and NO options for upgrades. Some manufacturers substitute off-brand components for name-brand parts, thus cutting costs. BEWARE of rebuilt units.

Other factors to consider when purchasing a computer are extended warranties and customer support. Check to find out how the manufacturer handles service. A one-year warranty is standard. Will a service representative come to your home/office or does the computer have to be returned to the place of purchase?

Technical Support
The other critical service often included in a warranty must be considered carefully. Customers today are becoming increasingly frustrated

with technical support, as customer service continues to go downhill. The norm is a long waiting time to reach a tech support representative who can help solve a problem. Some companies now charge an hourly fee for technical support during the warranty unless it involves a hardware defect. Other computer manufacturers charge tech support fees when the original warranty expires. Fees range from $35 per question to $2 per minute with a $30–$35 charge limit.

Additional Resources for Buying a Computer

Several Web sites provide useful information to assist you with the purchase of computer hardware and software.

A MUST VISIT site for PC Buyers

For additional information, connect to *PC World's* online Buyer's Guide (**http://www.pcworld.com**) for excellent information on the best PCs to purchase: PC World's picks of the top 20 power desktops; top budget desktops for under $2,500; and an interactive page that becomes your personal advisor for finding just the right match.

Macintosh users will find these two Web sites useful: MacUsers **http://www.zdnet.com/macuser** has up-to-date information on Macintosh hardware, software, and much more.

MacWorld (**http://www.macworld.com/index.shtml**) has an online Buyer's Guide, links to free Macintosh software, and daily news.

About ISDN (Integrated Services Digital Network)

Normal telephone lines are low-bandwidth analog lines. ISDN lines are digital lines that can handle large amounts of information very quickly—up to four times as fast as the standard 28.8-Kbps modem. An ISDN line is a single phone wire that makes it possible to download Web pages, send and receive faxes, and talk on the phone—all at the same time. An ISDN line is divided into three channels: two B channels and one D channel, thus making it possible to surf the Internet with one B channel and have the other two channels available for phone calls or faxes.

Before you can use ISDN, you must have the following:

- ISDN service in your community (check with your local phone company)

- an account with an Internet service provider (ISP) that offers ISDN access

- modem dial-up conversion from an Internet account to ISDN

- a *terminal adapter* (similar to a modem) that allows your computer to connect to the ISDN line

- a high-speed serial card (not necessary, but helps to achieve maximum speed from the ISDN line)

- an ISDN line installed by your local telephone company. You pay a monthly fee (in addition to your ISP fee) for the use of the ISDN line. Fees vary between phone companies and may range from $30 to more than $100 per month. Options usually include a flat monthly fee for a specified number of hours of usage, then an additional hourly rate if the allotted hours are exceeded.

INDEX

ABC.com, 54
Academic institutions home pages,
    181–82
Access date, 109
ActiveX, 20, 43
Address. *See* URLs
Address location field, 22
Administrative address, 59–60
Adobe Acrobat reader, 45, 192
Airlines on the Web, 198–99
Algorithm, relevance ranking, 90
All Business Network, 144
AlphaWorld, 71
Alta Vista, 79, 91
Alternative Entertainment Network,
    54
*American Psychological Association
    (APA) Publication Manual,* 110
America Online (AOL), 16, 55, 70
America's Job Bank, 135
    exploring job opportunities on,
        150–53
Andreessen, Marc, 5
Animation, 42
Apollo, 145
Apple QuickTime Plug-In, 45
Applets, 42
Archeological link, 92–93
Argus Clearinghouse, 86
ARPANET, 4
Artists Underground, 54
Art online resources, 93
ASCII text, 140, 141
Ask An Expert, 100
AT&T College Network, 135, 164

Audio, streaming, 42
AudioNet, 54
Auto Channel, 54
Awesome List, 28

Banners, scrolling, 43
Bartlett's Familiar Quotations, 100
Berners-Lee, Tim, 5
Best Bets for Extending Your Search:
    Other Internet Job Guides,
    132–33
Best of the Web, 28
Beyond Mail, 7
Bookmarks, 25, 26, 82
    adding to folder, 31
    copying, 31–32
    deleting, 32
    exporting and saving, 32–33, 39
    importing, 33–34
    modifying name of, 31
    organizing (Netscape Navigator)
        28–31; (Internet Explorer)
        34–36, 37
    saving favorite Web sites, 28–36
    using Internet Explorer, 34–36, 37
    using Netscape Navigator, 28–34
Boolean logic, 84
Boolean operators, 82
Boston Globe, 136
Britannica Online, 100–1
Brown University, 182
Browser(s), 5, 6, 9, 11, 13, 42
    basics of, 20–4
    customizing, 39–41
    integration with desktop, 20

Browser(s) (*cont.*):
  plug-ins and viewers with, 43–44
  and saving favorite Web sites, 28
  upgrading, 24
  and Usenet newsgroups, 62–63
Browser folder, 109
Browser page, frames on, 36
Browser war, 5, 19, 20
Bubble viewer, 45
Bulletin boards, 8
Bulletin board system (BBS), 61
Business online resources, 93–94
Business Web Site Directory, 145
Buzzwords. *See* Geek speak

California Institute of Technology,
  182
Career City, 135
Career Connection, 135
Career Doctor, 139
Career Magazine, 135
CareerMosaic, 136
Career Path, 135–36
Career Resources Home Page, 136
CareerSite, 136
CareerWeb, 136, 154–55
CCMail, 7
CERN, 5
Chaco Communication, 46
Chat room, 70
Chat rooms, private, 71
Chat rooms, public, 70
Chats, 8, 55, 70–71
  See also Internet Relay Chat(s)
Chat software, free, 55
Chat worlds, 70, 71
Chicago Manual of Style, 110
Chicago Tribune, 136
Chronicle of Higher Education, 138
CIA World Fact Book, 101
City.Net, 159
CNET.com, 28, 55, 71, 76, 191
CNN Interactive, 39, 54
Cold war, 3
Collaborative computing, 6

Collabra, 20
College Grad Job Hunter, 136
Comic Chat, 71
Commercial Sites Index, 129, 145
Communication network. *See* Cyber-
  space; Internet
Communication tools, 12–13
Communicator Suite, 55
Composer, 20
Composition and grammar resource
  sites, 181
Compressed file, 42
Compression programs, 10
Compression utility, 47
CompuServe, 16, 55, 70
Computer History Web Site, 6
Computers, buyers guide, 224–29
Conference, 20
CoolTalk, 20, 74, 75
Cosmo Player, 45
Criminal justice online resources, 94
CU-SeeMe, 75
Cybersleuth guidelines, 81
Cyberspace, 3, 4, 15, 56
  and career planning, 125–27
  See also Internet
Cybertown, 54
Cybervdo, 54

Dartmouth College, 182
Databases, 8
Data highway. *See* Cyberspace;
  Internet; Net
Delaware, University of, MBA
  program, 93
Delayed response media, 56
Delphi, 16
Desktop, computer, 6
Desktop videoconferencing, 55, 56
  See also Videoconferencing
Dial-Up-Networking, 16
Dictionaries & Thesauri, 101
Digiterati, 5, 54
Direct Internet connection, 16
Directory buttons, 24

Discovery Channel, 39, 54, 55, 70, 71, 76
Discussion forums, 16
Discussion groups. *See* Listserv(s); Listserv mailing list(s); Mailing list(s)
Diversity University, 72
Dow Jones & Company, Inc., 130
Duke University, 4, 182

Electric Library, 103
Electronic discussion groups, 56
    See also Listserv(s); Listserv mailing list(s); Mailing list(s)
Electronic highway. *See* Cyberspace; Internet; Net
Electronic mail, 8, 11, 12, 56
    and commercial online service providers, 16
    services available on, 6–7
    See also Email
Electronic media, referencing, 110–22
APA style, 111–22
Electronic Newsstand, 129
Electronic resumes. *See* Online resumes
Electronic tools, on Internet, 11–13
Electronic workshops, 7
Electronic Zoo, 202
Email, 58
    referencing information from, 119–21
    See also Electronic mail
Email address, 9
Email hyperlink, 141, 142
Employment:
    finding jobs on the Net, 146–67
    accounting, 150–56
    environmental, 156–65
    management, 146–49
Employment Opportunities and Job Resources on the Internet, 133
Encryption, 5
Encyberpedia, 87, 101

Environmental online resources, 94–95
Environmental Web sites, 156–58
E-Span, 136, 164, 165
ESPN SportsZone, 54, 202
Eudora, 7, 9, 16
Eudora Pro, 7, 8
Evaluation guidelines, for Internet resources, 106–8
Exchange, 7
Excite, 69, 76, 79, 81, 85
    searching with, 87–89
Excite Reviews, 28
Exploratorium, 202
Explorer, 9, 16
    entering a URL with, 27
    features of, 21–22
    See also Internet Explorer; Microsoft Internet Explorer
Explorer 3.0, 5, 43
Explorer 4.0, 20

Farrell, Paul B., 193
Files, compressed, 42
Files, self-extracting, 11
File Transfer Protocol (FTP), 6, 9–11, 12
    See also FTP
First amendment, 5
Fodor's Travel, 202
Frames:
    bookmarking, in Netscape, 38
    navigating with, 36–39
    printing, 39
Free-Nets, 8, 12
FTP (File Transfer Protocol), 11, 14
    referencing documents and, 116–18
    See also File Transfer Protocol
FTP sites, anonymous, 9

Galaxy, 79, 81, 86, 145
Gamelan, 43
Geek speak, 5, 49
    glossary of, 209–15

Geography resources sites, 95
Gibson, William, 4
Globe, 71, 76
Gopher, 11, 12, 14
Gopher sites:
    referencing, 114–16
Government online resources, 96, 189
Graphic image, 42
Groupware, 6
GTE Super Pages, 145

Hardware, 5
    selection guidelines, 225–27
Harvard, 182
Helper(s), 5
    installation of unlisted, 50–53
    working with browsers, 43–44
    See also Helper application(s);
        Viewer(s)
Helper application(s), 42, 46
    installing, 47–53
    See also Helper(s); Viewer(s)
Help wanted. com, 136
Hip, Hot, 'N' Happening, 145
History list(s), 26, 38
History online resources, 96–97
Hits, 82, 159
Hobbes Internet Timeline, 6
Holmes search software, 137
Home page(s), 13, 21, 25–26
HotBot, 80, 91
Hot Business Sites, 145
Hot Wired, 54, 71, 76, 191
HTML (Hypertext Markup Lan-
    guage), 14, 15
    posting resumes in, 137, 140
HTTP (Hypertext Transfer Protocol),
    14, 15, 27
Hypermedia, 11, 42
Hypertext links, 62
Hypertext Markup Language. See
    HTML
Hypertext MUD (HTMUD), 72
Hypertext Transfer Protocol. See
    HTTP

Icon(s), 25, 38
Illinois, University of, 5
Image Surfer, 79, 91
Image viewer, 43
Infobahn. See Cyberspace; Internet;
    Net
Information superhighway. See
    Cyberspace; Internet; Net
Infoseek, 79, 82, 85
    searching with, 89–91
Infoseek Guide, 89
Infoseek Professional, 89
Infoseek Ultra, 69, 76
    features of, 90–91
Inktomi, 80, 92
Integrated Services Digital Network
    (ISDN), 228–29
Intel, 6, 75
Intelligence At Large, 45
IntelliMatch, 137
Interactive mailing list. See
    Listserv(s); Listserv mailing
    list(s); Mailing list(s)
Interactivity, 42, 43
Interesting Business Sites, 129, 145
Inter-Links, 87
International Standards Organiza-
    tion (ISO), 110
Internet, 3, 4, 6, 13, 19
    career planning on, 125–31
    connecting to, 15–17
    content regulation on, 5
    employment opportunities on,
        131–40
    evaluating information on, 105–8
    finding providers, 16–17
    guidelines for research on, 81–81,
        105
    history of, 3–6, 189–90
    as new communication tool,
        180–81
    recording information resources
        from, 109–10
    as reference library, 100–03
    resources and tools on, 11–13

resume exposure on, 143
World Wide Web and, 13–14
Internet account, 15, 25
Internet business collections, 144–46
Internet Career Connection, 137
Internet Chat, 76
See also Chats
Internet collections, 80, 92–100
archeology, 92–93
art, 93
business, 93–94
criminal justice, 94
the environment, 94–95
geography, 95
government, 96
history, 96–97
literature, 97
mathematics, 97–98
music, 98
news, 99
science, 99–100
Internet communication, 56
Internet Explorer, 5
and bookmarks, 34–36, 37
and plug-ins, 44
and Usenet newsgroups, 65–69
See also Explorer; Microsoft Internet Explorer
Internet Online Career Center, 137
Internet Phone (IPhone, by Vocal Tec), 74
Internet phones, 13, 56, 72–75
hardware for using, 73–74
software for, 74–75
Internet Protocol address. See IP address
Internet provider(s), 62
finding, 16–17
See also Internet service provider(s); Service provider(s)
Internet Public Library, 103–04
Internet Relay Chat(s) (IRC), 4, 13, 56
See also Chats

Internet research tools, 80–81
search directories, 80–81
search engines, 81
Internet resources, 16
college planning, 170–80
financial aid, 171–74
information publications, 178–79
standardized tests online, 179–80
job-related, 144–46
Internet service provider(s) (ISP), 8, 15–16
See also Internet provider(s); Service provider(s)
Internet services:
Web sites for, 206–7
Internet Services List, 87
Internet tool(s), 7, 11
IP (Internet Protocol) address, 73
IPhone (Vocal Tec), 74
IPhones. See Internet phones
IRC. See Chat(s); Internet Relay Chat(s)
ISDN, 228–29
ISP. See Internet provider(s); Internet service provider(s); Service provider(s)

Jargon, computer. See Geek speak
Java, 42, 43
Java Center, 43
Jobhunt, 133, 137
Job interviews:
investigating companies on Net, 144–46
Job search:
accounting, 150–56
environmental employment opportunities, 160–65
environmental technology, 156–60
management, 146–49
JOBTRAK, 133, 138, 164, 165
JobWeb, 138
Jumbo, 10, 43

Kabacoff, Rob, 87
Keyword(s), 69, 81, 82
  identifying subject with, 83
  in resume building, 141

Lamda MOO, 72
Learning Adventures:
  career planning and job search,
    165–67
  exploring virtual communities,
    75–76
  using Internet for research, 123
LibCat, 104
Libraries, software, 16
Libraries online, 7, 8, 182–83
Library of Congress, 87, 104
LibWeb, 104
Link(s), Web, 9, 10, 26, 82
  exploring, 39
Link structure, 11
List, The, 129, 145
Lists. See Listserv(s); Listserv mailing
    list(s); Mailing list(s)
Listserv(s), 55, 56–62
  functions of, 56–58
  tips for using, 69
  and Usenet newsgroups, compari-
    son, 61–62
  See also Listserv mailing list(s)
Listserv mailing list(s), 11, 12, 76,
    111
  and career planning, 130–31
  referencing information from, 119,
    121
  See also Listserv(s)
Literature links, 97
Literature resources online, 188
Live audio, 43
Live events, 55, 70
Live objects, 42
Live3D, 45
Local area network (LAN), 7
Looksmart, 87
Los Angeles Times, 136
Lotus, 7

Lycos, 69, 76, 79, 91
Lycos Top 5% Sites, 28

Macintosh:
  compressed file extensions in,
    9–10
  and full-duplex sound, 73
Magellan, 79, 82, 86
Mailing list(s), 56, 57–58
  finding, 60
  joining, 58–60
  See also Listserv(s); Listserv mail-
    ing list(s)
Mailing list administrators, 57–58
Mainframe computers, 56
Mainframe supercomputer, 8
Maps online, 190–91
Maryland, University of, 195
Massachusetts Institute of Technology
    (MIT), 182
Mathematics online resources, 97–98
McCahill, Mark, 5
MCI, 75
Medsearch, 138
Megaconverter, 101
Messenger, 20
Microphone, 74
Microsoft, 5, 6, 7
Microsoft Internet Explorer, 7, 11, 13
  and the browser war, 19–20
  See also Explorer; Internet Explorer
Microsoft Network (MSN), 16, 70
MIME (Multipurpose Internet Mail
    Extension), 43–44, 48
MIME type, 52
Minnesota, University of, 5
MLA-Style, 110
MMX-technology PC, 6
Monster Board, 138, 154–56, 164
MOOs (Multi-User Shell, Object Ori-
    ented), 8, 13, 70, 71–72
Mosaic, 5
Mouse, 38
Moviestar, 45
MTV, 54

MUDs (Multi-User Domain), 8, 13, 70, 71–72
Multimedia environment(s), 5, 9, 42, 54
Multimedia Web sites, 54
MUSE, 13
Music links, 98
My Virtual Reference Desk, 101

NASA, 203–4
National Archeological Database, 93
National Business Employment Weekly, 130
National Center for Supercomputing Applications (NCSA), 5
National Employment Job Bank, 138
National Geographic, 54
National Public Radio, 54, 192
National Science Foundation, 4
Net, 3
    See also Cyberspace; Internet
Netguide Live's Best of the Web, 28
Net phones. See Internet phones
Netscape, 6, 9
    entering a URL with, 27
    features of, 21–22
    and plug-ins, 44
Netscape Communications Corporation (NCC), 5, 19
    and CoolTalk, 75
Netscape Communicator, 6, 13
Netscape Communicator Suite, 19–20
Netscape Media Player, 45
Netscape Navigator, 5, 7, 11, 12, 16
    and bookmarks, 28–34
    and the browser war, 19–20
    and Usenet newsgroups, 63–65
Netscape Navigator 2.0, 36
Netscape Navigator 4.0, 20
    and plug-in install feature, 47
Netscape 3.0, 5
Net Sites for Job Seekers, 143
Net surfer, 5, 25
Network connections, 15

Network servers, 4
Neuromancer, 4
New Rider's WWW Yellow Pages, 145–46
New Scientist, 158
Newsgroups:
    tips for using, 69
    See also Usenet; Usenet newsgroups
NewsLink, 192
News online resources, 99
NewsPage, 192
Newspapers, online, 16
News publications online, 191–94
News reader, 63–68
News server, 64, 66
New York Times, 136
New York Times, 192
Nickname, 70
Noble Citizens of Planet Earth, 102
Northwestern University, 182
Nova Southeastern University, 87
NSFNET, 4
NYNEX Interactive Yellow Pages, 146

Occupational Outlook Handbook, 163
Oikarinen, Jarkko, 4
Omniview, 45
OneLook Dictionaries, 102
Online Career Center, 146–47
Online recruitment services, 136
Online resume(s), 134–35
    preparing, 139–43
Online service providers, commercial, 16
Online services, 55
Online sites for job seekers, 135–39
Open architecture, 11
Open Text, 80, 92
Otis Index, 192

Page display, 21–22
Palace, The, 55, 70, 71, 76
Password, 15

Pathfinder, 70, 71, 76
Path statement, 111
PBS Online, 192
PC, and full-duplex sound, 74
PC compression, 9
PC decompression, 9
Personal computer, 4
    See also PC
PKZIP, 9, 42
    and file decompression for Windows, 47
Places to See Winners Page, 28
Plug-in(s), 5, 24, 42
    installing, with Netscape Navigator, 46–47
    obtaining free, 47
    special installation of, 50–53
    Web developers' choices, 45–46
    working with browsers, 43–44
Plug-in applications. *See* Plug-ins
Plug-in installer, 20
PointCast, 5–6
PointCast Network, 45–46, 192, 193
Point-to-Point Protocol. *See* PPP
Pop-up menu(s), 22, 23–24, 38
PPP (Point-to-Point Protocol), 15–16, 17
Presentation page, 11
Princeton, 182
Prodigy, 16, 55, 70
Protocol(s), 14, 110
Public Broadcasting System—History of the Internet, 6

Quarterdeck Corporation, 74
Query, 82
    refining the, 83–85

Rail, The, 28
Rand Corporation, 3–4
RealAudio, 46, 52, 53, 54
Real-time chats, 16
Real-time media, 13, 56
Real-time transmission, 55, 72
Reference Center, 102

Reference Desk, 102
Reference Indexes, 103
Reference resources online, 100–3, 183–84
Reference Shelf, 103
Research guidelines, online, 81–82
ResearchPaper.com, 103
Resume(s), online, 134–35
    preparing, 139–43
Resume builder, 140
Resume home page, 140
Resume services, 140
Retrieval path (Internet address), 110
Routers, 15

Saludos Web, 138
San Jose Mercury News, 136, 192–93
Screen name, 70
Search directories, 79, 81, 82–87
Search directories, subject-oriented, 86–87
Search engines, 69, 76, 79–80, 81, 82
    job hunting with, 150
    and resume building, 142
    working with, 87–92
Search tool, 159
Security, 5
Self-assessment, for career planning, 126–27
Serial Line Interface Protocol. *See* SLIP
Server pathway, 115
Service providers, 70
    See also Internet provider(s);
        Internet service provider(s)
Shareware, 10, 43, 205–6
Shareware Web site, 48
Shockwave, 46
Shockwave Gallery, 54
Silicon Graphics, 45
SLIP (Serial Line Interface Protocol), 15, 16, 17
SLIP/PPP, 16
Smithsonian Institution, 104–05

Software, 5
  service providers and, 17
Software client, 70
Software program, as helper, 53
Sound, full–duplex, 73
Sound card, 73–74
Sound files, 42, 43
Speakers, 74
Speeches and speech writing online,
  185–86
Stanford Research Institute, 4
Stanford University, 138, 182
Status bar, 22
Streaming audio, 42
Streaming video, 42
StudentCenter, 138–39
Study abroad resources online, 194
Stuffit Expander, 10, 42
  and file decompression for Macin-
  tosh, 47
Subject directory, 82, 83
Submission address, 59, 60
Substance abuse resources online,
  194–97
Summer Jobs, 139
Sun Microsystems, 42
Super-computing centers, 4
Survival Guide for College Gradu-
  ates, 133

TCP/IP (Transmission Control Pro-
  tocol/Internet Protocol), 3, 4,
  16
Technical support, 7, 17, 227
Telnet, 4, 6, 7–8, 9, 11, 14
  and chat worlds, 70
  Internet services with, 8
  with MOOs and MUDs
Telnet sites:
  referencing, 118–19
Text-based environment, 7
Text documents, 58–59
Threads, 62–63, 64
3D chats, 70
3D chat worlds, 71

3D environments, 70
3D video, 42
Tikkiland, 71
Time Warner, 55, 70, 71, 76, 192
Toolbar buttons, 22
  navigation of Net and, 22–23
Tripod, 134, 140
Tucows (for Windows), 10, 43

UCLA, 4
Ultraseek, 86, 89–90
Uniform Resource Locators. *See*
  URLs
United States Department of
  Defense, 3
URLs, 9
  correct usage of, 27
  index of, 90
  for newsgroups, 62
  organizing, 28–39
  as resource link, 20–21
  retrieving documents with, 14–15
Usenet, 56
  See also Usenet newsgroup(s)
Usenet newsgroup(s), 4, 6, 11, 12, 55,
  76, 81
  and browser support, 62–63
  categories of, 61
  for job hunting, 129–30
  and listserv, comparison, 61–62
  posting resumes on, 143
  reading with Internet Explorer,
  65–69
  reading with Netscape Navigator,
  63–65
  referencing information from, 119,
  121–22
  and URLs, 14–15
  See also Usenet
Username, 9, 15
Utah, University of, 4
U.S. News and World Report, 181

V-Chat, 71
Video, streaming, 42

Video, 3D, 42
Videoconferencing, 13, 56
    See also Desktop videoconferenc-
    ing
Viewer(s), 24
    working with browsers, 43–44
    See also Helper(s); Helper applica-
    tion(s)
Viewer applications. *See* Helper(s);
    Helper application(s);
    Viewer(s)
Viewer software programs, external,
    42
Virtual communities, 16, 55–76
    hands-on exploration, 75–76
Virtual libraries, 103–105
Virtual reality, 70
    adventure games, 72
Virtual Reference Desk, 103
Virtual universities online, 198
Viruses, Internet, 5
Vivoactive, 54
Vivoactive Player, 46
Vocal Tec, 74
Voice technology, multi-user, 55
V R Scout, 46

Wall Street Journal, 130, 193
Wall Street News, 193–94
Wall Street Research Net, 194
Washington Post, 136
Weather online, 197–98
Web browser(s), 5
    See also Browser(s)
WebChat Broadcasting System, 71, 76
WebChats, 105
Web designers, 42
Web directory, 87
Web document, 19
Web links, 79
Web objects, 43
Web page(s), 7, 20
    multiple panes in, 38–39
    special effects technology for, 43
    and URL information, 26

Web site(s); 79
    academic institutions home pages,
        181–82
    composition and grammar,
        181
    connection problems, 27
    environmental careers, 156–58
    finding changed addresses of,
        221–24
    government, 189
    history of computers and Internet,
        6, 189–90
    humanities and literature, 188
    Internet services, 206–7
    libraries and reference, 182–84
    maps, 190–91
    miscellaneous surfing, 198–205
    news publications, 191–94
    saving with bookmarks, 28–36
    for shareware and software,
        205–6
    speeches and speech writing,
        185–86
    substance abuse resources,
        194–97
    study abroad, 194
    surfing to, 27–28
    virtual universities, 198
    weather information, 197–98
    writing resources, 186–87
Web site(s), after-hour, 24
Web site(s), business, 24
Web site, shareware, 48
Web standards, 6
Web Talk, 74, 75
Wet Feet Press, 130
Whiteboard, 75
Window. *See* Web page
Windows, 6, 13
Windows operating system, 20
Window title bar, 21
Wired, 39
Wired magazine, 70
Wired Source, 80, 92, 103
World's Chat, 71

World Wide Web, 5, 6, 7, 11, 12
  chat sites on, 71
  finding companies on, 129
  and Internet, comparison, 13–14
World Wide Web home pages:
  job hunting and, 142
World Wide Web sites, 81
  referencing, 111–14
  See also WWW sites
World Wide Web Tour, 28
World Wide Web Virtual Library,
  87
World Wide Yellow Pages, 146
Writer's Block, 187

Writing resources online, 186–87
WWW servers, 14
WWW sites:
  URL linking to, 27
  See also World Wide Web sites

Yahoo, 55, 81
  searching with, 82–85
Yahoo Chat, 71, 76
Yahoo Employment Resources, 134
Yahoo Internet Life, 28
YahooJobs, 139
Yale University, 182
Yellow Pages, 145